A SPECTRUM BOOK

Prentice-Hall, Inc., Englewood Cliffs, New Jersey 07632

MIKE CANTOR

OPEN AND OPERATE YOUR OWN SMALL STORE

Library of Congress Cataloging in Publication Data

Cantor, Mike.
    Open and operate your own small store.

    "A Spectrum Book"
    Includes index.
    1. Stores, Retail.   2. Small business.   I. Title.
HF5429.C284   658.8'701   82-5265
ISBN 0-13-637496-4   AACR2
ISBN 0-13-637488-3 (pbk.)

This Spectrum Book is available to businesses and organizations at a special discount when ordered in large quantities. For information, contact Prentice-Hall, Inc., General Publishing Division, Special Sales, Englewood Cliffs, N.J. 07632.

1   2   3   4   5   6   7   8   9   10

Permission to reprint "Small Businesses Face Tough Sledding," by Glenn Ritt (Associated Press) is gratefully acknowledged.

ISBN 0-13-637496-4

ISBN 0-13-637488-3 (PBK.)

Prentice-Hall International, Inc., *London*
Prentice-Hall of Australia Pty. Limited, *Sydney*
Prentice-Hall Canada Inc., *Toronto*
Prentice-Hall of India Private Limited, *New Delhi*
Prentce-Hall of Japan, Inc., *Tokyo*
Prentice-Hall of Southeast Asia Pte. Ltd., *Singapore*
Whitehall Books Limited, *Wellington, New Zealand*

CONTENTS

OPERATING SUCCESSFULLY

PREFACE

Mike Cantor grew up observing his parents operate small stores. After law school and law practice, he returned to retailing as an executive in Macy's in New York City, and later shared operations of a small department store as a merchandising specialist. Since 1978 he has been teaching business courses at New School For Social Research and counseling entrepreneurs at the Executive Volunteer Corps of New York.

AMERICA: "THE LAND OF OPPORTUNITY"

Our parents said it—our politicians shout it—and the new breed of wealthy entrepreneurs proved it! The impoverished Vietnamese "boat people," Koreans, Cubans, and Eastern European refugees are showing so clearly, again and again, that regardless of our economists' most dire agitation over America's economic picture, the opportunity to make a living, and MORE, is HERE—NOW!

Your Own Store
IS This Opportunity

Do you need to be unusually talented, be a college graduate or have any kind of special genius to own a successful, profitable store?

Generally not; but don't downgrade the need for education because it will make you *more observant*, and help you learn from the successful merchants all around you. A talent for retailing will give you an "instinct" for decision making in merchandising, choosing the "way to go" that results in a minimum of the early mistakes in most business. I can't vouch for any "special genius" because I've never encountered any. . . . I only see bright, talented people who *plan* to do what they have learned in practical experience, some with more school background than others, following consistently with hard effort the kinds of guidelines I will offer you.

It is *not* the "easy way" to earn a living; but with good drive, some capital, and some luck a store owner can earn *more* than a "living," makes *his or her own* decisions and *enjoy* the small store with its personal touch. The friendly relationship with neighbors and customers builds for storeowners a place in the community and security for their families. I have seen it happen many times.

In 1905 my father and mother opened and operated just such a small store (with $900) after a learning experience with my grandparents. Their success eventually built it into a small department store which operated (always profitably) through 60 years, a period that included several depressions.

The small store plans a limited volume at the outset, and small profits. Success is not a sudden happening, and as you proceed through the text you will realize that this professional advice anticipates acquiring profits . . . and growth . . . in the orderly accession in time. It is a basic trait of entrepreneurs to have the ability to make correct decisions as to *when* to further invest their profits for growth. I will help you to recognize the signs, and the timing as well.

A small store has a special charm, a personality, a close relationship with its customers, developed by the *unusual* service to them—a unique connection that can be both a joy and an advancing personal success. There is always a gamble, a monetary risk in any personal venture and now you must decide:

- That your philosophy will no longer happily tolerate working under another's direction despite the consoling benefits of a recurring paycheck.
- That you are ready and able to make *your own bold decision with your own monetary security on the line*—and,
- That your *training* and *background* fit into the step-by-step scheme of planning for your store I have prepared for you.

I have *no intention* here to ask that you analyze yourself for doubts as to your readiness to proceed.

I will not place statistics before you to show that a certain percentage of new business ventures fail because of enumerated management deficiencies. The emphasis here is on *how to succeed.*

Appendix A is a short historical background of many famous stores which began in the way you are urged to ... small shops with good ideas ... "mama-papa" stores building huge success on a personal appeal.

USE OF THE APPENDICES

The Appendices are specially digested material aimed at clarifying and augmenting the text in special subjects or showing forms that are helpful as examples. This is *not* intended to interrupt the narrative of the chapters but only to augment it with some interesting background, explain a procedure in more detailed fashion when you are ready to use it, and show examples of specialized merchandise stores you may be interested in. It is aimed at avoiding the necessity of reading other reference works while offering *all* the material to attain your goal. It may help your professional as a reminder of special circumstances in personal agreements.

Free advice and counsel concerning your store plans is available at SCORE (Service Corps of Retired Executives) or the Executive Volunteer Corps (city-sponsored) in certain cities. They will likewise help you secure appropriate legal (or accounting) professional assistance through their local Referral offices. Advice on population and areas is available at local chamber of commerce offices, and from the Small Business Administration office on financing.

A consensus of Professional Management Consultants agrees that the most frequent reason for failure in new retail ventures is poor planning and the resulting indecisions. Think and plan with these chapters to attain your goal. There is more material here than any one retailer needs now; but once having read it through and planned with its guidance, you may find it a good reference work for later problems as they arise.

GOOD LUCK AND HAPPY RETAILING!

"THANK YOU's" from Mike Cantor

Steven Sahlein for suggestive writing direction
Randy Duchaine for excellent photography
Joanne Baer for typing, cooperatively and pleasantly
Marge Gale for helpful office work
Daniel Cantor for objective reading and suggestions
Delia Cantor for another point of view on stores
Eric Emory, (Sacred Heart University) management
Bill Berner, helpful on fine jewelry stores
Seymour Miller, sportswear stores, chain management
Max Kligman, furniture retail and distribution
Sol Edelman, retail furniture stores
Guy Weill, helpful on menswear stores
Irving Mishkin, menswear stores trends
Ken Robins, small giftware stores
Felix Lilienthal, buying offices
Ed Groner, insurance broker
Seymour Mantell, attorney, business forms and agreements
Herbert Raskin, novel stores of today
Sidney Fidlon, for encouragement to retail teaching, writing
Commissioner Sidney Kushin Executive Volunteer Corps of N.Y.C.
Delia Kuhn, suggestions and author guidance
Kermit Klaster, book review
Sanford Felberbaum, control advice

STARTING UP

1

PLANNING
YOUR STORE

. . . first thoughts . . .

> I know that I would enjoy owning a store . . . I know good things when I
> see them . . . I know I could make it a success!

Many such personal thoughts and store plans originate with not much more than
being interested, being curious, being a careful and exacting shopper—shoppers
observing with a keen eye for quality or fit, noting reliability, experiencing that
special service, or just being pleased by a friendly way of doing business. All
these impressions of business dealings we admire add up to a pleasing sale and a
happy moment for buyer and storekeeper—and success!

You think, "If I had a store I would do it better."

You certainly *can* if you *plan*.

Basically the retail business is very simple. You buy appealing, needed items for customers that you would normally expect to shop in your area. You buy at a price you call *cost* and "price" it so that it is inviting to your customer and leaves you a profit, which is the difference between your cost and the selling price. (Retail price minus cost is your *gross* profit; subtracting other expenses equals *net* profit.) Profit is the very essence of your business because it pays you and your help, your rent and other overhead expenses, *and* it leaves you with a small residue that you may use to expand your business and grow financially. Without profit—the key word in business—your business is not satisfying and will not last very long.

Of course, even though this idea sounds simple, we have all seen some stores grow and multiply, and others wither and die. Many were influenced by outside uncontrollable factors, but the single most important factor to retail success is the guiding, driving force of the owner. Therefore, there are things that *you*, the owner, must know or learn to be a success. Start by thinking out your goals. Write down

- What *kind* of goods or services you want to offer.
- What you *know* about this kind of merchandise or service, and
- What you *have* of the other elements necessary to open the store.

The elements of success are here. Each discussion will make you aware of these elements and how much more you need to be successful, as well as how your financial resources (capital) fit your plans.

KIND OF STORE

Your thinking should start with what you are interested in . . . the kind of store, goods, or services you admire or really know about . . . or a kind of store you perceive as being *needed*.

YOUR CHOICE, YOUR WAY   Your interest may lie in what you wear, what other family members wear, home products, or perhaps what you admire but can't afford. You may love to *compare* quality in some special kind of goods, brands compared with unknown names, high with popular price makes. At one time you may have given some thought to *ways of selling a product, displaying it, or advertising it* that you believe is better. The strength of this belief in a way of selling a product, or the drive to do it better, is helpful to a new store owner in finding an appeal, a niche for your store. If you possess a particu-

4

lar skill or talent, it can be the basis for a special service that you offer with or without merchandise. Your small store and its special, personal relationship gives you a big advantage over the impersonal chain stores.

PRODUCT KNOWLEDGE   You *must* know your product very well. If you don't have the intimate knowledge of the product, its quality variety, price lines, seasonal variations, sizes, colors, supply sources, and what kind *your* customers want at any given time of year, you can learn this information from several sources.

- Similar store experience; working in the field is the best source of knowledge.
- Complete market study of the stores that are successful in these items and the sources where they buy them, noting brand names and assortments.
- Trade shows where many lines are displayed and can be compared.
- Help from professional buyers, other store owners, or professional buying offices who will represent you for a fee.

RETAIL STORE WORK IS BEST   The very best background for merchandise expertise is your own working experience in a similar store, even part-time, weekend, or holiday employment. If that is impossible, study the many retailers around you; shop and compare the selection of goods offered by department stores, discount stores, and specialty stores, noting the price lines featured as well as the sale prices. Shop the stores that are known for their merchandising skill in this line, their displays, their promotions, and their advertising; copy down trade names of the merchandise you note as superior. Spend time comparing quality and price; discuss lines and retailers, source firms, sales people, and factory personnel.

WHOLESALERS AND SHOWS   Some of the lines are available at distributors who can be helpful in offering quality comparisons to add to your knowledge. Enlist the aid of any friends who have some experience. Retailers in areas away from your planned store may discuss lines of goods if you ask. Often a visit to trade shows can be helpful; they show many lines at one time that can be compared. Some department store training programs suggest a visit to factories to compare component raw materials, their quality, and the labor.

RESIDENT BUYING OFFICES   For a fee, you can obtain help at resident buying offices, professional buyers (see Appendix P) who know the lines, the up-to-date style leaders, and the best sources available. For stores away from the source markets, their help, especially in fast-changing style lines, should not be underestimated. They also exercise more powerful "buying clout" for your small quantity buying in the source market by joining orders.

The Unique Quality

After absorbing product knowledge, you will be faced with a major question about your own store that is critical to a favorable opening, a good first impression.

How can I make my store "unique," a different or better store so I can attract and build a loyal clientele?

One way is to project a "unique quality" to your trade.

One of the ways that a new store can be *better* is to know or learn the needs of the neighboring clientele by studying the life-styles, the buying habits, and the homes (see the area study in Chapter 2) of those living nearby. If you are going to please these nearby customers, you must know their needs. As Marshall Field of Chicago proclaimed, "The customer is always right! Give the lady what she wants!" No one will be there to tell you the price lines, the quantity or the timing, or when to have it in stock for her. If you don't have it, she may not give you another opportunity soon again to make her a customer. But she *will* respond to a feeling that you want to please her and will return.

The unique quality of your store may have been *the very idea* that prompted you to think of a store of your own. This "reason for being," added to a fine assortment of needed goods, has made most of the world famous stores draw customers from far away and capture the loyalty of the nearby residents as well. Many of these stores were tiny mom and pop operations with *good ideas* when they opened.

A UNIQUE IDENTITY   Many great stores started with or developed a unique identity that people *recognize* as very special, and you can adapt some of these ideas for your own use (see Table 1.1).

"IN" SHOPS   Some stores are unique because of management alterness to fashion trends or changes in life-style. They consistently offer new or the "off-beat" merchandise and have become the "in" places to shop. A good example is "Bloomie's" (nickname for Bloomingdale's) in New York. Buying volatile, "trendy" styles is very speculative because these "hot" numbers often die as quickly as they rise, leaving reorder stock stuck in inventory. But the chance to become the "in" shop is often taken because the publicity of newspaper and magazine articles is much more effective than any advertising for reputation enhancement.

Other Ideas

UNUSUAL ASSORTMENT   Full specialized store assortments are sometimes unique. Many stores in recent years have opened with complete assort-

TABLE 1.1. Developing Store Identity

Some Unique Ideas	Originating Store(s)
Famous brands sold at truly lower prices; some known as "discount" stores."	Korvettes (early) K-Mart Woolco Caldors Syms
Small home appliances sold with manufacturer's and your own repair shop guarantee.	local stores
Timed automatic markdown of prices as fashion goods age in stock (intrigue for bargain hunter).	Filenes (basement), Boston Syms, New York
Store-sponsored community projects (nonmerchandise): parades, senior citizen groups, teen clubs, flower shows, scouts, sports teams with printed t-shirts.	Macy's (all stores) Dayton's, Minneapolis-St. Paul
Luncheon and tea-time fashion shows (tease the appetite).	G. Fox, Hartford, Connecticut Bullocks, Los Angeles Marshall Field, Chicago
Neighborhood fashion show working with churches or charities to make local people aware of them.	local stores

ments of a particular category. The examples of "Athletic Feet" and "Lamps and Lighting Shops" are included in Appendices I and G. These assortments were unique in themselves at first, but more recent openings have highlighted entrepreneurs who added their own special touch as well.

Very Top Quality

Stores can also be unique in certain areas by offering a selection from only the very top quality of all the lines, examples are Nieman-Marcus stores and Hightowers (Oklahoma City). Many of them give a personal service to their customers that caters to their every whim, and a few stores thrive on snob-appeal development of the name (Gucci, for example) over the years. The honest value inherent in superior design and craftsmanship has made buyers flock to Tiffany's in New York and Gump's in San Francisco, whose museumlike appearance hasn't changed in well over a century.

Finding and featuring your unique identity is worthwhile. Doing it *better* supplies the theme for advertising and displays, creates enthusiasm that spreads around your area, helps to presell customers, and encourages loyalty to your shop. Your local paper is gnerally interested in your unusual way and will run a story. (Eugene Ferkauf of Korvettes attributes much early success to news "interest" articles—Appendix C).

Gimmicks

A store owner on a very busy low-end shopping street, who has a very large clientele for closeouts, seconds, damaged goods, and such, puts it this way:

> I wouldn't consider opening a retail store today without a gimmick!

His customers, like flea market shoppers, love to uncover some treasure among the vast array of goods in many categories, accepting the possible need for cleaning or repairing the low-priced bargain.

The "ideas," "gimmicks," reasons for being "special" are many and varied. There are new ones every day, and they may have a limited life. Gimmicks that were great "drawing" ideas years ago may no longer have the same effect. Words like *discount* that used to be surefire have much less power today. And stores have to *continually* prove their allegiance to a concept to grow with it. People later did not believe Korvettes as a discount store while K-Mart and Caldors proved they lived by the concept, and their success continues.

Many stores still offer consistently lower prices than their competition, especially in promotions, and their reputation for reliability enhances the pulling power. "Marshall Field advertises in a whisper, but draws like a fire sale."

Years ago such stores as Sams in Detroit, Goldblatts in Chicago and Kleins, Ohrbachs and Loehmanns in New York built reputations by buying up manufacturer's closeout stocks of fashions and selling many pricelines of the closeouts at one low price. Policies with customers varied from "as is," no refunds, to a five-day return privilege, and all were successful. Some of these stores no longer exist because the conditions that encouraged manufacturers to sell off huge stocks to meet pressing financial needs have changed.

HOT CONCEPTS AND WORDS   Many stores now feature lines of goods with a much different appeal. The word *designer* has conjured up in the public mind a transformation from ordinary style and make to the "extraordinary," resulting in the wearer becoming more attractive, sexy, and desirable. This advertising appeal is similar to that in cosmetic, perfume, and health foods, and although effective now, it is bound to be diluted in time by the addition of so many new names with a similar story. Be aware that the current appeal of this or other new images may be transitory, and watch for signs of a change. Richard Marcus (Nieman-Marcus) said, "the rising consciousness of things 'TEXAS' is a happy coincidence (for us), but this too shall pass. . . "

YOUR WAY WITH YOUR TALENT   Be *creative* in the "idea" for your store, using any special talents or individual capacity that will appeal to your area people. Some stores (Hinks in Oakland, California) have become known for their personal sentimental ads of poetry on Valentine's Day, or for religious noncommercial expressions at holidays. Customers generally love sentimental personal appeals, and their response may reward you financially and personally.

Your idea, doesn't have to be *new*. There are really very few *new* ideas in retailing that someone else hasn't used before, so look for the good ones everywhere and use them. If you can make expert garment alterations, understand fashion, health, diet, sports, or other interests of your customers, try to incorporate that skill into an activity connected with your store.

Creative ideas usually find their way into print. Read daily newspapers, *The Wall Street Journal,* the Fairchild Retail publications, *Women's Wear Daily,* or *Daily News Record* to find ideas for your store and to keep aware of changes and trends in customer needs and sources of goods.

LIFE-STYLES OFFER A TARGET   Think of changing social trends, ways of life that are different, the new mode that perhaps can use a special appeal from you; the unmarried couples, the needs of senior citizens, childless couples who have suddenly started having babies; separate households and clothing for executive women. Today's life-styles demand new assortments. Can you supply needed services to those on exercise programs, fitness through diet, food supplements, vitamins, natural foods, or homewares that are a thoughtful addition to this life-style? The strong fervor for causes, the "born again" philosophy, the rekindling of interest in nostalgia, and the new clothing trends toward the sexy, as well as the interest in the romantic, may be a niche for you and your store.

Whether you are considering a health food-vitamin store (Appendix F), a fashion boutique, jogging and athletic equipment, designer jeans, novelty t-shirts, or any other merchandise, you have all those successful stores around you to study. Talk to their salespeople, walk around the busy big store departments and look for ideas that may account for their popularity. Their magnets should remind you of the "different" approach. This unique theme will elevate you above the average.

Other sources of ideas are manufacturer's sales reps and jobbers, especially on display at trade shows. Go to flea markets, too; observe the appealing merchandise and what motivates shoppers. Farmer's markets or garage sales may remind you of a motivation.

Some of the newer product lines are keyed to our everyday life-styles that get news space and attention by the "now" generation, are shown in the following list below.

"Harem duds for he-ing and she-ing."
"Chic threads for disco dancing."
"Roller disco-wear that's there!"
"Health food and vitamins for the inner-you."
"Babies are In! *Berley's Babes* caters babies before birth."
"Weddings are *in*!"
"We give that extra little service—"

- "Our Wedding Party Plans are Free!"
- "Visit our Salon Tuesdays at Five for Free Home Decorating Advice!"
- "Free Make-up Counseling—Health Hints."

STORE OWNERS AND STOREKEEPING

Working in a store that is similar to your own interests helps your knowledge and timing of buying your own merchandise, and you may even discover your "unique" idea. Working for someone else will also teach you storekeeping and allow you to profit from the owner's abilities, errors, and omissions. It will be helpful, even on a part-time basis, to observe store safety in money handling, display, maintenance, and other everyday management. Merchandise pricing, marking, and stocking are always easier after the first time. If you don't know storekeeping, know your merchandise "timing" thoroughly, and plan your finances carefully; it can be very costly.

To illustrate inexperience, poor planning, and inefficient storekeeping, here is a true tale of woe:

A few years ago, Laura Dolgins came in to discuss a proposed investment with two women friends in a fashion store. They each contributed $30,000 to the corporation and felt that their years of knowledgeable personal shopping was enough background to supply the expertise needed for success. I disagreed and was no longer consulted as they proceeded with the opening.

THE EFFECTIVE OPENING   There was much excitement created in their suburban town as their ads promised a new source of "true high fashion women's dresses and sportswear." The local newspaper ran a public relations story about "these bright educated women" who were deserting the "recreation circuit" to involve their lives in this wonderful store because of their "love of fashions and a genuine desire to offer something better to women who appreciate quality."

At first the response to their ads was encouraging, but as the first half-year passed, they found an overstock of past season's favorites and a shorter supply of funds to buy current new styles. A lack of new styles hurt sales.

Laura admitted that they had spent too much of their capital on building and decorating the store and that the *timing* of their buying always seemed to be a "little late" (see Chapter 3 on money and timing). They had also made some mistakes running the store, some cash had disappeared, and because their capital now seemed insufficient, the partners began blaming each other and were becoming slightly disillusioned about their investment. Laura felt that none of them was enjoying the business any longer, certainly not as a "hobby," and that even their prepaid buying trips no longer held their original charm.

ALL-IMPORTANT TIMING   The store has now been sold, and the partners will each receive about $6,000, all that remains of their investment. Professional training would have helped them perfect their timing in buying, one of the absolute prerequisites in fashion merchandising. It is as important as any quality or style element. The overspending in the original store plans left too little capital to operate, and buying errors used up more. With a depletion of capital, the loss of operating cash was even more serious when some of it disappeared. Store operations training probably would have safeguarded this money (Chapter 9—Security). And perhaps the less-than-total commitment of the partners contributed to their loss, especially after the novelty wore off.

So, for a more successful store operation:

- Plan to open a store selling merchandise you know about.
- Understand buying, stocking, promoting your goods, and storekeeping as we illustrate them to you.
- Plan to open a store that is in some way unique, different, or better, or one that is *needed* in your area.
- Plan the use of your money in a store you can afford (see Chapter 3).
- Think out and write down your overall story, unique concepts, strategies, and merchandise lines, as you would tell them to a friend.
- Create a financial plan and company formation in the light of what this book offers you.

Don't rush in. There are always retail opportunities, so wait until you feel confident in your understanding of the business. Every day people invest their money and lives in new stores, and some will have the success you seek. In one *New York Times* survey of successful business starts, several new immigrants from Korea, who had founded retail ventures, were quoted as saying:

"This is a country of more, and more, and MORE OPPORTUNITIES, knowledge, and wealth for the little man."

Remember—retail opportunities are always there. These people succeeded in very small capital fruit and vegetable stores by featuring "freshness." They shopped daily before dawn at wholesale markets. Other Korean immigrants have opened electronic specialty, stereo, and fabric stores based on their observations of these trades in Korea (sponsored by American firms).

You have a good opportunity, too. Take it with your best *planned* shot!
You have OPTIONS:

- A new store
- An existing store
- A franchise

A New Store

For the new store you build as you wish, you need

- Maximum merchandise experience with expert planning.
- A keen eye to analyze customers needs in the area by observing housing, schools, offices, factories, etc., to chose your location . . . a suitable premises to fit your plan.
- A good planning "feel" for structural design and fixtures because you must deal with architects, contractors, plumbers, painters, and others. These people do not offer credit terms, so cash is required.

A new store is closest to the ideal of the store planner, and if capital is no problem, professional assistance is usually available. Use that help unless you have confidence in your past experience. You may then choose a store with the traffic pattern that is perfect for your planned estimated volume.

Buying a Store

If you have only *some* background experience, you may want to buy an existing store, where the owner wishes to sell store, fixtures, inventory, and "goodwill" for one price (see Appendix K for a study of how to buy a store). The price is most always considered to be subject to some bargaining, depending, of course, on seller's and buyer's "poker playing." Why is the owner selling? Buyer's anxiety to take over will bring the price up. Sellers who wish to be rid of the store and retire may be glad to lower the price.

Generally, buying a store has four principal advantages over starting a new store:

1. You are "in business" and sales will be made the first day you open the doors.
2. With a less experienced background, you will have merchandise to observe in the operations, and your customers will help you learn.
3. You will not have to learn about store construction or buying fixtures, two skills required when you build a store.
4. You know the total cost of getting into business and the terms at once. When you build, your final costs are often inflated over original estimates.

Some of the drawbacks of buying a store are:

- The merchandise you bought in the inventory may be older or less saleable than you estimated (see Resident Buying Offices, Appendix P).
- The "goodwill" may be an illusion if the former owner antagonized customers or created a poor image to the trade.
- The fixtures, front, and physical store may be old and need replacement or expensive repairs.

- The figures on sales, profits, and such are not guaranteed and may not be accurate.
- An extreme downtrend because of local conditions, housing, and other factors may be difficult to reverse.

WHERE TO LOOK FOR STORES   The usual sources of stores (see Appendix K) for sale are newspapers, trade papers, or business agents. Salespeople and others in the trade often hear about stores for sale. If you buy through a business agent, the seller is normally expected to pay the fee. An exception is an agent whom you assign to "find" a store for a fee. Always get your attorney's advice before you sign. Selling prices of stores are rarely firm and an attorney or other professional can help you "bargain" to get the best price. A key to the deal is usually the owner's reason for selling. Other storekeepers in the area may offer an opinion on the store, so walk around the area and talk to neighbors.

If the price is within your means, check the area potential and get a professional opinion on it and the value of the inventory. Do not hesitate about using professional help on this "one-shot" large investment. The professional will more than justify the expense in the bargaining and will get you a more accurate look into the previous owner's operations. Even if the owners are unwilling to confirm stated profit figures by showing their IRS tax returns, your lawyer or accountant may be allowed to review it with the owner's lawyer or accountant. Your attorney must review and confirm what property you are getting for your money and that it is free of liens or other encumbrances. The lawyer should also check compliance with "bulk sales" laws in your state, requiring public notice and payment of sales taxes applicable.

You must do some investigating yourself to check the area potential and its sales and profit trends. A walking examination is most effective. Talking to other merchants, banks, realtors, and insurance brokers can help you evaluate the owner's claims. Bankers have information they may share with a professional, accountant, or lawyer about trends.

If you have little or no merchandise or store experience consider the third option:

Franchises

Retail franchises provide a semi-independent mode of operation by a "franchisor" to you, the "franchisee," with special expertise more or less guaranteeing success for the fees paid. The franchisee is required to make a large initial payment and pay a large percentage of receipts "off the top" in return for expert training before and guidance during the operation of the contract. Your own way of operating is restricted and contract renewal may be difficult (see Appendix K).

CHECK THE CONTRACT AND OTHER FRANCHISEES   Each franchise offering (by franchisor) should be carefully studied by an attorney to explain the contract rights and liabilities of the franchisee (you). Only after careful evaluation of the franchisor's financial stability, training programs, and the experience of several franchisees in operation should any contract be signed or down payment be made.

Without previous experience and without expert assistance, buying another's store may be risky because of a lack of ability to judge the business potential or condition of the store's inventory. A franchise may be the only way to get a training program and open a business without any prior expertise. There are many good franchises, but there are as many unworthy ones—therefore, examine each carefully on its own.

Most states are now adopting legislation (see Appendix K) to insure more equitable treatment to franchisees. Without this legislation, many franchisors often insisted on unreasonable modes of operation, which gave them a greater return, on the threat of establishing competing franchises near the franchisee or canceling the contract on a technicality. Franchise sellers are trained professionals; some may take advantage of an eager novice to obtain a signature or down payment.

Some local colleges have business courses that study in depth many of the skills that are helpful in a small retail store. Personal conferences are offered free by former professionals at the Executive Volunteer Corps (see Appendix Y) (or SCORE) in many cities. A combination of some retail store background and the advice offered here should suffice, however, to insure success in opening and operating your retail store.

Baylor University in Texas has a course on "how to begin a business" that most MBA's do not get in their course.

Other colleges offer courses in entrepreneurship, more relevant than "big corporate management." Some of the other colleges where it is taught are Emory, Harvard, University of Hawaii, M.I.T., Purdue, S. Illinois, Baylor, University of California, and Babson College (Wellesley, Mass.) with credit toward a Bachelors or Masters degree.

RETAIL STORES: NEEDS, AIMS, AND PROFITS

Whether they sell appliances or the service of appliance repair; whether they sell cosmetics or operate a salon for hair and skin, *all* stores have some things in common. To really succeed, they must:

- Keep *thinking* and *planning* as time goes on.
- Maintain clean, inviting premises to best present their wares.
- Produce enough dollar volume with a total profit to pay for all overhead and selling costs, and have a profit left over, a *net profit*.

THE PROFIT GOAL

It is unsatisfactory to do $100,000 in sales of goods that cost $75,000 when your overhead and selling costs are $30,000. It is just as unsatisfactory if those goods cost only $50,000, but your overhead and selling costs are $55,000.

In both cases, you show *no* profit; in fact, you show a loss.

The important goal of a business is profit—*net profit*—after all expenses are paid, and any business that cannot give profits is a "loser." It does not give satisfaction, or bonuses, and it does not last long. It is harder to solve the problems of *why* a business has not produced profits after you have started a course of operations; it is easier to plan for them beforehand.

TURNOVER   In discussing overall store profits, retailers talk about *turnover,* which refers to buying and offering for sale goods (or services) that sell at a profit (from cost to retail price); then taking this money and replacing those goods with new saleable products that sell and make another profit . . . over and over. You sell enough in any given time period so that the total profit on the goods sold is greater than the total expenses of doing business during this period, and so you have a net profit.

Turnover is used in planning and comparing your operaton with similar stores carrying the same lines of merchandise. For instance, the basic total value of your stock, your average inventory, turns over a normal number of times in a given year, according to what similar stores historically have done. Even though you may stimulate sales to greater volume through promotions, you will find that the ratio between your total inventory average figure at retail and your yearly sales figure will be fairly close to the traditional turnover ratios chart (Table 2.1, also in Appendix Z). Thus, if you are planning to do a sales volume of $100,000 a year, and the chart reveals a 3.2 time average turnover normally associated with variety stores of your type, you probably need from $28,000 to $30,000 (retail value) to do this volume. It is not exact, but it is a guide. Comparing with other retailers gives you reason for pride, especially when your greater turnover produces greater profits.

COORDINATE BUYING WITH CUSTOMER'S SEASONAL WANTS The keys to profitable buying and turnover are *planning* and *coordinating* your seasonal buying from the best sources with the customer's buying urges—what he or she needs and wants at this time. If you choose, you can also stimulate some extra urges (by promotions) to greater buying with advertising and offering goods you promote at a special price incentive. You give a customer an extra stimulus to buy more, and this turnover of more goods delivers more profits to match against expenses, and leaves you more net profits.

Management strategy for the control of expenses to help the profit is a very important subject to be dealt with later in each subject chapter.

To know how well you are doing, compare store figures, profits, and percentages with the Table 2.1.

How to Figure Profits

In retail stores (unlike manufacturers and distributors), all profit figures are based on the *retail price.* For each item your gross profit is the difference

TABLE 2.1. Retail Stock Turnover Ratio* and Others: Average of all stores sampled

Merchandise Kind of Store	Inv. Turnover	Year Net Proift %	Net Profit % on Net Worth
Childrens-Infants	3.5	4.8	18
Mens and Boys cloth'g & furn.	3.6	4.5	17
Department stores	4.6	2.0	9
Family clothing stores	3.3	5.1	16
Furniture stores	4.4	4.4	16
Hardware stores	3.3	4.5	16
Auto and home supply	5.1	4.3	22
Household appliances	5.1	3.6	20
Jewelry	2.4	7.7	20
Misc. general mdse.	4.0	4.1	14
Paint, glass, wallpaper	6.1	5.5	25
Radio and TV	4.9	4.0	22
Retail nurseries, lawn garden supplies	5.6	4.5	19
Shoe stores	3.3	5.2	20
Variety stores	3.2	3.7	13
Women's ready to wear	4.5	5.0	19
Grocery stores	15.4	1.8	20
A Ratio of	$\dfrac{\text{Av. Mo. Inventory}}{\text{Net Sales}}$	$\dfrac{\text{Net Profit}}{\text{Net Sales}}$	

*Reprinted by special permission of *Dun's Review* October 1979. Copyright © 1979 Dun & Bradstreet Publications, Inc.

between your cost of the item and your selling price (also referred to as your *markup* on this item). All profit (or markup) percentages on this item is found by dividing this profit by the retail price. For example:

> An item bought for $2 each sells for $4 each. The gross profit is $2, divided by the $4 selling price, giving a profit percentage (or markup percentage) of 50 percent. When the total of all merchandise invoices for the year is $60,000 and total sales are $100,000, the gross profit is $40,000 and the gross profit percentage (40,000 divided by 100,000) is 40 percent.

When profits of a business are discussed, we are talking about net profits—what is left after *all* expenses are deducted. This is the only kind you take home. To produce net profits, you should plan a price strategy.

Price Strategy

How you markup the goods from cost to selling price (sometimes also called "mark-on") and your overall profit plan depend on the merchandise itself primarily, its traditional profit margins, sources, types of promotional appeal to your trade, local competition, and necessary physical store requirements. Salons or restaurants, for instance, have high costs for premises and overhead and require different thinking and strategy.

Selling prices are no longer dictated to store owners by manufacturers (see Fair Trade Laws, Appendix O) even though some brands would deny a relationship to stores that sell below their list prices. (In some states alcoholic beverages are still controlled.) There are very few government limitations on price except during war periods and extreme shortages (for example, oil products). Therefore you may charge what you like! Well, not exactly. . .

You price your goods with a planned policy that you hope will induce customers to keep coming and buying, and yet priced high enough to include the profit margin you need so that overall gross profit on all goods bought and sold for the period is enough to leave you a net profit . . . after *all* expenses have been paid.

Pricing goods should not be a mechanical process. Some merchandise will be advertised and promoted perhaps at no profit; some at a slightly higher then regular markup (a special lowered cost price from the manufacturer perhaps). Pricing is *not* a regular mathematical percentage always, but an exercise of your thinking about a price that serves your entire operation best—your thinking based on observation and experience, demand and supply of the goods, competition, and perhaps a desire to do more volume. Superior "instinct" about price policies separate the *merchants,* who usually produce bigger profits and growth, from the average storekeepers.

Markup strategy does not always remain the same. Good merchants are aware of the factors that serve the store best and they plan price strategy changes in response to a need for more volume or more profit margin as they consider their customers' reactions to price changes they are contemplating. For example, with the rise in wholesale prices of your goods during an inflationary period, you must decide whether inventory on hand bought at the lower price should be raised to the selling price of new goods bought now. Will such a raise hurt your "image" with local trade? You must judge whether the price raise that increases your profit margin will perhaps lose some sales or possibly even some goodwill.

SALES PLANNING, ETC. There is one influence on pricing strategy that is common to all stores—the domination of sales volume by the calendar, the time of year. This creation of peaks and valleys variation by seasons and holidays has the greatest influence on planned operations of the store owner, who must always be ready for the consumer "buying urge." Do you make the most of the expected buying urge through price promotions that will increase the customer's appetite, or do you use extra bait in the off-season to increase the otherwise anticipated slow sales volume?

PROMOTION STRATEGY   As an example, toward the end of winter, in later January or February, there is a traditional consumer buying urge letdown as people tire of looking at dull winter clothes and unpleasant weather, and find repugnant the necessity of still paying for that extra gift bought during the seduction of the holiday period. At this time, stores use Washington or Lincoln's Birthday sales to lure buyers into the stores with "crazy bargains," giveaways, prizes, below-cost loss leaders, and so on, hoping to sell all items in the store, including regular markup goods not advertised. The additional sales volume, even at a lower overall markup, has a good effect on the profit/loss of the period because a store's constant overall expenses (rent, other overhead, salaries, and long-term costs) are not any less in periods of lowest sales volume. (This help to the *cash flow* will be noted later.)

The contrast of the needs and the aims of one store to another carrying different merchandise should, therefore, be quite apparent in planning your new store. (See Appendices A through J for history, beginnings, and merchandising many kinds of stores, illustrating the changing ways and opportunities of today.)

BUYING PATTERNS   The difference between being a large store or a small one is especially evident at times, and "local" management has a vital effect. Your locally run small store has a distinct advantage over chain operations because large-store management cannot react to changing conditions as you can. To illustrate, here is a true story concerning men's wear:

For nearly half a century, nowhere in retail was the conservative pattern of buying and styling seemingly more impregnable to change than in men's wear and furnishings. After World War II, the servicemen returning home in the late 1940s seemed content to follow the old patterns and perpetuate the men's wear old giants. Then it happened—establishment, flags, traditions, the CIA, and dress-up clothes were stomped on. As the demand for clothes of the past dropped off and a whole generation started to wear jeans and tattered shirts, many "kooky" styles became immediate short-term hits, fooling the most experienced chain buyers and merchandise executives. The conditions in men's wear chains turned into chaos, and failures—(John Davids, Broadstreets, and many more)—were numerous. Many suit manufacturers perished with them.

But new chains began to take the places of the old, some with highly promotional different appeals. Many single (owner on premises) men's stores followed the changing demand with consistent on-the-job merchandising, and they still do well, at regular markups and profits. (See Men's wear, Appendix D.)

How are the newer men's wear entrepreneurs doing? For example, a promoter bought out Lacey's, an "old-timer" men's store in northern Westchester

County, New York. He brought in his own usual closeout junk, but advertised "going out of business" as though the store and merchandise was still Lacey's. By the end of the lease, he had "milked it dry" with all the phony price comparisons.

When I heard that Hy and Len Dorinson were opening a new men's store on the same premises, I asked, "How do you plan to overcome the bad feeling generated in that phony five-month 'going out of business sale'?"

"We only know one way," Len said. "Put in a good men's line, advertise it, but keep a low profile. We'll send out some flyers in the mail to let people around know we're here with good clothes, and hope they will appreciate the change. There are still people who appreciate good quality and honest service. We'll give good alterations and cater to I.B.M. and other company middle-executives who live around here and dress up to go to work."

That was in 1975, and while I admired their ideas and ambition, I had some doubts. But not long ago, Len Dorinson talked about how the store was doing in the face of all the "new economic crises."

"We're doing great in *both* stores!" he said "Two years ago, when the big men's store closed in White Plains, we realize that Hickey-Freeman and other great lines would be available to us in Westchester, so we thought about buying them. Hy talked me into the 'full line,' not to just 'try some of it and see if it goes.' It's been a great line for us. You know, things have changed in the last few years; everybody's dressing up again and we have the clothes for them! How's that for luck?"

We discussed words like *luck* in relation to *good timing* in business, and having *guts* as related to *risk*. Dorinson then spoke of a plan for perhaps one more store in Connecticut when "one of his people was ready to be manager" and after the recent alterations were paid off.

At no time in my most optimistic imagination did I envision the magnitude of this small store's success.

STUDY AND PLAN THE NEEDS OF THE AREA   What was needed to get the Dorinsons started on the road to small store success? For one thing, they had some previous store experience. They studied and became aware that their area had potential for dress-up clothes in the face of the seemingly overwhelming depression of the men's clothing world in that aspect. They realized that the national companies who had recently moved their main offices into the area were run by young executives on their way up, who needed to look like they "belonged." The "look" they wanted was neat, dressy, and trendy, to indicate being "with it." This look requires quality and fit.

A STUDY, A PLAN AND SUCCESS   They had examined their area carefully and noted I.B.M., Reader's Digest, American Can, and six other major employers. They spoke to real estate agents and local banks, who encouraged their investment because their plans were based on intelligent study. The realty people pointed out available stores and closed the deal. Len Dorinson said, "We only know one way! That *had to be* the way to go!" Their store was a concept of *need* for better dress clothing for this area. Study your area for just such a need.

SELECTING AN AREA

ANALYZE SHOPPERS   You may conceive of your store idea with a thorough area study. Walk around in all directions from the area to observe the kinds of stores, the kinds of people in the walking traffic during shopping hours, the people who work nearby. Talk to salespeople in clothing stores, supermarkets, and other shops; compare price lines generally for a guide to your own merchandise relative selling prices. The busy successful stores are your key. Shop and copy!

ANALYZE OTHER STORES   Will your customers drive to you? Is there convenient parking? How is public transportation for mass items requiring heavy traffic? Are there workers in offices, hospitals, schools, factories, or government buildings who may be potential retail trade? Evaluate the drawing power of your neighbors. The department store, furniture, and appliance stores (big ticket stores) draw from other areas, and their traffic helps you. Tradespeople, cleaners, stationers, card stores, and the like do not. A theater may draw from other areas, but its customers are intent on entertainment and the theatre's peak hours are usually when you are closed. However, for small pickup items like stationery, cards, drugs, cosmetics, or candy, perhaps a store can benefit from this off-hours traffic.

Competitive stores will not necessarily hurt your business if they bring people. Good restaurants, bookstores, and aggressive fashion-style stores bring people to your area. Tourists are helpful. Social service and other agencies or drug clinics may not be.

Each business can have site locations that are perfect for it, some that are adequate, and some that are not recommended.

THE DOWNTOWN COMEBACK   After World War II, downtown areas without parking dried up as middle America began its move to the suburbs. Shopping plazas became "the American way" to shop, and central cities were allowed to rot. Now, the government is concerned with saving the gasoline used to shop on the highways. The resurgence of many downtown areas with government-sponsored housing in the area has given the small store owner a real choice again. Realty developers are revitalizing buildings downtown, claiming that these "quaint interesting" areas bring a *warmer, more personal touch* to the customers!

After analyzing the area residents and housing, their income index, and the availability of a suitable size and roughly affordable store premises, you will have some idea of a place, and the first step has been taken to start figuring money needs.

CONSIDERATIONS TO REMEMBER–PAY MORE, GET MORE   In general, a store that depends on very heavy customer traffic to attain its high volume must expect to pay a proportionately larger rental to get that potential traffic. Downtown areas or those near highly concentrated housing produce greater walking customer traffic; outlying shopping plazas draw nearly all customers by automobile and so must have safe, adequate parking areas. There is a psychological advantage to parking spaces in front of the stores rather than behind them. Easy accessibility from highways without congestion is important.

New shopping malls may be very beautiful, and they usually make shopping comfortable and convenient–the ads say "shopping's fun again, like a festival!" Many have covered walks to stores, several levels, and draw from as far away as one hour of highway driving. These superattractive shopping plazas have a correspondingly high rental cost per square foot, plus a percentage of the store volume as well as a proportion of taxes and maintenance increases.

But you may get what you pay for–they do pay off! If you can benefit from the generated mall traffic and do the planned volume, you will grow and attain your profit goal. Don't forget that even as large as a 25% increase in rental will rarely amount to more than 2 1/2 percent of your volume. Some shops, such as art-hobby and natural food-vitamin stores (see Appendices D and F), do very well paying high rentals in malls.

Buying traffic is the key. It is still true: *More customer traffic sells everything greater than in direct cost proportion!* Eugene Ferkauf, founder of E.J. Korvettes, said, "Pay for it if you need it; traffic is the name of the game."

Know your people, too. You will want to inquire about social and religious groups in your proposed area, not only to help assess their tastes and wants, but also to assist you in choosing media to "let them know." (Media choices are discussed in Chapter 6.) Shopping mall tenants often advertise effectively as a group, the resulting traffic a benefit to all. Ads for the mall itself may be charged to tenants pro-rata. Watch for it in your lease.

RENT AND LEASE CONCERNS

Rents are often discussed on a square foot basis, Multiply inner wall (including front) dimensions and divide into rent per year. On main shopping streets, a "front foot" store width governs the price, too. Many store locations are selected through newspapers and trade papers, which may offer a physical premises suitable for your planned store. It is certainly an advantage to a tight budget to spend less for front or interior if it does not need rebuilding, only redecorating. In many newly built store plazas, the exterior will be finished to the entrepreneur's specifications.

REAL ESTATE AGENTS   If you are seeking a particular area of your city, a realty agent is often helpful especially when there are no obvious vacancies or ads. The alert agent will usually know property owners and the present lease termination dates and will make an appropriate offer for you for the store.

Leases, like store purchases, entail an amount of bargaining, during which an attorney or a realty agent can assist you. Be sure to check *beforehand* how much this professional help will cost.

Most desirable stores today require a proportion of realty tax increases to be added to rent yearly. Many add increases in building maintenance as well, and these can be costly over the term of the lease.

LANDLORDS' OBLIGATIONS   The landlord is usually responsible for maintenance of exterior doors, walls, roof, and the like, but not for the tenant's interior, display windows, or exterior signs. Permission to make major store interior alterations, display window rebuilding, or exterior sign changes should be obtained in writing at the time of lease negotiation. At some later time, this permission may be more difficult to obtain from landlords and may even be the subject of some bargaining for some clause they want.

LEASES AND CLAUSES   Most leases in many states are standard form documents that are known to contain a number of landlord-tilted clauses. There are also blank spaces for writing *before* you sign. No oral conversation differences from the written lease will ever be admitted as evidence should a dispute arise later, so write them in!

Any explanation of lease clauses for your store premises should not take the place of an attorney to represent you. A lease is too important a step without professional experience and advice; and these explanations should merely help you understand what to expect in your preliminary work.

Your professionals should make you aware of local zoning laws or other regulations affecting your operations (many are covered in Chapter 4).

OPTIONS AND OTHER CLAUSES   The leasehold period provisions in your negotiations should take into account your new store uncertainties and should be liberal enough to give you an *option*, after the original term expires. This option clause gives you the privilege of notifying the landlord near the end of your term that you wish to extend the term under the same lease conditions (if nothing is stated) for the option period. It sometimes requires you, the leasee, to pay an increased rental for the period, part of the landlord's increased land taxes, and possibly an increase in building maintenance costs. These latter two increases are often automatic *elevator* clauses in modern original leases. All building *restrictive* clauses, as well as those relating to your ability to sell any product you want, should be negotiated originally, giving you the widest possible latitude in the event you feel that a change in merchandise direction is desirable for your store. Your right to sublease or sell the store is an important clause to be negotiated and included.

CASH NEEDS   The usual cash deposited by the tenant with the landlord to guarantee fulfillment of terms of the lease is two to three months' rent. Some states require landlords to pay interest on this deposit. The deposit is usually reclaimed by the tenant by not paying the last few months of the term, even though legally it is a deposit to guarantee the condition of the premises at the end of your lease. You will also need deposits for electric and telephone service.

At this point, your figures should give you some idea of the cash needed immediately (see Appendix T and Table 2.2). You look at the appearance of the front, floor, ceiling, walls, electrical work, rest rooms, fitting rooms, employee dressing room, and outside sign to start calling experts for cost estimates. You may need additional telephone service, too. Any time you can move into the premises following a tenant who used a similar physical store, you can probably save some rebuilding costs—a plus!

Buying a going store would seem to save original building costs, except that the owner has probably figured that into your price.

ESTIMATED FIXTURE LIST   You will need to estimate the cost of shelving, tables, racks, counters, display cases, and the like, and some shopping is in order. Used equipment tables, counters, and other items (which, in fact, may be better made than new ones), including time clocks and registers, are generally available. Modern new registers (see "point-of-sale" registers, Chapter 11), although expensive, are helpful in reminding you of sales of certain stock categories to be reordered. See Table 2.2 and 2.3.

WINDOWS   If your store enjoys a generous walking traffic, your windows are your face and your fortune, and the alluring appeal of professionally dressed windows should never be underestimated. An artistic talent for displays, ability to paint presentable signs, and the organizing skills to match merchandise to current fashion leaders are very important to your presentation to the public. If you feel that you lack these talents, try to find them in a full- or part-time employee.

Remember that first-rate window displays require new backgrounds and floor coverings periodically, as well as expensive mannequins, stands, and/or

TABLE 2.2. Store Opening: Planned Open to Buy (at retail)

Opening inventory plan	Total at cost $_____	Retail $_____
Mdse. breakdown		
Item 1.	_____	_____
2.	_____	_____
3.	_____	_____
4.	_____	_____
5.	_____	_____
6.	_____	_____
7.	_____	_____
8.	_____	_____
TOTAL	_____ TOTAL	_____

other display material to best present your wares to the area trade. A high-priced window display professional used on a regular schedule is an investment in advertising and "image." That good first impression creates your image, which may or may not persuade the customer to enter the store.

IMAGE

Your store's image is a customer's view, an impression not necessarily conforming to the fact. This delicate feeling can "turn off" a potential consumer by inappropriate handling of a complaint or exchange, or an advertising emphasis on expensive store surroundings that seem to indicate overpricing. A store owner should be careful, if possible, to match salespeople to the consumer's socio-educated level, lest he alter his image up or down. Ads may offer personal messages to convey a friendly impression. Your ads and windows can influence your image by using private brands to project exclusive quality, national brands to upgrade the quality impression of your medium-priced assortment, and an early presentation of the latest fads to show you are a fashion leader.

In a small store you cannot be all things to all people, so aim for your chosen clientele and convey the feeling that you care.

FIRST MERCHANDISE PLAN   The basic aims of your store, your target customers, location choices, product lines, and general pricing strategy should point the way toward a portion of the source market best for you. You will need time to shop for the best suppliers (vendors) of the right merchandise you envision for your store opening, and the form outline for Store Opening (Table 2.2 and repeated in Appendix S) should aid in breaking down these needs by category. The first three month's sales projections, the basis of your store's

TABLE 2.3. Planned 13 Week Quarterly Inventory and Open to Buy (retail)

Week	Holidays	Last Year Sales	Plan Sales	Actual Sales	+ or − Plan	Opening Inventory	
1.	——	——	——	——	——	——	Open Inv. ____
2	——	——	——	——	——	——	End Inv. ____
3	——	——	——	——	——	——	
4	——	——	——	——	——	——	
tot. mo.							
5	——	——	——	——	——	——	+
6	——	——	——	——	——	——	or
7	——	——	——	——	——	——	−
8	——	——	——	——	——	——	
9	——	——	——	——	——	——	+ sales ____
tot. mo.							
10	——	——	——	——	——	——	=
11	——	——	——	——	——	——	Open to Buy. Retail
12	——	——	——	——	——	——	
13	——	——	——	——	——	——	
tot. 3 mo.	——	——	——	——	End inv. ——	——	_____ open buy cost.

open to buy (how much you should order from suppliers to be delivered and ready for customer's demands during the period), will be a complete subject discussed in Chapter 5.

MARKET CREDIT   Time is needed for your source market's approval of a credit line for your store. This is the assessment by market (and credit agency) financial people of your credit worthiness up to a credit rating, a limit. It allows you to buy from these manufacturers on regular trade terms instead of cash, giving you 30 or 60 days to pay invoices after shipment to you in accordance with this supplier's terms. The efficacy of the financial aspects of your business plan is discussed in Chapter 3.

PROFESSIONAL HELP REGARDING YOUR RATING   The most experienced business people consider it a wise investment to use professional realtors and lawyers to guide them into a particular area, make store selections, advise on lease terms, and give a third party view in negotiations. It is also important to consult local bankers regarding their estimate of an area's potential because they are privy to information about businesses there. In anticipation of your new accounts, business and personal, bank people can be very helpful in estimating your future financial needs and give you added confidence in your estimates.

The local building contractor can help in estimating the rebuilding or redecorating of the store. A contractor's knowledge of all the trades involved, local licenses and permits needed, and zoning restrictions will keep you out of costly building violations and give you a more accurate physical cost forecast.

CAPITAL, MONEY, AND FINANCING

Your *capital* is the total of all the money needed to start your business, whether it is your own or borrowed money.

Probably the most misunderstood notions of new entrepreneurs are those concerning the total money needed to go into business and the true facts about borrowing possibilities at the beginning of their ventures.

This is typical "capital" talk:

John and I have this good idea for a store with special unpainted furniture. How much money do we need and where do we get it? We have a little money, and I understand the government wants to help small business. . . .

Experienced business advisors talk about *capital, cash,* and *business planning* with blunt advice.

You need cash now, *your money,* other capital later, and good credit to open and operate your own small store. Start planning with *your* money!

If you have a *small amount, don't plan a large business,* or you may turn your first step into a quagmire of problems—A DISASTER.

Don't expect others to finance your business if you have not invested in it yourself.*

Those who look to government, banks, or others to supply start-up capital are usually disappointed!

In November 1979, the head of the Small Business Administration made this statement: "Since 1977, S.B.A. has had almost no funds to loan and has made only loan guarantees with banks, and these only on existing companies, not new ones." (See Small Business Administration, Appendix Q.) You *may, indeed,* be pessimistic about being able to borrow capital funds for your store from banks or the Small Business Administration. Instead, at the outset, let us proceed with what you have.

FIRST STOCK ASSORTMENT COST   Surely if you can invest more in your stock assortment, you create a greater buying urge in more of your trade. but you must conceive of a realistic investment in your merchandise and the physical premises to match your capital. Our discussion here aims at adding up the first money needs of your store, how to apportion your money now and later, how to use the cash in your operations so that you will not run short, and how to understand the flow of this invested capital into profits and growth.

FIRST FIGURES

At first, you need capital money for:

1. Your physical store—to build or rebuild the premises, or to redecorate, repair, and rehabilitate the store, to buy fixtures, display materials, signs, and so on.
2. The opening merchandise inventory to present to your customers.
3. An estimate of your merchandise needs for the first few months.
4. Recording the opening overhead deposits (rent, power, telephone), business formation, permits, professionals, insurance costs, and the estimated running expenses of a store doing business as it is planned with you here.

Following the first figure forms (Appendices S and T) will remind you of other inquiries to be made, besides your landlord, utility company, insurance broker, contractor, and suppliers, for other expenses. You will also need "running money" for everyday operating cash.

*Some sources: Kentucky Highlands Investment Corp., "Securing Small Business Financing"; S.B.A. MA 235; Bank of America Vol X #10, Vol XIII #7; N.Y. State Dept. of Commerce "Your Business."

TABLE 3.1.

Money Plans: Needs, Estimates

USE	DEPOSITS cash now	est. month	est. year		USE	CASH NEEDS		
					Store prep			
Rent					**FIXTURES**	estimate	$	final
					Shelves, cabs, wall cases			
Telephone								
					Showcases, counters			
Power, electricity, heat								
					Hang racks, tables, etc.			
Petty cash: travel, entertainment								
					Wrap, cash counter			
Stationery, supplies								
					Register, safe			
Licenses, registrations								
					Floor			
Owner draw					walls			
					lights			
Other payroll					internal signs			
					carpenter			
Taxes, soc. sec.					plumber			
					electrician			
Operatg cash					paint, paper			
					toilet			
Audit & legal					fitting room			
					clean-up labor			
Maintenance, misc.					Machinery, carts			
					delivery equipment			
Advertising, PR.								
Insurance					FRONT: sign			
					glass			
Interest and Installments					walls			
					lights			
Other professional fees:					floor			
Contractors (realty)					display: Manneq.			
Architects (display)					stands			
					decor			

TOTALS   month _____ year _____

          cash now   .... cash now ..

Opening Plan
Merchandise   cost _____ retail _____

Wrapping, bags,
hangers,   total
selling supplies _____   now: _____

First Figures to Total for Capital Needs
- Fixture List
- Cash Deposits, etc.
- Cash for store fixup
- First Inventory
- "Running money" needed

(These first figure forms are duplicated in Appendices S and T so that they may be separated and used in your preopening work.)

PHYSICAL STORE: BUILD OR REMODEL

The physical requirements of one store may vary greatly from the required setting of the merchandise of another store, and, therefore, each must be examined, studied, and planned according to your own concept. Certainly it is easily understood that a medium to better fine jewelry store (see Appendix E) requires a more exotic presentation with more expensive fixtures and front than does an appliance store. Tildens, a fine jewelry store, planned 25 percent of its capital of $100,000 for physical premises.

If the store you are considering needs rebuilding (not just decorating) it would seem wise to get figures on rebuilding from a professional contractor who knows all the trades and permits involved, unless you have enough personal experience in construction. Most new store planners seek advice and professional blueprints from store architects, who can then supervise the construction to make sure they get what they pay for. Store architects plan this new store layout with you and then work with contractors they know, fixture suppliers who are reliable, and aim at a money total cost within your budget. An architect's fees—which, it is hoped, are affordable—can be considered insurance to get what you want within your price. You need to have these reliable building cost figures within your budget, and these professionals can help you get them. If you spend too much on the physical premises or other opening costs, you may wind up short of the running money your store needs for continuing operations (as discussed in a story of business failure in Chapter 1).

For less demanding presentations of merchandise, low-end budget stores, discount stores, appliance, or service stores (the no-frill stores), anywhere you want to convey the impression of money saving, from 10 to 15 percent of capital is suggested. As already mentioned concerning window display, the higher costs of mannequins and other expensive display fixtures is justified where your merchandise appeal changes often with style. The advice and use of professional display people to plan windows may save money and help your store attract attention on opening day and later.

YOUR VISION OF THE PREMISES YOU WANT   Study the physical stores you admire and rough out your store layout drawn *to scale* so that you can sketch in counters, register, wall fixtures, and front to give you an idea of what your store will do to present your goods. Leave room for the flow of traffic in busy times and plan counter displays to entice customers to buy additional goods.

USED FIXTURES ARE AVAILABLE   For those opening small stores with less than 10 percent of their opening capital that can be spared for fixtures, a visit to auctioneers and used fixture firms may be productive. Watch the ads for going-out-of-business sales to make a deal with the store owner for fixtures you need. Owners will get very little from dealers at the close and will probably be obligated to move everything out for the landlord, thus putting pressure on them to dispose of cases, counters, registers, and so on, helping you get them at a saving. Measure the fixtures and make cardboard scale models to fit onto your scale drawing.

Although a fine jewelry store might aim to spend between 25 and 30 percent of their opening capital for the plush setting that would best present these luxury items, a hair salon or restaurant would spend an even larger part of the invested capital on the physical plant. A "price" or discount store would best be advised to make a very plain setting, in line with the psychology of price buying.

When you have all your prices from building contractors, redecorators, electricians, plumbers, and fixture suppliers assembled with the merchandise costs, you are ready to make some decisions. Start to figure the opening merchandise costs to be ready for opening day (see Appendices S and T).

INVENTORY/SALES PLANS

OPENING MERCHANDISE INVENTORY PLAN   How much total stock should you plan to buy for your opening inventory? We have already discussed the relationship between the average stock retail value and the volume of sales as calculated in the turnover charts for various retail stores. (Average turnover of merchandise times average stock equals estimated yearly sales.) You can understand that where a fine jewelry store estimates its turnover at 1.0 to 1.25 per year, a stock of $50,000 retail ($25,000 cost) will usually produce sales of $50,000 to $65,000, rarely more than $75,000. Consider, then, the turnover of your type of store, your planned volume, and the estimated stock that will normally be necessary to produce it. Assume that your early selection is professional and that it will turn over effectively. Where you buy a going store, you must consider whether all the stock is saleable, current, and desirable for turnover.

This estimated sales volume will generate a gross profit based on your normal average markup from cost to retail. It will also generate a certain amount of net profit calculated by subtracting all the other expenses of your business. Most successful retail stores net between 3 and 8 percent of sales per year (jewelry close to 8 percent), and you can consider the likely profits in planning the first inventory investment.

Take the planned buying of the quantities needed in the assortment, colors, sizes, and such that you first feel necessary and make a total value at retail for comparison using the turnover chart (Table 2.1). You may want to adjust this total up or down, based on these estimated figures as compared to your goals. Make certain that your fiscal selections and the goods needed to replace them are ordered in sufficient time to insure a full assortment of your stock at all times. (Sales forecasts, buying plans, and open to buy will be discussed in Chapter 5.)

TABLE 3.2. Store Opening: Planned Open to Buy (at retail)

Opening inventory plan	Total at cost $____		Retail $____	
Mdse. breakdown				
Item 1.		____		____
2.		____		____
3.		____		____
4.		____		____
5.		____		____
6.		____		____
7.		____		____
8.		____		____
	TOTAL	____	TOTAL	____

OPENING STORE INVENTORY PLAN

Plan to buy your opening quantities of each category of merchandise as you visualize all the goods necessary to satisfy your customers. Each category will have several price lines and the breakdown in sizes and colors. The totals are then carried to the right at cost, and the retail value is the result of placing a retail price on each item bought on these orders and adding all of them. Your markup can then be calculated by dividing your gross profit by the total retail value.

QUARTERLY SALES PLANS–YEAR-END INVENTORY, NEW YEAR START   With an estimated year's sales already considered, it is wise to plan seasons and months in quarters in order to have comparative figures to plan with and to compare with other retailers who report their figures.

It is easiest to start to plan your yearly sales by conforming to most retailers' planned inventory-year-end at a time of a store's estimated lowest inventory. In most stores selling consumer goods, this is usually the end of January or July. It is probably preferable to end your fiscal year (contrasted to the calendar year, January 1 to December 31) on January 31; and stores do this to take advantage of their greater ability to reduce inventory through January promotions before the end of their tax year when the stock is counted. Some stores prefer January to July because there is less help during employee summer vacation time. If a store ends its year on December 31, while the large volume of holiday selling, exchanges, and refunds is still taking place, the ability of a store owner to plan a year-end inventory figure is complicated by the busy time. Therefore, most owners use January 31 as the year end.

Owners have the month of January to reduce the inventory figure in contemplation of profit taxes (see Chapter 8 and 11 on profit taxes) and the attainment of the final year's lowest inventory figures is sound planning. It also gives the owner a postponed tax obligation if incorporated to May 15, for the business and to the next tax year (personal taxes) for any *January* bonus he or she may take prior to the end of January.

QUARTERLY SALES PLANS BASED ON ACTUAL FIGURES   After you close your books at the end of the fiscal year, or when you have a starting figure ready to open, you have an actual starting inventory figure to use in the plan, and you break down the sales year into four quarters or three-month periods of 13 weeks each, as follows: February 4 weeks, March 5 weeks, April 4 weeks starting Monday and ending Sunday; May 4 weeks, June 5 weeks, July 4 weeks; August 4 weeks, September 5 weeks, October 4 weeks; November 4 weeks, December 5 weeks, January 4 weeks ending with the year-end inventory counting (see Tables 2.3, 3.3, and Appendix S).

Department stores report their monthly figures (by department) to the Federal Reserve District where they are located, compared with the same month last year. The Federal Reserve District Reports appear in daily newspapers. This gives you a chance to compare your own sales performance against the reported summary of the average of the district as a whole, and to understand when your performance is superior to other stores even if your sales are slightly behind your own of last year. This, too, gives you the factor of *trend* based on local economic health for the period to use in your plan of future sales.

Sales peaks and valleys of the year are forecast based on your rough estimate of the year's sales and of each quarterly period. This estimate is based on the holidays that influence the buying urges of your customers and is planned by the seasons with their weather influences. For example, the first period

TABLE 3.3. Year Planning: Sales Calendar (in fiscal quarters)

Sales Volume Percent Projection	$ Sales	Holidays	
1st Quarter		Ground Hog Day	
_____%	Feb. _____	Lincoln-Wash. B'day	_____
_____$		Valentines Day	
		St. Patricks	
	Mar. _____	Pre-Easter Fashions	_____
		Palm and Easter	
	Apr. _____	Dressup	_____
		Home Fixup	
	Total 1st Q. _____	Total	_____
2nd Quarter		Mother's Day	
_____%	May _____	Pre-Summer Fashion	_____
_____$		Summer Furn.	
		Memorial Day	
	June _____	Brides and Weddings	_____
		Father's Day	
		Summer Hot Promo.	
	July _____	July 4 Sales	_____
		Clearances	
		White Sales	
	Total 2nd Q. _____	Total	_____
3rd Quarter		Pre-Campus Events	
_____%	Aug. _____	Fall Fashions	_____
_____$		Back to School	
		Stationery Needs	
	Sept. _____	Labor Day	_____
		School Days	
		Jewish Holidays	
		Columbus Day	
	Oct. _____	Coat Sales	_____
		Fall Fashions	
		Home Furnishings	
		Halloween	
	Total 3rd Q. _____	Total	_____
4th Quarter		Area Promotions	
_____%	Nov. _____	Pre-Holiday Gifts	_____
_____$		Veterans Day	
		Thanksgiving Home Dressup	
	Dec. _____	Policy Ads-Gift Wrap	_____
		Gift Ads	
		Last Minute Pickups	
		Post Christmas Sale	

TABLE 3.3. Year Planning: Sales Calendar (in fiscal quarters) **(continued)**

Sales Volume Percent Projection	$ Sales	Holidays	
	Jan. _____	New Years Event	_____
		Jan. Clearance	
		Pre-Inventory	
		Crazy Clearance	
		Giveaways	_____
	Total 4th Q. _____	Total	_____
	Total Year	Year Ad	
	Sales _____	Budget	_____

(February-March-April) has pre-Easter spring dressup for both clothing and the home, and the sales of those weeks prior to Palm Sunday are usually higher. The fall periods have an expected buying urge for cold weather clothing (usually higher priced), home preholiday fixup, and the strongest period of sales in most stores, the gift-giving months. For clothing stores (or outdoor furniture), the influence of summer weather assures the planner that a well-prepared stock of warm weather fashions can bring high sales for the period. The buyer should be aware that an adverse cool period can result in leftover stock of unsaleable summer clothing at the end of July, the normal waning of summer demand, so the owner should be ready to plan an extra promotion in July to reduce that stock.

It may be necessary to get the guidance of experienced retailers as you plan your first period of sales to aid your confidence in your own planned buying. After you make the first few sales plans, you will find that instinctively you include all of the influential factors relating to the sales trend. You will also be governed by promotional factors if the particular time is one that your type of store benefits from advertising "specials" to bring in added customer traffic. In such periods as February-Washington's Birthday-Lincoln's Birthday sales, most retail stores plan two weeks of advertised price promotions to increase customer traffic and sales for this otherwise dull period. (Advertising, media, and your planned year-long promotional calendar are discussed in Chapter 6.) The benefits of off-season stimulants to increase sales in dull periods is an accepted principle of retailers because it keeps cash flowing in a period when less business is expected. Since the overhead and long-term expenses (interest, insurance, audits, and so on) on the business continue during this period, there is bound to be a net loss and less cash available. Despite the extra promotional expense, and perhaps smaller overall markup for the period, the increased sales do benefit the lifeblood of the business—the cash flow.

Total the capital need for opening your store by using the reminder lists supplied (see Appendices S and T), entering the facts or estimates that your research with landlords, power and telephone companies, insurance agents, contractors, and first merchandise plan have given you. It is then time to make your first comparison of these totals with your own money and decide whether your store goal is right or too expensive, needs to be altered, or that you need a source of additional capital.

The strategy in a new store is different from purchasing a going business, where the terms of the seller may be bargained or the length of the payment term increased.

Where your total on the planning sheets are obviously too high for the capital, you can:

- Try to squeeze more money out of personal or family sources.
- Accept a co-owner with capital (and perhaps expertise).
- Use some personal assets (real estate, life insurance policies) as collateral for a loan.
- Try to secure some long-term financing from a bank or other lender. (Few banks make start-up loans to retail stores.)

The securing of additional capital to finance your store from any source requires a complete mastery of the figures related to sales volume planned, profits expected, the cash flow projected into the coming period, and a profit and loss forecast. The lenders want to be assured that you know the source of the money to repay the loan. This is a part of a comprehensive story to tell potential creditors, who will be judging your credit worthiness and financial stability.

COMPREHENSIVE BUSINESS PLAN

The elements of a comprehensive business plan (see Appendix N) include the story of your intentions and store goals, financial and others. It tells your potential creditors how you intend to run your business profitably. The plan has words and numbers, needs the thinking ahead logically involved in sales and expense forecasting, and may require an accounting professional to help you. It should include:

1. Name, location, general description, and form of business.
2. Why your store aims for this goal, here, your customers, merchandise, and services (as you might relate them optimistically to a friend).

3. Your background expertise and training, your unique reason for being better or fitting a special need, and your strategy (other owners, if any, and background).

4. The total capital need and your own portion, plans for the inventory and category breakdown, physical store, and planned employees. Need for additional capital, why, and how it is to be used.

5. A sales plan, cash flow projection (see Cash Flow below) and expected profit, for first year, plus a profit and loss projection. Creditors and agencies often require a personal business history, bank references, and credit statements.

When you have mastered the art of forecasting the sales-to-be for the coming period, the cost of the merchandise expected to come in during that time, and the logically expected expenses to operate, you will be able to forecast the problems relating to the cash that must be available when needed. This is called a projection of the cash flow of the business.

Cash, Cash Flow, Profit

Cash is the lifeblood of a retail business, as distinguished from profit, the result of good management of money—a generated product.

Understand *cash flow* just as the words themselves seem to aptly describe: the flow of actual cash (in contrast to what is owned or due later) into and out of the business during operations. Every item of business expense to be paid in the period, from overhead to a messenger's services, needs cash to pay for it, and it affects cash flow. Every due invoice, whether for merchandise or store cleaning supplies, uses cash, and every due tax obligation must also be part of the cash need. All cash sales, all money from customers from past sales, interest from banks, dividends, or other earnings affect the cash supply coming in. Any interruption of the incoming money supply, or sudden unexpected swelling of expenses, results in the store having less cash for invoices and all other payments due, and it creates a dangerous, tense incident called a *cash crisis*.

Fixed and Variable Expenses

Many expenses of a business are considered *fixed* because they are not controlled, or are always about the same (rent, telephone, power, and other overhead costs that vary little from month to month). Others are called *variable* because of the wide fluctuation in cost from one month to another as you control these expenses by deciding what you want for the sales expected at this time. Employee cost, advertising, and the cost of merchandise due in during the period are examples of expenses that are controllable and that affect the outflow of cash. Without a plan based on a sales forecast and the buying of merchandise to match the plan, a store might exhaust the cash supply by ordering too much stock to come in during the period, or use too many employees for the amount of expected sales.

The use of a budget in each of the variable expenses is referred to as a cash budget to spend in relation to sales (cash inflow) expected. By putting these figures on a chart with the various forecasted figures (fixed expenses, sales, and such), a store operator should be able to anticipate and plan for any cash situation ahead—too little to operate or too much on hand. This forecasting of possible crises allows time to make adjustments in the forecast as the actual sales (or actual expenses) differ from the projected figures and show a different trend. The owner can then alter the variable expenses for the next period ahead to bring about a change in the end result to balance the newly adjusted, expected inflow of cash.

PROMOTIONS, TOO   The owner can promote extra business to increase the cash supply with a special sale of merchandise. Or, if a cash shortage is forecasted, go to the bank to ask for a loan for that time in the future. Without planning for the cash shortage ahead, the banker can hardly have confidence in the operation's solvency if the owner suddenly appears and asks the bank to be bailed out.

Too Much Cash on Hand

On the other hand, keeping too much cash on hand cheats the business of growth potential and gives the owner less return on the total money invested. Extra cash can better be used to earn interest for the business when invested in short-term interest certificates, or to produce extra volume of sales through an investment in a wider or deeper assortment of store products that builds permanent growth and profits. It is just as important for your cash flow chart to foresee the happy event of too much cash on hand as it is to foresee a shortage that forces you to cut expenses drastically or look for personal assets to use for collateral for a loan.

THE GOAL IS FINANCIAL CONTROL   Your first cash flow projection chart, or any other forecast will not be as accurate as your later ones, but keep in mind that adjustments to correct for any errors in predictions have the effect of financially controlling your operations, which is all you are really seeking. Adjustments and planning make you more knowledgeable concerning the technical inner workings of your business, and that will impress potential creditors or their agencies who will have confidence in you as a professional merchant, not just a storekeeper.

Look at the cash flow example (Table 3.4) and take your figures from your first figure forms and your anticipated variable expenses to get the feel of what will happen to the cash in a few months, if your sales forecast becomes a reality. Try changing the sales projection to an actual 20 percent drop to see the effect on your cash supply and a crisis-to-be. Perhaps all of these headings may not apply to you, but generally they will be understood for use in other circumstances.

TABLE 3.4.

CASH INTAKE	• Estimated net cash receipts (sales forecast)
	• Cash expected from past credit sales
	• Bank interest, other income
CASH OUTFLOW	• Overhead expenses (fixed—rent, power, telephone), interest (other fixed) on loans, dividends to stockholders
	• Audit cost, insurance, dues, subscriptions
	• Installment payments on fixtures, auto, register, etc.
	• Variable—salaries, wages, FICA taxes due
	• Other taxes, maintenance, window trim, selling commissions, special professional services
	• Invoices for merchandise or supplies received

OPERATING CASH ON HAND—RUNNING MONEY   In discussing too much cash on hand for the best return on investment for the store, the question is often asked, "how much is the ideal amount?" Many merchants suggest the simple formula of a sum equal to one month's total cost of running expenses, overhead plus salaries, and so on, all your cash outflow as noted above. Retail stores are subject to changes in fortune or disasters from storms, fires, floods, or theft, and the running money on hand can cover any delay in insurance payment (if you are covered) to keep you operating without a lapse of time, which could prove costly (see Chapter 10 on insurance).

USES FOR EXTRA CASH   Where you have an oversupply of cash on hand, there are other programs in addition to the outside investment for income, or the new increased assortment of stock to bring in additional volume. Often, it is a rebuilding of the physical premises that offers the best chance for permanent growth, or adopting a newer, more costly advertising or promotion program to change your image or increase your appeal to a larger clientele. The choice of vehicles to propel your business to greater volume of sales and profits is the growth on which your personal financial goals are based. The extra cash on hand is a first sign to alert you to the choice of methods or strategies to attain that growth and success.

TABLE 3.5. Cash Flow: Year Projection

CASH (beg. mo.)	FEB.	MAR.	APR.	MAY	JUN.	JUL.	AUG.	SEP.	OCT.	NOV.	DEC.	JAN.	TOT.
On Hand													
In Bank													
Other													
INCOME (month)													
Sales													
Other income													
Credit sales													
TOTAL													
Purchases due													
Expenses													
Salary													
Wages													
FICA													
Taxes													
Overhead													
Maint. etc													
Ins./Prof.													
Transp./Petty													
Interest													
Other Cash													
TOTAL													
End month													
Cash Flow excess.													
Months cumulative													

Profit and Loss

Another projection required in your comprehensive business plan concerns profit and loss items, which are much more inclusive than those elements in cash flow. These include all items on an "accrual" basis, when income, costs, and expenses are incurred, (happen) rather than just when the cash changes hands, as in cash flow, which merely monitors your liquid cash position at any moment.

Working on projections gives you financial know-how. With an understanding of profit and loss and the prepared projection, you will have a clearer understanding of your true net worth (net value of the business), a projected net profit, a general financial estimate of the future, and any tax liability. Unlike cash flow, these profit and loss items to be projected on a chart include deferred payments or receivables from customers, depreciation items on front, fixtures, machinery, and the like, and bad debts—when customer accounts are no longer deemed collectible. (See Appendix W.)

Break-Even Point

For theoretical purposes, some storekeepers discuss a breakeven point in their sales volume below which their business is losing money. This study, which has more relevance in the manufacturing business, takes an average markup (see Chapter 2) for all merchandise in a given period, and by projecting sales and probable expenses for that period on a graph, meets a point below which there is a net loss to the business. Because of the natural unavoidable peaks and valleys of the year's sales at retail and of the common fact that with a fiscal year ending on January 31, the break-even point is rarely attained until approximately December 1 (if not later), the calculation of this figure seems relatively unimportant.

Vendors and Credit Agencies

It is to your advantage to be thoroughly familiar with your financial data as you are interviewed about your financial structure by vendors (suppliers) and their credit agencies. Your market of manufacturers, jobbers, or distributors—your vendors—subscribe to credit agencies (such as Dun and Bradstreet) to exchange up-to-date information on their customers, including you. Your application to D&B for a credit rating, submitting your business plan, will invite a visit from a representative to personally review your data, discuss any phase the agency wants explained, and return with an opinion on which your credit rating will be based. Smaller supplier firms that subscribe to Dun and Bradstreet, for instance, depend on this rating almost entirely, and they check it from time to time. Larger firms use the rating as only a portion of their credit manager's evaluation of your credit limit of their merchandise (credit line) when you place an order.

A good rating is essential as an alternative to paying cash before delivery (C.B.D.) or cash on delivery (C.O.D.) when you place orders. Most better sources will not sell for cash or C.O.D., and a good rating is, therefore, or greatest importance to your lifeline of supply. Your credit worthiness is reviews periodically or whenever some subscriber notifies the agency of some negative information. A good credit rating is worth the effort to upgrade with such agencies as Dun and Bradstreet by submitting latest information from your accountant. "Best" market sources have superior styles and quality and sell only well-rated accounts. It is worth the cost of borrowed money to pay and discount your due invoices to retain a superior rating.

Credit agency ratings reveal an estimated net worth of your firm as well as provide an estimate of how promptly you pay invoices. You may often be called to supply recent financial data because in recent years Dun and Bradstreet has been criticized for offering data on debtors too out of date to be reliable. Any subscriber can request a complete report on a business firm to secure more detailed information about executives, dates, and general evaluation by the agency's staff. These reports (usually obtainable at your bank) figure in considering the background of a future partner, associate, or management employee.

YEARLY FINANCIAL REPORTS   Yearly financial reports are expected by credit agencies to bring the file up-to-date, and your accountant will prepare them at the end of your fiscal year. Toward the end of this period, your accountant's professional advice is very valuable for merchandising decisions to save year-end taxes and to guide operations so that the final data on the statements are more favorable. For financial strategy discussions with your accountant on an even plane, you should be familiar with expense control, inventory totals, elements of profit and loss, and the cash flow chart. If you have no accountant, you should, on your own, be familiar with the reasons to effect inventory reduction, for example, for the benefit of the year's overall performance record and your tax obligations.

Cost of Living Budget

During their busy preparations for a new store, new owners often neglect accounting for their own personal income needs, or they expect to draw a salary at once, even before the store opens. But, drawing funds before actually making profits has the effect of reducing the capital invested, and it is unwise. A new store is always "tight" for cash—it shows little profit. If you are otherwise employed, you should try to remain on salary as long as possible during your preparations and your personal living requirements should be accounted for by working with a cost of living budget (see Table 3.7 and Appendix X).

TABLE 3.7. Personal Living Budget

Monthly Payments

Rent (or house)	_____	Invested	
Car cost paymt.	_____	other income	_____
Car, other insur.	_____		
Appliance furn. pay	_____	Part-time work	_____
Home impv., loan pay	_____		
Health, life ins.	_____	Int.	_____
Misc. payments	_____	Misc.	_____
Total	_____	Other Income	_____
Household:			
Food	_____	Minimum monthly	
Clean, supply	_____	NEEDED	
Telephone	_____		
Power, gas, water	_____		
Maint., repair	_____		
Drugs, clothing clean	_____		
Aver. Dr. and dentist	_____		
Travel, auto upkeep	_____		
Mags., papers, dues, personal petty	_____		
Dining out	_____		
Fed., state taxes	_____		
Other taxes	_____		
Clothing or house purchases	_____		
TOTAL EXPENSES	_____		

LOANS AND BORROWED FUNDS: EQUITY VS. DEBT

The ownership in any piece of property is known as your *equity* in it, or your share of ownership. Therefore, when a lender requires a share of ownership, a part of your equity, as a prerequisite to granting you a loan, it is called "equity financing." Normally, you would sign over some shares of stock of the corporation to represent the agreed loan amount, and the lender would hold those shares, hoping for a financial advantage from this type of investment, possibly even selling them back at many times the original loan (venture capital lenders).

EQUITY LOANS   The major advantage to your company of an equity loan is that the business is not usually burdened with the necessity of making immediate cash repayments of principal or interest, which might be a drain on the cash from a fledging operation. The principal disadvantage, of course, is that you are sacrificing some of your independence, some of your schemes and strategy, your plans and expertise, as well as hard work. You are selling some of your financial future without even getting expertise labor that taking a co-owner might add, as well as the capital infusion you seek.

DEBT LOANS REQUIRE PAYMENTS REGULARLY   Other loans made to your company on terms of a regular repayment schedule of interest and principal (amortization, scheduled repayment of principal) are called debt loans, the usual loans made by banks to businesses. Here, the strict requirements of the repayment schedule can be too much of a drain on the cash and can act to block the cash flow and natural growth of the operation. During periods of very high interest rates, both borrower and lender must ask:

> Can this business afford such a loan? Can the expected sales generate enough profits over expenses to repay on this time schedule as promised without hampering operations?

Overburdening at the outset often discourages a new owner or may sap the financial strength of the business before it has time to generate the profits needed to move ahead. For original capital loans, as contrasted with short-term operations loans, most banks consider new retail firms too risky and will require outside collateral, as well as personal signatures of the principal owners (personal guarantee with all personally owned property in jeopardy).

JUSTIFYING LOAN INTEREST EXPENSE   Operating loans related to expansion of facilities—a promising new advertising program, a new merchandise direction, or depth of inventory related to increasing volume and profits—are always the more pleasant and possible loan prospects. Increased profit will justify the loan cost. A plan for a new direction or expansion is the very essence of the judgment skill of the operator who develops an intuitive sense of restlessness with the status quo, a yearning to build and expand on yesterday's victories. An expansion program that logically promises growth impresses the banking community and gets your loan.

Seasonal Need for Funds: Short-Term Loans

At the peak sales periods of the year, such as holiday gift-giving times, your sales projection plan will show that you anticipate needing higher than normal inventories to meet these sales. At the time that the invoices for this extra merchandise are payable, there is often a shortage of the cash in the bank to cover them, and your local bank will set up a revolving credit to have money available as needed. You arrange for this months in advance.

DISCOUNT BILLS TO RAISE YOUR CREDIT RATING The wise course of borrowing to discount all bills will be reflected in the reputation and rating given you by the credit agencies used by your suppliers. Anticipation of these needs long in advance at your local bank insures that no crisis will appear during your busiest season. Maintaining a good credit standing with the best suppliers is well worth the cost of interest charges. (Loss of credit rating because of over extension is one reason for the collapse of E.J. Korvettes, see Appendix C.)

It is important to note that in any analysis of the credit worthiness of a new business, the evaluation includes your own personal credit record down through the years. Your personal integrity in your dealings is one of the first general aspects involved. If you have never borrowed and repaid loans, or have never been extended personal credit and proved worthy, it may be more difficult to assure the creditor or agency that they should take the risk, because of your "no record." It is often suggested, therefore, that while still working in a salaried job, you take a bank loan and repay it promptly to create such a record. In today's world of charge cards, most people, however, have left some credit mark.

Bootstrap Financing

Starting with a tiny amount of capital and reinvesting constantly without draw until your capital has grown to normal size.

Bootstrap financing was quite common and possible back in 1905 when my parents opened their little store with $900. But even then, that was considered a shoestring beginning. Starting with too little capital is very difficult, but if you must do it, "stretch your shoestring" by buying minimum make-do fixtures, and such, making the most out of every dollar you have. Carefully select only fast turnover goods in weekly quantities. Test out merchandise and ideas in flea markets. Buy with great restraint and rebuy as needed, using all cash receipts. Do everything yourself, disciplining yourself to use little expense and reusing all money for cash flow generating profits. If you can continue to operate in this manner without business flow interruptions, you will be building up capital by the super effort of pulling yourself up to a successful start.

Government Help

Many eager store planners become convinced that "big brother" government is waiting with cash to help them get into a new small business. Most have heard stories and assume that the Federal Small Business Administration is just such an agency with sums sufficient for their needs at special lower interest rates as soon as they sign. Unfortunately, that is not true. The S.B.A., since disclosure of the scandal in 1977, has had little or no money of its own to lend and remains largely a guarantor to bank lenders *to certain* specific classes of borrowers (women and minorities such as blacks and other native Americans), very strictly administered by cooperating banks and S.B.A. jointly. Since 1977 applications sat for over a year of delay, but the Federal Government has recently received word of the cooperation of some of these banks and the S.B.A., offering more efficient handling procedures. Most banks still find small business loans too time-consuming to be profitable, so they avoid them, and others require a minimum loan amount of $15,000. Other bank policy says that *any* loans to stores (without very solid collateral) are available only to firms with several years of solid performance that can be proved—no new ventures (at prime interest rates plus 1-2 percent).

VENTURE CAPITAL AND GOVERNMENT-SPONSORED SIMILAR GROUPS*   Venture capital lenders are individuals, groups, corporations, banks, insurance companies or any others delicated to taking higher risks than other lenders and gambling with expectation of high capital gain returns rather than simple interest. They supply long term growth capital with an investment in the equity (corporate stock) of the borrower concern in the hope of a return many times the invested capital in three to five years. These capital sources are rarely available to small retail stores, except perhaps the government sponsored agencies for minorities.** They invest in promising growth manufacturing.

Other very high interest sources of capital are commercial finance companies and small loan companies, whose demands for collateral and/or cosigners rule out many of the new retailers even if they are willing to pay the interest rate between 25 and 30 percent. The only collateral interest in a retail business is the value of the lease (if any), the cash register, safe, and other machinery, or a car. Still, on rare occasions some loans have been made where the loan officer admires the business plan and the management (who must sign personally).

Despite the discouraging service to entrepreneurs seeking start-up capital without any other recourse, many do go to banks who will make special cases out of unusually promising business plans and superior personal expertise. You will have a better chance of securing a loan by following what is suggested for any loan request:

- Anticipate for many months; loans take time and last-minute pleas are never accepted.
- With your prepared business plan, be ready to explain the special need for money over your own capital (Living expenses do not qualify.)

*Federal M.E.S.B.I.C.S. (Minority enterprise Small Bus. Investment companies.) The S.B.A. refers you.

**Some states have agencies, such as the Small Business Investment Company of California.

- Show a projected profit and loss statement for each of the years of the duration of the loan.
- Show a projected cash flow table for the first 12 months of the loan period and be able to explain it.
- Explain the use of the loan proceeds in terms of generating profits that would be available to repay the loan.
- Always include ample funds in the first request because no later added "need" plea is usually considered.
- The terms of the loan are more easily agreed upon when related to cash flow and projected profit.

When you are seeking loans, don't hestitate to use all your personal connections, introductions, and business associations that may give you preferential treatment. Your turndown at any bank should not prevent you from asking that loan officer if he or she knows of any other loan source. Often attorneys and accountants are able to assist in finding lenders.

Alternative Ways of Adding to Capital: Co-Owners

Most new entrepreneurs who require additional starting capital that has been denied them in the usual lending sources consider a working partner (or a co-stockholder in a corporation) one of the most practical solutions because it promises additional responsible management happily wedded into the opera tion. Expertise in some other phase of management should, indeed, be one of the very important motives behind the invitation to join together, because the mutual respect of two contributing working partners (see Appendix M, Partnership Agreements, and Chapter 4) will go a long way toward preventing slight personality differences from erupting into chaos. Be aware, though, that many co-owners who start out on a very friendly social plane develop animosities as the business progresses and their personal expertise becomes secondary. At that time disruptive problems often arise as the result of petty social jealousy involving spouses and children maturing to possible roles in the business.

The working co-ownership should only be entered after some investigation into background and extensive open conversation into modes of opera 'tion so that differences can be uncovered and compromised (in writing) before the alliance is seriously welded and legal agreements closed. A Dun and Bradstreet report on the business background of any prospective partners is the first step to uncover any possible character flaw (honesty, integrity). Hold conversations with former associates where possible. The fact that a new partner may be related by family ties does not obviate the necessity for investigation and for effective written agreements (see Appendix M and note "Escape Clause"). (This subject is also discussed in Chapter 4.)

Loan Plans Preparation: Fraud

Some companies may offer to prepare a loan plan to the Small Business Administration directly, or to a bank requesting an S.B.A. guarantee commitment to the bank. They also may offer great assurance of success. But, remember these facts:

- The average fee for such preparation should be approximately $400-$500.
- No preparing service company can *guarantee* the delivery of such a loan (despite several exposed fraudulent companies' verbal guarantees to that effect).
- In many cities, agencies like S.C.O.R.E. and the Executive Volunteer Corps. will prepare such loan presentations free, or will direct you to a government agency especially constituted to prepare the loan presentation without charge (S.B.A. program special for minorities).
- California recently indicted the Peoples Financial of California (P.F.C.), based in Los Angeles, for fraudulently taking $1,500-$3,000 to deliver loans, with S.B.A. guarantee, to many companies. The oral promise to get the loan was never kept; the fee was.

FORMING
THE COMPANY

A retail business needs a legal form; its financial future (and yours) will be affected by the form you choose. Therefore, study the choices, which are basically three—sole proprietorship, partnership, and corporation (with variables)—and select the one that is best for you.

You are undoubtedly becoming aware by now that running a store requires a variety of knowledge and skills. You may be able to "go it solo," or you may find it desirable to take a *co-operator* to help you. The word *co-operator* is fitting because whether this co-owner becomes a partner or a co-stockholder in a corporation with you, it is essential that there be *cooperation* between you.

After reviewing this book and the basic demands of your store, consider the following carefully:

- Do you have all the skills of administration, sales, promotion, display, advertising, and others that you feel would be desirable, besides knowing the merchandise?

- The need for additional capital may be a motive to seek a co-owner but there are other considerations: do you want to be tied physically to the full schedule of store hours without relief? What if illness strikes; who will "watch the store?"
- What about personal liability to creditors of the business should things go wrong? Would you risk your personal savings or home?

Remember that the form you choose at the outset may be changed later, if you feel it desirable.

Table 4.1 shows advantages and the characteristics of each of the forms to consider when you discuss possibilities with legal counsel or others.

TABLE 4.1.

I. SOLE PROPRIETORSHIP	The very simplest form, easiest to get into and out of, *your* money or your "family's." *You* own it, make all decisions, take the risks, and get benefits. Your other property is *at risk*. Pay taxes individually.
II. PARTNERSHIP	Two or more co-owners operate *dependently,* each being fully liable for liabilities of the business. Taxes paid individually. Inexpensive registration in county (D.B.A.).
III. CORPORATION	One or more individuals prepare "Certificate of Incorporation" according to each state laws, strictly controlled and taxed where you operate. Cost most to use, special taxes, but gives owners limited liability for failure of the business.

I. SOLE PROPRIETORSHIP

With the sole proprietorship form, you can start your business using your own name, as it is, or under a D.B.A. (Doing Business As) certificate, which is filed for a fee in the county of operation. Buy three copies of the form in a commercial stationery store, complete, and take to your county clerk with cash or a certified check (amount varies from $25-$50). In most places you do not have to file any certificate if you use your name "as is." In most areas banks will not give you an account in the business name without showing a copy of the certificate you have filed. With the D.B.A. registration, you may call yourself "Company" or "Co.," but not "Corporation," "Inc.," or "Limited," as these are reserved for corporations under state law. When you choose a name, check your local phone books to eliminate possible conflicts with other firms and try to use one that helps to identify your specialty.

For example, under a D.B.A., you may use "John Smith Co." or "Joe's Perfect Pizza." Without it, you may use "John Smith" (if that is your name), even adding descriptive words such as "modern art design" under it.

The ease of getting into business—you can be registered and "in business" in a few hours—is matched by the lack of notice necessary to leave it. Just pay the creditors and the landlord, close your doors, and you're free. A sole proprietorship is a very effective way of opening up quickly and operating with your own money. It is very satisfying to those who love to "do it their own way," especially when working with or for others presents problems. Personal satisfactions are matched with ways of building up one's personal assets over the years. Although all profits of the business are taxed as personal earnings of the owner, there are accounting methods that are helpful in the accumulation.

LENDERS AND SOLE PROPRIETORSHIPS   Sole proprietorship does not much interest lenders of capital because of the very nature of "doing it alone" without a back-up helper. Lending to a sole proprietor becomes a personal loan. There is hardly a feeling of stability or continuity in a business where all the skill rests in one individual and his or her health. Some lenders insist on life insurance policies and look to the person's other assets for security. This type of ownership is hardly attractive to very capable employees unless there is some offer of future share.

The principal drawbacks to the sole proprietorship are the requirement of being expert in all phases of your business as you grow and the lack of coverage when you cannot be there. In the other forms of ownership you have someone to help you, but of course, divide the gain.

II. PARTNERSHIP

Two or more individuals can enter a voluntary arrangement to operate a business together under descriptions in the Uniform Partnership Act. Registration with the county is very similar to sole proprietorship filing using a D.B.A., except that the form denotes the partnership name of the business, address, and such, for a similar charge. The clerk will stamp and return two copies of this form, one of which you use to open a business bank account. The other you use for all licenses, sales taxes, and the like.

GENERAL PARTNERS ARE PERSONALLY RESPONSIBLE   Profits of the partnership are distributed as per *their own agreement* (see Appendix M), and each pays income tax as an individual on that share and any other income.

Each is fully responsible personally for any unpaid debts of the partnership unless he or she previously registered as a limited partner in accordance with the regulations of the state. There must always be at least one general partner who is fully liable. A partner is a "silent" partner when there is a contribution of money, but no participation in the running of the business (usually registers as a limited partner). Limited partners' losses are held to the amount of original investment.

Investing and working together require planning, investigation, and a formal written agreement called a partnership agreement (see Appendix M). This covers contribution to capital, responsibilities, distribution of profits, and any other item on which there may be possible later disagreement. It must always include a "buy/sell" clause. The advantages of copartnership and co-operators of a corporation are similar in the sense that two heads are better than one when they cover for each other and add the skills of each. Some of the advantages of a partnership are:

- Pooling of capital funds, larger total without the need to repay.
- Joining of talents hopefully complementary.
- Dividing of responsibility: physical covering for store hours, relief, vacations, illness; executive duties divided, performing tasks more skillfully covering what each does best.

Capital fund loans cannot be made as equity participation to partnerships because lenders would become liable as partners.

PARTNERS ADD HELP AND MONEY   A pooling of funds often avoids the need for outside financing and avoids the necessity for allotting funds for repayment. This consideration of getting added capital should be augmented by the benefits of additional expertise.

Hardly anyone is gifted in all the phases and skills necessary for a successful store. The best reason for merging the talents of a prospective partner with yours is the happy meshing of divergent abilities that will complement each other.

Well-chosen partners may be a great boon to the business and each other. If you are not imaginative or creative, try to find these abilities in a partner who will need your solid, persistent steadiness while your company benefits from his gambling touch. Your partner may admire your instinct for pricing or merchandising; you may like your partner's patient selling technique of making friends for the store. Who will know store maintenance best, have a flair for display, handle employees, keep records? The benefits to your business are obvious where both operate in their most expert sphere of work. Important, also, is dividing the burden.

HAPPY PARTNERS WITH FULL TRUST AND SHARED BURDEN
Happiest is the partnership when the long schedule of hours may be shared, the enjoyment of a relaxed vacation planned, and the coverage during illness assured. The division of responsibility of management and the use of the acknowledged talents of each promise a happy mutually respectful partnership that is most able to endure. The company needs and the use of partners' special abilities help both to overlook glaring differences in life-styles, political viewpoints, or other personal traits.

But—partnerships have problems, such as:

- Partnerships are automatically dissolved by death, bankruptcy, and possibly by imprisonment of a partner, thus affecting longevity (although an agreement may provide for continuation).
- Partnerships are subject to personal turmoil, disagreements, mistrust, and jealousy.

KNOW OTHER POSSIBLE PROBLEMS   When strangers are brought together without thorough investigation, where talents and work habits are unknown, it is easy to see how one could describe partnerships as highly speculative ventures. You must, therefore, approach such a decision with the thought in mind that:

- As a partner you are responsible for all the misdeeds and debts of the business with all your personal wealth. In a partnership, because of the close personal relationship, you are responsible for all your partner's actions as well as your own. Therefore, you must, as far as possible, be able to trust your partner.

Look up your prospective partner's history in business with a Dun and Bradstreet report at your bank. Check him or her with the Better Business Bureau and the Chamber of Commerce. Check his or her personal credit through the local credit bureau (store subscribers or bank subscribers have access to their files). Check with former neighbors, co-workers, and competitors, and then spend as much time with the prospective partner discussing past experience, goals, and how they are to be attained.

Investigate a person thoroughly before even considering a merger. If this is your idea, you might propose a time span, an "engagement period," to make certain it is happy for you, the prime mover. (See Partner/Stockholder, Appendix M with the "escape clause" feature.) You (and your attorney) must make the decision based upon what you have learned. Balance out the good features with the other facts. Discuss any doubts with your prospective co-owner and compromise your differences *before* you take the elements of your partnership agreement to your attorney to finalize all points.

After you have settled into a successful merger of your talents, you should be aware of the tendency to develop personal animosities over the years, especially when tensions are heightened during bad business periods. Personal social contact, especially involving spouses or children as workers, has soured many working, cooperating partnerships.

As in marriage, there are some risks.

III. CORPORATION

The corporation form of business for retailers is the most popular because of the limitation of the business liability to the assets it owns, reserving the owners' property from jeopardy. Corporate debts are not chargeable to officers or shareholders personally. The corporation is a *separate "entity,"* controlled by legislation in the states where it does business and is *taxed there* for profits, *even though it was formed in another state.* Its assets and property are separate from the owner's and the transfer of property to or from the corporation must be properly accounted for to the state in the corporate books (taxes paid where due). It acts, does business, hires you as an "employee" and pays taxes as a separate "being." Call it "Corp.," "Inc.," or "Ltd."

- A corporation has rights and privileges differing from the rights and privileges of those who own and operate it. It survives them and preserves those rights for transfer to others, as well as the continuation of its own identity.
- It can increase or decrease the number of owners (shareholders) without altering the nature, purpose or rights of its operations. (See Subchapter "S" later in this section)
- It confers on stockholders "equity" ownership without any management responsibility . . . nor are they liable for any unpaid debts of the corporation. Corporate officers are responsible for unpaid wages or withholding taxes.
- The incorporation of a business is more expensive.
- It is more difficult and technical, often requiring an attorney. (See Appendix L, Corporate formation without an attorney.)
- It requires more bookkeeping, records and tax filing than other forms.
- It must pay state fees, franchise taxes, profit taxes (exception Subchapter "S") and sometimes City taxes.
- It is regulated by state and federal governments, which control issuance, sale, and transfers of stock, and other inner business relating to stockholders.

Each state in the United States (and province in Canada) has its own regulations for setting up, or incorporating, a business: Some laws are very simple, inviting to the small business entrepreneur to do without an attorney. Stationery stores, for example, have corporate kits containing Articles of Incorporation, which must be completed and sent to the state department of corporations (in the state capital usually). (See Appendix L.)

In all corporations, an investor's portion of the total value of the company is represented by shares. When a corporation issues 200 shares of stock and you have invested in half of the total capital, you normally would be issued 100 shares of stock to indicate that ownership. Shares are issued, bought, and sold in accord with federal and state regulations, but those laws do not set the price of shares. The ease of stock transfers and sales has made the buying of equity in public corporations on the stock exchanges of the world a very popular investment for the general public.

A small company whose shares are all issued to its few investors is called a closed corporation (sometimes family held), because no shares are available for the public to buy. To sell shares publicly, corporations must adhere strictly to the regulations, and legal advice is needed. Corporations who are listed on stock exchanges conform to the exchange regulations as well. Buying or selling shares does not affect the running of the business until stockholders at their meeting (at least once a year) elect directors, who in turn give new officers the control. You must do the same in yours.

States differ on fees for a new corporation charter; some charge less than others, but may charge more for income taxes on yearly profits. Many states, such as New York, have a minimum tax on profits made in the state, which is called a franchise tax. For example, a Delaware corporation operating in New York State is subject to income tax on profits made in New York and must pay the minimum yearly franchise fee ($250) even if no profit was made.

A corporate entity accounts to the state in its reports, and therefore a corporation form is easier for lenders to deal with. Because of regulations requiring sworn financial reports and because the funds are segregated from those of the owners, a lender can feel more secure in following the operations of the borrower corporation. For venture capital lenders who want to hold shares of stock (equity) in the hope of reselling them to the management later at a large capital gain, this form is ideal. Banks, too, look favorably on the fact that death or incapacity of owners will not impede the continuing life of the business since the stock can be transferred.

Corporations are subject to state and federal income taxes on profits. Because of this and other state regulations, the standards of bookkeeping for the corporation are more exacting. Federal taxes on corporate profits begin at 16 percent for the first $25,000 and go to 46 percent when over $100,000. Estimated prepayments are required quarterly. State taxes are a smaller percentage, but most states charge a minimum even when no profits are made. Some cities do, too, such as New York, with a $125 yearly minimum.

Stockholders of corporations receive some of the profits regularly, called *dividends,* on their shares and must pay an individual income tax on this corporate profit. Since the corporation also pays a tax on the same income, it is often referred to as "double taxation," a great source of irritation among taxpayers. The subchapter "S" is one type of corporation that avoids the double tax on profits.

Subchapter "S" Corporation

This form of corporate structure is often referred to as "small" because it lends itself to fewer stockholders and a simpler kind of business. Here are reasons that may make it good for you:

- There is no corporate profits tax; owners pay their own individual income tax on the share of the profits. No untaxed profits remain in the corporation.
- Stockholders report their individual share of ordinary corporate losses and charge them against other income.
- Long-term capital gains are reported as stockholder's own.
- Stockholders may add the corporate charitable contributions (their own share) to their own for tax purposes.
- Stockholders benefit from fringe benefit plans with qualified pension and profit sharing, sick pay exclusion, and accident and health insurance.
- Owners benefit by using a fiscal year for the corporation rather than calendar year to postpone personal income tax liability or stretch it over a two-year period.

There is no limit on the volume or profits to be eligible under Subchapter "S" 2553 of the I.R.S. code; but there must be less than 10 stockholders, issuance of only one class of stock, no relationship (ownership) of any other corporation, no nonresident aliens as stockholders, and not more than 80% of receipts from outside the United States in one year. The corporation may not have more than 20% of its annual receipts in "passive" income such as dividends, rents, royalties, interest, or sales of securities.

All stockholders must agree and any new stockholder must sign an assent at once. The request to the I.R.S. must be made within 30 days of the beginning of the fiscal year of the corporation *after* it is legally in existence.

Taking a co-worker as a partner or costockholder is very much the same in advantages and disadvantages, and the agreement between them becomes a stockholder's agreement (see Appendix M) when you choose to incorporate. The same reason for seeking an escape clause is present, and the other clauses that are agreed upon may call for the issuance of a *different* number of shares than the percentage of total capital calls for. You and your coowner may agree to any arrangement of money contribution, work load, ownership of shares of stock, bonuses, or any other phase of the operation, and it is no concern of anyone else. But be sure it is in writing because the *uncertainty* of rights between the coowners often produces more disharmony than the right itself.

P.C.: PROFESSIONAL (PERSONAL) CORP.

P.C. is the more recent development of the use of incorporation to protect individuals and/or partners who perform professional services from the threat to their own property of malpractice suits. In addition to this personal protection these professionals are given free use of corporate rented or owned assets, (cars, apartments, and others) charge cards, and other imaginative "perks." The advantage of their use is obvious over payment with their own after-tax dollars. The I.R.S. has been promising more stringent control.

REGULATIONS, REGISTRATIONS, LICENSES, TAXES

The store owner must be aware of the zoning regulations of the community, sign and building restrictions, and special permits that may be required to do business. Property, zoning, and business permits vary. City hall is the best source of information; a contractor or attorney should know the physical limits, and the business advisor should be helpful as well (Appendix Y).

Many cities limit door-to-door selling, canvassing, and distributing of ad material; others license it. Most cities require permits to do alterations in your premises, special licenses to qualify plumbers and electricians, and may even restrict your doing other work yourself.

Each state has a list of business operations it controls by licenses, fees, qualifying examinations, and such. Most apply where health, food, liquor, drugs, or treatment on face, hair, or skin is involved. Some states have added auto inspection and repair, and television or home appliance repair licensing to attempt to control poor service. States control real estate selling, billboards, vending machines, and, of course, legal and medical qualifying licenses. (A complete list is available in state offices and at the local Chamber of Commerce.)

Cities have attempted to cover areas not covered by the states in their consumer affairs testing and licensing offices. The list controlled is huge, some requiring a large yearly fee. New York, California, and other states try to insure legal behavior by requiring a large deposit for pushcarts, street vending, auctioneers, bingo games, catering, refuse removal, employment agencies, home improvement contracting, pawnbrokers, second-hand or used dealers, locksmiths, laundries, and all kinds of cafes and entertainment premises. (The local list is available at the city office of licenses.) Generally, you must be over 18 years of age, be qualified if skill is involved (proof of minimum working experience), and be a citizen or have secured a green card (indicating intention of becoming a citizen), submit business registration, and state any criminal record. States also have a large list of business activities controlled through licensing.

58

Sales Taxes and Other Regulations

Many states have enacted sales tax legislation making stores responsible as collectors of varying percentages of the sales of many items. The usual exception is food and drugs, but many states collect taxes on certain foods, such as candy, and only except prescription drugs.

At the local office for this state levy, you register by showing your certificate (sole proprietorship, partnership, or corporation) and receive authority to collect the tax. In certain states (California is one), you must deposit a sum as a sort of bond to guarantee your compliance and payment of the collected tax. You will also receive a resale certificate allowing you to purchase from sources without paying the tax on the theory that you will be collecting and paying tax on this item to the authority later. In order to sell to anyone and not be responsible for the tax when you do not collect it, you must list the customer's name, address, and resale number. You will receive forms regularly and are responsible to complete them properly and forward the taxes collected. Banks are authorized to receive sales taxes. Some states require you to segregate these funds as collected, with social security and withholding from employees in a separate account.

States and cities have certain special taxes. A few cities, such as New York, have enacted "occupancy tax" regulations, which charge any business premises with a percentage of the rent up to 5%, to be paid quarterly. The state of New Jersey has a personal property tax that applies to inventory, fixtures, and other capital assets.

Employer Responsibilities

Every business that employs people on any basis, except that of independent contractual labor, must obtain an employer identification number from the local I.R.S. office of the federal government, using form #SS4 (10-67). This registers responsibility to collect all proper social security payments and federal, state, and city taxes prepaid by all employees as prescribed by these authorities. In the case of corporations, all persons are employees even if you are the only worker, the only owner. (Always get an invoice to cover independent labor from whom you have not deducted social security.)

All officers of a corporation are responsible for wages and for withheld deductions just as they would be in a sole proprietorship or partnership, with all their personal assets. Your company is not responsible for the deductions for labor that is performed as an independent, for particular tasks of separate labor that is billed and can be proved to be as claimed. The state and your city hold you responsible, too, for taxes not deducted from employees.

Your local I.R.S. office will send you forms regularly instructing you what percentage of social security deductions to take from wages paid, based on total pay, employee dependents, and where employees reside (in case of resident vs. nonresident). Most employers find it easier to use a current tax chart, which is carried by commercial stationers for about $6. The business firm is responsible for a payment of social security itself equal to that of its employees, and it pays all of this usually to its local bank as a collecting agent for all the taxing authorities. It also pays federal unemployment tax.

All corporate employers (with even one employee—you) must carry Worker's Compensation and Disability Benefits Insurance for employees, in most states. There are labor regulations governing number of hours, rest periods, and minimum wages applying to each class of workers (male, female, under age 16), which the state labor department will send you to post on your premises. These are in addition to any labor union regulations you may contract for. You are responsible, too, to conduct your business free of safety hazards under OSHA (the federal Occupational Safety and Health Act of 1970), which is usually more applicable to manufacturing plants, and you must be careful to comply with the stringent federal regulations governing discrimination against minorities, women, and senior citizens in hiring practices.

Manufacturers are primarily liable for labeling of "content" of garments and for the washability of these products, but the customer who has a relationship with you always holds you responsible. Be aware of these Federal regulations for the protection of your customer and for knowledge of the characteristics of the different fibers to help her make best use of your products. Learn from your manufacturers the proper care (and fitting) of the products you sell; keep your employees informed so your store may serve your clientele in their best interests.

OPENING DAYS

5

CREATING THE PLACE TO BUY IN

MERCHANDISE ASSORTMENT

Buying the opening inventory for your store is a very delicately planned undertaking requiring every bit of your merchandise background, a detailed study of your area and people, and systematic market shopping in plenty of time for delivery, stocking, and display. The breakdown of your merchandise into colors, sizes, ranges, and price lines, in addition to style trends and choice of top sources in each, may require the professional help of a buying office (see Appendix P). You will be following a comprehensive plan, expressing the uniqueness of assortment and strategy that sets you off from the other stores in the area.

Will your merchandise concept and strategy work here? Do you know the customers well enough to predict their future needs as well as those of the present? If you are not sure, pick a store for a model and copy its style, goods, displays, ads, and other features you admire.

63

STUDY YOUR MARKET   A new business starts with a lack of knowing for sure, a disadvantage you must overcome. Prior to shopping, you need to study your market and buying public; this will give you a "feel."

- Who are you aiming to please in this area?
- What do these consumers need?
- What will tempt them to buy more?
- What is the unusual feature to bring them in?
- What is the area competition doing?

Your intuition and experience may be very good, but with a market study, it will be better. Talk to all your neighbors, even your competition-to-be, for hints of local tastes, peculiarities, trends in housing, and forecasts in population movement. Talk to walking customers, local officials and suppliers. Read local newspapers and learn from trade associations and local banks. Pick the brains of those you find most knowledgeable and assemble the impressions.

Gamble a little in your assortment and merchandise varieties that your instinct tells you is the trend. These decisions will give you more pleasure when successful, as well as more profit and more stature in the community. Don't aim at a middling, mediocre business; aim high, start strong. You must overcome the inertia of a dead start. Don't imitate the competition unless you give your customer some advantage. Watch the successful area stores but *do it better.*

Watch living styles and the earnings level. The changing social movements are creating exciting new merchandise desires that can help to make your shop the "in" place. Considering the age level, life-style, marital status, work life, educational background, and ethnic origin of the local people should complete your view of likely merchandise demand. Examination of earnings level should produce a fair estimate of factors in your sales projection, plus some evidence in demand for price lines, low, popular medium, or luxury. Then buy:

- The best-known market sources, who nearly always have the winning styles. Good advertised brands are already presold.
- Today's headline fashion styles, some even a little extreme. (Watch the fashion publications, magazines, Women's Wear Daily, Daily News Record, and National Retail Merchants "Stores" magazine.)
- A balance of needed staples, the "needs" people buy once they are in your shop, with a good depth of sizes, colors, and such.
- Loss leaders to advertise and other promotional goods of proven drawing merit for excitment.
- A few of the coming season's trendy styles to evoke a feeling of time-liness about the store.

One big misconception in the choice of the basic assortment of a store's stock is an attempt by some to live and grow on a specialized "all bargains" promotional assortment with no staples. In heavy traffic areas, however, "one price" shops are often successful—"88¢ stores" or "all dresses $15." Macy's (New York) failed in their attempt to successfully replace an existing department store with an "all-promotional" assortment of goods with great fanfare in upstate Syracuse, New York, in 1939. That big costly flop was liquidated soon thereafter. Even a store like Korvettes, which rose to great heights on the discount principle, always had some regular staples in the luggage and leather goods stock. As soon as the over-extended financial management tried to live on past reputation, make back some needed higher profits, and mark goods with no bargain discounts under their competition, their patrons started to desert. Many manufacturers had long since ceased to ship to Korvettes because of slow invoice payments, and so their choice assortment narrowed. Suppliers who watched a successful French company buy out the 44 Korvettes stores (in 1979) wondered how they would make a comeback. They couldn't, and they closed (most of the stores shut down in 1980). Meanwhile, other discount merchants like K-Mart, Woolco, and Caldor grow stronger as they remain faithful to their merchandising principles.

When you are buying the assortment of promotional goods, you will probably be offered closeouts of last season's leftovers at substantial savings over this season's line, which will have price inflated along with everything. Don't corner the market on such offerings; buy reasonable quantities based on outside consultation with experienced merchants. Merchandise bought at prices way under the regular price is no bargain to you and no advantage to your store, unless it is readily saleable *now* in the regular operations as you proceed and at the profit you plan. Don't buy now to pack away for next year. Most goods held over until next year never look quite as appetizing to you, your employees, or your customers when you reopen them. If you can, sell them out now!

It is important to have established a credit line before doing your market shopping for the opening. This takes time (see Capital, Chapter 3) and will be effective only if the proper presentation, your comprehensive plan, is made well in advance. Check with the Dun and Bradstreet representative to know your own rating before shopping. Have extra copies of the financial documents ready for credit managers of the larger branded firms, who may require them before giving you a credit line.

TRADE SHOWS   One of the easiest ways to compare lines of a category of merchandise, prices, quality, style, and novelty is to attend a well-organized merchandise trade show. These shows are announced in *Women's Wear Daily,* other publications, and vendors' showrooms, or dates and places can be obtained from sales representatives. Most trades have a showing about twice a year, usually six months in advance of the season in market cities, giving their company representatives a chance to meet buyers who had no previous view of this company's goods, or get another chance to convince attending retailers of their superiority in a perfect setting for comparison. Trade shows contrast the value of best lines and show new lines, new modes of operations display, and the like. Many new unadvertised lines need exposure, and buyers like you may not be adequately covered by the sales force in the beginning, so a show serves both. At many shows, the trade organization sponsors helpful instructive talks about merchandising the product, stocking, displaying, or forecasting the future for the attending retailers.

STORE OPENINGS AND STORE ATMOSPHERE

Store openings are happy events, and your local patrons will be delighted to participate if you let them know good reasons to buy from you on opening days.

No one can select all winners in your regular or promotional assortment of stock for the opening. Fortunately, if you have a good crowd for your opening days, your customers will buy some of everything in the atmosphere of competition. It will be up to you to be ready to move the less desirable stock to the most advantageous display for traffic.

EVERYBODY LOVES A BARGAIN, A PARTY, A UNIQUE SERVICE All customers have some bargain hunter instincts, which the very attractively priced "hot" item of the season will bring in. Once in the store you can hope to secure the buyer's continued loyalty with your unique assortment that you know is better than stores around. Shoppers enjoy looking at the latest extremely styled goods even when they are too exotic for their taste, and to be offered trendy goods at least gives them the feeling that your store is with it.

CATERING TO YOUR SHOPPER'S WANTS IS SPECIAL   Most of all, shoppers will be captivated by a feeling of being wanted and catered to in a friendly courteous atmosphere. They all know that the big stores and chains advertise price or assortment temptations, but those stores do not project your one-to-one touch. In your small store, you can offer the something that money can't buy and stores don't sell, that personal warmth projected by an interested store owner to a guest. This appeal is not a secret ingredient, nor is it new. Many famous stores started humbly (see Appendix A, B), featuring this personal element that helped them attain the success and growth that is your goal. Absentee management is always seeking this in vain. The buying power of the national chains will often provide the basis for a lower price on some of the same items you offer, but customer loyalty gives you a chance to compete if you are aware of the competition, and you may even override a small price difference with your service. You offer help, *not* self-service.

Keeping customers is like keeping friends. Be aware of their needs in a pleasant way and they will reciprocate. Serve them new, interesting fashions at a fair price and they will be happy to pay you a fair profit and show loyalty. Be different, innovate, and they will always want to see your next offering.

EMPLOYEES WILL DO AS YOU DO   Stores operate with a feeling generated right from management—you, which means they will mimic pleasant and unpleasant owners. The very operating atmosphere and policies you feel comfortable with may be the basis for your success or failure. Not all stores thrive on the same kind of customer-employee relationships. Choose your way, do it yourself, train your employees, and the store policy will probably be followed.

SERVICE

Friendly service does not mean that you have to encourage your store as a hangout, an oasis downtown where people can come in to chat with employees to pass the time. These activities can often be counterproductive, diverting attention from a buying interest and corrupting the work habits of salespeople from the floor. If you take an honest interest in customers' wants, listen to their problems with a sympathetic ear, and take an interest in community projects (that you can afford), you will project an interest in your customer. This sincere interest should guide, not dominate selection. Treated as a V.I.P., the customer should enjoy shopping because the selection is available, ready to take or be delivered, gift-wrapped, of if wrong, cheerfully exchanged with apology. Consider these services:

- Layaways and bank credit cards.
- Mail, phone orders, and delivery.
- Easy payroll check cashing by adopting a secure routine (personal checks only for regulars you know).
- Store hours set for customer's convenience, enlarged as you see the demand.
- Free alterations where possible (or at reasonable cost).
- A posted clear policy on exchanges, refunds, and repairs. It should always be *pleasant* and *prompt*. (One unpleasant incident can negate all the inviting image established by time, values, or costly advertising.) It is wiser to give in to a troublesome customer, even an unreasonable one, where the exchange or repair is not a substantial cost to the store. Some local stores do exchange branded goods even if not purchased there, as a service that can make a friend.

Ventnors, a very successful gift store, has a liberal policy for exchanges (but no refunds). The shop is well known for a great assortment of branded crockery, tableware, printed cloths, cookware, luggage, and handbags normally priced except for discounts on key branded lines. The cut prices marked by Peter Ventnor are balanced out with the gift sets to give him an excellent average mark-on for the year on a volume in excess of $400,000. His merchandising policy of constantly adding and displaying popular wedding giftware of crystal, party serving pieces, and Americana linens gives him a fresh *look* that melds very effectively with the price image to keep consumers loyal. His employees follow his lead in a friendly relaxed atmosphere where he allows known shoppers to charge personally as well as use bank cards. Stores using Visa or Master-Card pay 3 percent–6 ½ percent depending on their total and average sale. It is negotiable.

Ventnor says that charge account losses are less than the charges that the bank cards cost him. He adds that he does not figure the cost of money for his own charge accounts because his capital has grown in 20 years to accommodate it without borrowing, and he feels that customers have a more personal feeling for him when he charges them personally.

GIFT WRAPS HELP SELL GIFTS   Ventnors simple gift wraps are free, but customers are offered a descriptive list of elaborate gift wraps for a separate price, which more or less balances out all gift wrap cost.

CATALOGUES AND FOLDERS EXTEND REGULAR STORE BUSINESS   Peter Ventnor has a small advertising budget for newspapers, uses radio rarely, and concentrates on folder enclosure to his charge account and long-term mailing list. Twice a year his slick paper, colorful catalogue of gifts brings in mail, phone orders, and a great deal of traffic on the floor. Much of the branded gift item catalogue expense for these mailings is paid for by the manufacturers, who share the cost of producing and postage. He has a brochure of colorful gifts given by local fraternal, social, and country clubs, who are enthusaistic about his selection. Some local manufacturing firms work with Ventnor for their annual gift-giving to customers. It is these extensions of normal store business that has him planning the use of an upstairs loft to facilitate packing and shipping mail orders (with part-time employees). The catalogue gift business he sees as his profitable growth in the future. Ventnor and his wife participate in a local gourmet cooking club, where he is able to show many of the latest appliances from his stock. The club sponsors a famous chef to judge finalists with personal cooking masterpieces and gift prizes from Ventnors. These extra offerings have all contributed to growth.

Peter Ventnor was a former salesman calling on retail gift stores for years before deciding to have a store of his own. After some part-time holiday experience in the store of one of his most successful merchants, he was pleased to have the owner offer some capital and expertise as a coowner in a store similar to his. After several successful years together, Ventnor began buying back the stock of his coowner according to plan suggested as an option in their original stockholder's agreement. It has been an amicable, profitable arrangement for both partners, and they still trade marketing information and save through joint volume buying.

PROFESSIONAL DISPLAYS SELL ASSORTMENTS, NOVELTY AND VALUE   Ventnor says that if he were to open a store today, he would place an even greater emphasis on store display inside and out, spending the capital for a "jewellike" setting. He feels that it is possible to get a three-time turnover or more if the stock is augmented on a regular schedule, with regular market visits and good delivery. The store is in a local area, not any kind of shopping center, but Ventnor feels that an expenditure of 5 to 6 percent can be justified in a shopping plaza with good parking. A net return after a modest salary can be about 6 percent a year (of volume) after a year or two. In 1980 he reported almost $60,000 income from the store. *Timing,* he says, is one of his most important assets. For example, the popularity of Silverstone coated pans was grasped as a sure winner the first time he saw them because of their effective use without fats, recommended by all the diets. He sent out a folder to his customers before most the competition had any stock on hand and received free publicity in a story in the local newspaper, with pictures of his display—far more valuable than any ad would be. The store was busy for a week. Headline styles may beget publicity and local talk.

OPENING DISPLAYS AND ORDERS   In your opening assortment, feature a current favorite with an unusual price, as Ventnors did. Where you find an unusually attractive window display, seek the trimmer for your store if merchandise in a plush setting is important to you. Most display specialists work on a free-lance basis and may have open time for you. You must be willing to pay more for a talented artist.

After your first few days in operation, you will find that there are important missing items you need to satisfy some of your first shoppers, and you must try to satisfy them. Don't take orders for specifics unless you know the availability, and don't promise delivery that you cannot produce. Serve, don't disappoint. A disappointment can affect your future with the customer. Most retailers would rather be short of some things as the alternative to being overstocked. You will hear it said in many ways:

- Mother said, "Always be a little hungry for goods!"
- Macy's management said, "You can always *buy* merchandise!"
- Dun and Bradstreet said, "You can't do business from an empty wagon."

You should always be "open to buy" some 15 percent of your planned purchasing for the coming period; never be completely bought up. When new things are offered, be open to buy to take advantage of the novelty.

Figuring for your opening purchases, "retail" the invoices, total the retail value contrasting it to total cost, and get a mark-on percentage to work with. Experience and your shopping have shown you the approximate cost and retail price of each of the categories of the opening stock. The profit is divided by the retail price to give you a mark-on percentage for the first open to buy.

Buying plan figures. Let us say that for category A you planned to buy $1,000 total cost, and on writing all the retail prices on each order copy, you reached $1,500 retail total for all the orders you placed. You show a $500 profit on $1,500 retail, or a 33 1/3 mark-on percentage for the category. This percentage multiplied by the projected volume of sales for any given time period will give you the profit in dollars. Subtract this from your retail to figure the amount of goods at cost you need to buy in that category, which you will need for the amount of business projected.

In the three months after the opening, let us say that you have projected approximately $10,000 worth of business, of which category (A) is thought to be 30 percent, or $3,000 at retail. Category (A) mark-on percentage is 33 1/3 (retail sales times mark-on percentage equals profit; subtract profit from retail to give you cost of goods to do these sales), and you easily calculate your open to buy for the three-month period at $2,000 to do that amount of business. If business in the first month is higher than planned, you will have to go into the market to buy more merchandise to cover the increased business. For example, if the first month's business in category (A) was $600 more than estimated, multiply your mark-on percentage of this amount, subtract that profit from the retail increase, and you see that you should order $400 of goods at cost to cover the increased business (and still be prepared for the next few months estimated sales.)

Financial health requires buying controls. For a safety margin, if you want to leave yourself a little "hungry" for goods and not chance being overbought, order about 15 percent less than the $400 figure you felt was your increased open to buy, or $340 at cost.

Planning the amount you are open to buy in each category and keeping your purchases total within these figures are the only ways to insure enough money to pay bills currently and keep suppliers interested in serving you.

(Chapter 8, Merchandising and Inventory Control, discusses open to buy, as related to inventory planning, in greater detail.)

SHOPPING BAGS AND SUPPLIES   Want to make your customers carry your message all around the neighborhood? Work out a stunning, colorful design and message on a shopping bag (the plastic kind) and use it in place of plain tan or gray paper sacks, the usual store cheaper kind. These shopping bags have become an art form and are very effective advertising; customers thank *you* for allowing them to carry *your* message as they use them over and over. One large source of these bags, Container Corporation of America, reports that stores establish a basic logo that identifies them so definitely in an area that they refuse to change designs drastically in the new printing as supply runs out. They retain portions of the design and change it only partially and gradually, so that the immediate recognition is not lost. Equitable Bag Company is another good source. The National Paperbox and Package Association in New York City can supply names of other companies for large quantity purchases. For smaller amounts of packaging paper, gift wraps, poly bags, all sizes of regular garment carriers and boxes, twine, cord, and such, see your local paper jobber. But, of course, shop around, as prices vary.

For delivery to customers who insist on it, despite your attractive shopping bags, consult your yellow pages for a local delivery firm who can pick up from you perhaps a few days a week. United Parcel Service is excellent for out-of-town, especially for mail orders. It takes much of the business parcel post once had, but is a little expensive for local delivery.

PROFESSIONAL PROMOTION COMPANIES   Depending on what kind of store image you wish to create with your opening barrage promotion, you might use contests, promotional stunts, giveaways and souvenirs, or store "dress-up" to get your clientele and employees in the mood. Every area has promotional companies who create stunts and gimmicks to help the excitement, and you could have them submit sample plans to choose an appropriate one. The alternative is to select your own ideas from what you have seen elsewhere, buy streamers, flags, paper signs, corsages for your employees, souvenirs and prizes, and run contests with advertising agency help (as discussed in Chapter 6).

ADVERTISING AND PUBLIC RELATIONS

The purpose of advertising and public relations is to give the public a message, to make them act, to come in and buy.

"It pays to advertise" says the slogan, whether you are building public acceptance for a product, a service, or a store. But does it really always pay? Probably not. We are all bombarded day and night with the "superior" attributes of MacDonald's restaurants, American Express cards, Coca Cola, Perrier water, and so on, the dramatic pitch for thousands of products to capture our interest, and so most people pay less and less attention. Your store ads, therefore, must be well conceived, and perhaps even clever, to be noticed. How well you do it, then, is what really counts.

Here are some things to consider in advertising plans:

- Prepare well ahead.
- Know the right merchandise for the ads.
- Select the proper media, day, and copy for these customers.

- Know when customers are interested.
- Be sure your ad cost is affordable.

To make the best use of its ad money, a store must plan a campaign that is consistent with the philosophy of its merchandise buying, with an understanding of it's ad appeal to these customers, and must place the ad in the media best calculated to reach them. The timing must match the ready-for-sale condition of the store's stock. Customers will always be more responsive when ads are timed to seasonal buying urges. The total cost of advertising is usually preset in a budget figured as a portion of the overall expense budget. Whether the theory of cost control for advertising involves a percentage of the sales projected or the amount calculated to produce a particular goal result, it is a reasonable amount of expense fit into the overall store plan.

ADVERTISING COPY

Your copy can be general ads based on the unique appeal of the store, or specific merchandise appeal based on the known response power to bring them in.

YOU NEED TIME AND SKILL   Do you have the ad writing skills, and the time to use them? It is not always possible to be professionally intuitive about item selection and effective in writing advertising (or public relations) in view of retail demands. Time is an important element as well, and if you have made a sizeable investment in premises and merchandise, perhaps the time invested in struggling through a mediocre presentation is not in your best interests. An inquiry to nearby media will bring you suggested professionals whose competency may be proved by their past programs. Make inquiries to their other clients and be certain there is good working rapport between you.

BE DISTINCTIVE   A small store ad program should attempt to be different, distinctive on sight whether you adopt a fancy border, an emblem, or unusual script type. Perhaps you can copy some feature you have seen in your travels. Ask your agency to come up with something unique that will blend well with your aims and the image you want to project.

YOU CAN DEVELOP YOUR OWN SKILL   If the expense of an advertising professional does not appear logical, *you* may be able to handle it yourself after some research and a little practice. The same basic ability needed to produce a comprehensive business plan may well translate into competent brochures, leaflets, handbills, and newspaper layouts. Using one of the many advertising technique books along with some imagination *may* develop a different approach with a *personal* touch that will show excellent results and satisfy you personally. (An example is the personal "homey" ads by Frank Purdue on chicken.) Look for inexpensive assistance from:

- Art or photography students or recent graduates for illustrations and lay-outs.
- Ad staffs of newspapers, radio stations, or other media for advice on lay-out and mat services.
- Newspaper blowups of your ads to use in windows, displays, or mailers.
- Vendor-prepared ad campaigns from brands.
- Books such as *How to Get Big Results From a Small Advertising Budget* by Cynthia Smith (Hawthorne, 1973) or *Advertising Copywriting* by P. Burton and B. Kreer (Prentice-Hall, 1962).

Advertising copy response power, classified

X—Immediate response expected, short term (super-X, loss leaders, excite-ment created).

Y—Fashion or current popularity, some immediate response expected, longer period.

Z—Institutional general store copy, image created, long-range benefit.

GOALS   Stores measure the response to X ads by the plus over normal (P.O.N.) business in that category that is generated by the insertion in the days immediately following it, within the week at most. Copies of all ads are saved and the results always tabulated to have records as a later guide. The normal hoped-for P.O.N. is approximately 10 times the cost of the ad, and it is realized that some long-term effect always remains to benefit the store.

For Y ads, the expected response is calculated over a longer period, per-haps two weeks, and it is usually a source of more long-term favorable feeling for the store, affecting, perhaps, when customers will return regularly. The image of the store being "with it" is emphasized when your ads are timed with a national campaign of great strength (as in designer brands), thereby lending prestige.

Z ads are part of a long-term, well thought out campaign for image build-ing, or making consumers aware of a new category of offerings or services that are not commonplace. You might be participating in a local cause, sponsoring an athletic team, offering senior citizens some help, giving prizes for winners in a "mutt parade" (children marching with nonthoroughbred animals), or some nonretail activity calculated to make the public "feel at home" with you. Macy's annual Thanksgiving Day parade is said to produce more editorial lineage than the parade cost could buy in advertising. Fashion shows with local student models have the added objective of selling the styles and the store to future customers and admiring families.

1. *Store Opening Budget:* a separate allocation.
2. *The Regular Budget:* the long term year plan broken into quarters with other expense budgets.
3. *Special Campaigns:* for special purposes, new directions.

1. Store Opening Budget

Your store opening is a special combination of merchandise buying coordinated with advertising and other events as an assault on the consciousness of people nearby to notice you and rush in. It is basically a short-term plan involving X and super-X items and promotional strong copy, the cost of which need not be based on a percentage of sales expected for the period. It is a management decision to invest money in the blast-off excitement, which will often include prizes, contests, and other inducements to turn the shopping footsteps your way. The super-X loss leader items brought for your opening should not detract from the general image of the store you would like to convey (for example, seconds are naturally inappropriate for a Nieman-Marcus opening), and merchandise must always give the wearing service up to standard.

2. Regular Budget

This long-term, yearly plan is broken into quarters with other expense budgets. It has the overall long-term objectives in mind, as well as holiday and off-season promotions, and so must include all manner of response-expected merchandise and ideas. Basically, it is closely coordinated with the expense budget, which is founded on being reasonably tied to the sales plan of the periods. The longer term objectives, which will be carried by the Y and Z items, are usually funded by making a management decision for an investment in this goal of a given amount. In this way, a reasonable sum can be reached and the more difficult breakdown into time periods, media spaces, and merchandise content can be started. In any long-term ad program, most experts put the emphasis on *consistency.* If you decide to spend the money and then stop the ads inbetween, the on-and-off process may negate all the benefits.

3. Special Campaigns

This sum for advertising is an investment to inform the trade of a new direction, category, or service you are offering, or it may tell them about your newly rebuilt store. You may want to take on a new famous brand line, with or without some vendor-paid ad assistance, this calculated to bring a whole new segment of

TABLE 6.1. Year Planning: Sales and Advertising Calendar (in fiscal quarters)

Sales Volume Percent Projection	$ Sales		Holidays	Advertising $ Budget
1st Quarter			Ground Hog Day	
_____%	Feb.	_____	Lincoln-Wash. B'day	_____
_____$			Valentines Day	
			St. Patricks	
	Mar.	_____	Pre-Easter Fashions	_____
			Palm and Easter	
	Apr.	_____	Dressup	_____
			Home Fixup	
	Total 1st Q.	_____	Total	_____
2nd Quarter			Mother's Day	
_____%	May	_____	Pre-Summer Fashion	_____
_____$			Summer Furn.	
			Memorial Day	
	June	_____	Brides and Weddings	_____
			Father's Day	
			Summer Hot Promo.	
	July	_____	July 4 Sales	_____
			Clearances	
			White Sales	
	Total 2nd Q.	_____	Total	_____
3rd Quarter			Pre-Campus Events	
_____%	Aug.	_____	Fall Fashions	_____
_____$			Back to School	
			Stationery Needs	
	Sept.	_____	Labor Day	_____
			School Days	
			Jewish Holidays	
			Columbus Day	
	Oct.	_____	Coat Sales	_____
			Fall Fashions	
			Home Furnishings	
			Halloween	
	Total 3rd Q.	_____	Total	_____
4th Quarter			Area Promotions	
_____%	Nov.	_____	Pre-Holiday Gifts	_____
_____$			Veterans Day	
			Thanksgiving Home	
			Dressup	

TABLE 6.1. Year Planning: Sales and Advertising Calendar (in fiscal quarters) **(continued)**

Sales Volume Percent Projection	$ Sales	Holidays	Advertising $ Budget
	Dec. _____	Policy Ads-Gift Wrap	_____
		Gift Ads	
		Last Minute Pickups	
		Post Christmas Sale	
	Jan. _____	New Years Event	_____
		Jan. Clearance	
		Pre-Inventory	
		Crazy Clearance	
		Giveaways	_____
	Total 4th Q. _____	Total	_____
	Total Year Sales _____	Year Ad Budget _____	

PERCENTAGE OF TYPES OF ADS . . . RESPONSES			IMAGE BUILDING EVENTS
X	Y	Z	
1st Q. _____	_____	_____	_____
2nd Q. _____	_____	_____	_____
3rd Q. _____	_____	_____	_____
4th Q. _____	_____	_____	_____
Total _____	_____	_____	_____

people who believe in it. New scientific breakthroughs in merchandise, like the silverstone finished pans noted previously, may seem an ideal way to garner gift trade, the nutrition minded, or just the average cook who likes new things.

Budgets are the total money that must now be broken into the time and space allocations on the calendar for the time ahead. Large monthly calendars with big square spaces for each day make ideal visual plans on which to break down ad spending (available at commercial stationers).

On opening day, your enticements that bring people into the store must be followed by proof that you keep those loud promises and that you offer lots of other attractive things you have not advertised, and show that you are always offering unusual values. A most disappointed and disillusioned trade results from merchandise not being ready-for-sale in response to an ad. In opening ads, it can be fatal. Convey that excitement in the store that your ads are shouting, give them the service they will remember and the values they can believe in. Use reprints of the ads, signs, ribbons, flags, special flowers, and employee costumes in the store—make it fun. If you cannot decide on the most effective ad merchandise to use for your opening, follow the successful merchants around you by noting the ads they have repeated many times, and consult with other merchants you know. Price seems always to be the most effective bait, but when combined with latest headlines in popular life-styles, the response is bound to be augmented. Select a popular local craze for a theme, or refer to a local hero. A few effective headline themes—on fuel economy and home protection—might be:

- "Be warm at home even with the fuel saving, wear our robes and slippers."
- "Be snug in our wraparound sweater."
- "Weather-strip your doors by the yard; saves fuel and $."
- "Insulation at our prices installed easily by you saves big fuel dollars. We show you how."
- "Pick-proof locks feel more secure on your doors."
- "Alarm rings if window is forced; you can install it yourself."
- "Invisible ray alarm thwarts intruders."

MEDIA

Media are the vehicles to carry your communication to induce people to shop with you: newspapers, flyers, catalogues, circulars and radio, and television. Carefully choose the media for your trade because it is as important a decision as any element in your advertising. Charges for print media are set on a per line basis, based on circulation confirmed at Standard Rate and Data in New York.

National and Contract Rates

There are special contract rates for regular users within a time period, and the charge for one insertion (national rate) is higher. But more important to know is the effective circulation to you, since most of the media cover other areas too far from your drawing area. Many purchased lists for direct mail flyers and such contain names hardly useable, and so the percentage return is further reduced for mailings. Using your own maintained list is far more effective for you.

When you have determined that this particular newspaper or program reaches many of the customers you seek, start working with the calendar and insert a certain amount of lineage, the total of which approximates your budget. You will soon be able to figure the return from any media if the items are the X or Y response types; whereas it will be much more difficult with Z. You will discover that promotional merchandise, contests, and the like sell your store better in some newspapers than others and that allocations for various media may be a trial-and-error method for you. Keep an ad book with responses to plan future ads and lessen errors.

Work with local media ad people. Select the times on your calendar for your insertions, and by figuring space cost in each of the media, stay within the planned budget total. The merchandise for each ad is timed to the delivery into stock of the supply of the items and the seasonal demand. Occasionally, out-of-season goods are promoted in full assortment and discount priced very successfully.

Newspapers

Newspapers are the favorite for retailers because of the more effective graphic presentation of most of their items. Does your local newspaper reach your trade? You will have to study the coverage by the local daily or weekly paper because many do not sell well in all areas. If the circulation does not cover small districts that house recent immigrants or others who perhaps don't subscribe, that problem is usually overcome by house-to-house distribution of shopping papers or by mailing third class to "householder." Values clearly shown to this trade can often transcend any language difficulty. Local zone edition rates save money.

NEWSPAPER PROMOTION   Most newspapers offer free use of mat services with a variety of illustrations that can be used without the expensive artwork and photographs to portray your goods exactly. Special "shopper" papers that join many area merchants are assembled by promoters, who also may offer mats, layout, and copy assistance. Many of these papers notify consumers of an area event that promotes shopping centers or other organized groups of stores offering prizes or free goods for the time period, and the names and addresses on the coupons build a more reliable mailing list for later use.

VENDORS WILL COOPERATE   A well-run promotion can often secure free major name appliance prizes when run in conjunction with a major ad agency, which can supply the free goods in exchange for substantial publicity. Vendors will cooperate by paying for (part or all) ads of their brands in papers of substantial circulation, if you are a good customer and run it in your layout. Vendors get the benefit of your contract rate as they insert a prepared layout, which under national rates would cost them twice as much if not in your ad. These ads often result in more orders from other retailers, who play follow-the-leader convinced that "if Bloomie's sells it, it must be worth stocking."

Radio

Does radio reach your trade? In major areas where there are many stations, the ad thrust of any one seems too ill-defined to benefit a small store, except possibly for long-term Z copy. In small towns where the coverage seems to include your consumers, time spots run in conjunction with a favorite program seem more appropriate. The spots can be bought in lengths of 10 seconds or longer

TABLE 6.2. Advertising as Practiced by Selected Small Businesses

Type of Business	Average Ad Budget (% of Sales)*	Favorite Media	Other Media Used	Special Considerations	Promotion Opportunities and Warnings
BICYCLE SHOPS	1.5-2.0%	Newspapers (sports section)	Flyers, Yellow Pages, cycling magazines, direct mail		
BOOKSTORES	1.5-1.6%	Newspapers shopper Yellow Pages	Direct mail	Cooperative advertising from publisher	Autograph parties
DRUG STORES (INDEPENDENT)	1.0-3.0%	Local newspapers, shoppers	Direct mail (list from prescription files)		
DRY CLEANING PLANTS	0.9-2.0%	Local newspapers, shoppers, Yellow Pages	Store front, ads, pamphlets on clothes care		Specials on seasonal cleaning (sleeping bags, parkas)
EQUIPMENT RENTAL SERVICES	1.7-4.7%	Yellow Pages			
GIFT STORES	2.2%	Weekly newspapers	Yellow Pages, radio, direct mail, magazines		Open houses, demonstrations of product lines like cookware
HAIR-DRESSING SHOPS	2.0-5.0%	Yellow Pages	Newspapers (for special events), word-of-mouth		Styling for community fashion, beauty shows, conducting free beauty clinics at local high schools

HOME FURNISHING STORES	1.9-3.2%	Newspapers	Direct mail, radio	Cooperative advertising available from manufacturer	
LIQUOR STORES (INDEPENDENT)	0.5-0.6%	Point-of-purchase displays	Newspapers, Yellow Pages	Manufacturers do all product advertising; coop funds available	Caution: see Alcoholic Beverage Control's advertising and promotion regulations
MAIL ORDER FIRMS	15.0-25.0%	Newspapers, magazines	Direct mail	Displays ads, not classified, in publications	Firms spend up to 40% of sales on advertising some promotions
PET SHOPS	2.0-5.0%	Yellow Pages	Window displays, shopper newspapers, direct mail		Talk on pet care to schools, community groups.
PLANT SHOPS	1.3-1.5%	Local newspapers, word-of-mouth			Plant care clinics, courses in plant care, plant sitting, repotting
REPAIR SERVICES	0.8-1.6%	Yellow Pages	Signs on vehicles direct mail, shoppers		
RESTAURANTS AND FOOD SERVICES	0-3.2%	Newspapers, radio, Yellow Pages, transit, outdoor	Television for chain or franchise restaurants	Word-of-mouth relied on heavily by independent restaurants	"Free" advertising in restaurant critics' columns, specialty advertising, birthday cakes or parties for customers
SHOE STORES	0.5-0.8%	Newspapers, direct mail, radio	Yellow Pages (especially for specialty items)	Cooperative advertising available from manufacturers	Collecting outgrown (but not worn out) childrens' shoes for donation to local charity

*Slightly higher in new establishments; Statistics compiled by Small Business Reporter Bank of America.

and their use during special events seems well advised. Special segments of the populace—young men, homemakers, teens—are targeted by including the spot during what are thought to be their favorite programs. Sears, for example, uses commuting hour spots for auto supply merchandise.

Many stores allocate up to 25% of their total regular budget for radio when they have well-defined target segments and see results. Radio advertising people say "be brief and repeat your message over and over."

Franchisors, who include a minimum ad percentage of volume requirement of franchisees, prefer radio (and television) for prestige and wide geographic range. The local franchisee benefits from association with the expert professional preparation of these national advertisers (fast food franchises such as MacDonalds, Burger King, Kentucky Fried Chicken).

Many store ad executives consider radio as stronger for daytime over television, or over newspapers that are not well entrenched as a monopoly in the area. They feel that newspapers rarely cover more than 50 percent of most areas.

Television

The cost of programs on television is usually beyond the budget of single stores; one-minute spots sell from $400 up in metropolitan centers, without production costs. It is possible for an enterprising entrepreneur to feature the unusual, the hard-to-get, the rare thing that will arouse the interest of the daytime interview program participants, and persistent tactics may result in an invitation to tell the story on the show. This is worth many times the value of an ad to the store. Public relations pros use gimmicks such as awarding the daytime m.c. the "public servant of the month" placque, and during the ceremony the store owner explains the reasons for the award and in return is permitted to include "special things" about the store.

Flyers, Circulars, Catalogues

An artistic, colorful flyer is an excellent medium to tell a quick story, to arouse a public interest in any business with an out-of-the ordinary approach. Results of flyers for service businesses, restaurants, personal treatment salons, and unique merchandise stores are especially good. Hand-outs are excellent on the busiest corner in town (where allowed), supermarkets, outside factories, hospitals, schools, and hotels; people tuck them away if some later use is visible (calendar, train schedule, helpful hints).

Everyone with a charge account is accustomed to receiving flyers offering special merchandise regularly with billings and at other times. Taking advantage of the slightly captive customer list to offer mail order merchandise on glossy life-like colorful folders enclosed with the expected communication is like a foot-in-the-door tactic of door-to-door sales people, and it works!

APPEALING CATALOGUES DO BUSINESS   The circular or catalogue you mail to *your* mailing list is much more personal to the receiver than one distributed door-to-door or mailed to householder. The fact that this customer has been in your store and you have added the name to your list will give you a better percentage return from the mailing. Keeping your list up-to-date by extracting people who have moved away will augment that return further, and it is one of the store chores to be done when buying traffic is slow. With public (bought) mailing lists, it is important to test market their value to you because of the other expenses of mailings:

- Mailing list cost (whether bought or your own maintained).
- Printing costs (attractive productive pieces cost most).
- Cost of layout, artwork (production).
- Cost of postage (or distribution).
- Manual labor of handling (your own in slower periods or an outside service).

Maisons, a store bought from retiring owners at a high price, seemed to the new owners to resist expansion in their regular gift lines, homewares, and such. Through some personal contacts of one partner, they succeeded in getting orders for prizes in local schools and soon expanded this to social and country clubs in the area. They studied catalogues of firms supplying this merchandise and found that the markup was higher than their normal store profit and that this business seemed to augment their sales total advantageously without added costs. They have added to their mailing list and opened a second floor department for stocking and handling only mail order; and this department after three years is approaching their regular gift sales volume. The mail department sends flyers to local charge customers (including bank cards), which helps floor traffic, and some of these are paid for by aggressive manufacturer brands (cosmetic, table china, cutlery). The Christmas gift catalogue has had enormous growth, and Maisons production costs have been reduced by the participation of some of these vendors and the makers of branded luggage.

Mailing Lists

Many small stores begin their mailing lists with an area study of likely drawn customers, using the telephone directory as a start. You can use multicopy self-sticking pages of labels copied by high school or typing school students, who need not be employees on the payroll as they get typing practice and work for a minimum rate of so much a page. This is less expensive than the older production of Addressograph plates kept alphabetically in cabinets; new plates are needed to update the list. New copies of the list can be photocopied after changes are made to update. New phone directory issues help keep your list in good order and store event names and addresses can add to it. Special promotion phone directories for affluent suburban communities provide excellent yearly renewed lists.

WINDOW DISPLAYS COORDINATE WITH ADS   Window and interior displays augmented by signs are a real part of your advertising scheme. If you do not have the skills to produce what you consider acceptable displays or signs, make this one of the priorities in seeking employee or pro help. Most small stores who benefit from street and store traffic hire professionals as a necessary expense. Working with fine professionals may eventually build up a latent talent of your own and give you courage to do it yourself. Sign painting for interior use can be developed with practice, but be sure to work with the best equipment, brushes, paints, cardboard, and place to work, as the pros do. Most brands offer free display material.

Specialty Promotional Gifts

Printed inexpensive gifts, such as rulers, pin cushions, or paint stirrers, remind consumers of the store that offers a selection of home repair needs, stationery, sewing and hobby supplies, or decorating. These small promotion gifts are often kept and used. Members of social or service clubs can be given these and other useful tokens to let them know your connection. The variety of general gifts of this type is ever increasing, and a suggested source is offered in your yellow pages. The more useful and novel the gift, the more lasting the reminder effect for you.

The Yellow Pages, The Classified
Phone Directory

Most users of products or services are already mentally presold when they use the yellow pages. If you sell products or services that are out of the ordinary, rare, or that users need on rare occasions, listing them in the yellow pages may be worth the investment per year. The cost, added to your monthly phone bill, depends on the total circulation (phone users) of this local book. For consumer service businesses, restaurants, repairers of premises or maintenance, personal treatment centers, or any service not used every day, the cost of listing in the classified is considered as necessary as any overhead. Before subscribing, study your local book and your competition's use, and consider whether your trade is likely to be looking for your offerings there. The use of any other directory must be considered in the same light, although usually only the telephone classified directory is truly worthwhile.

Outdoor Billboards, Signs, and Transit Cards

People traveling around cities each day normally follow similar patterns, and the use of billboards, signs, and transit cards is aided by the fact that there is repeated exposure to them, whether driving or on public conveyances. The use of these stationary posters is being discouraged or banned as "eye pollution" by federal and state environmental groups. Benefits in small store advertising is limited to the long-term institutional Z effect, or your store's association with a name brand. Perhaps this brand will pay part of a billboard or car card for you.

Signs outside your store to identify you and call attention to your offerings are excellent sources of attention from passersby. Some manufacturers will co-op a sign cost with you if their brand is mentioned on it, and others will supply a sign (from their makers) at no cost to you. Try to carry out a distinctive emblem or identifying border throughout your ads, signs, windows, and displays.

Ad Effect

Stores do the most meaningful cooperation with communities by association with things naturally matched to their merchandise or service offered:

> Homeware and gift shops—cooking classes, homecare seminars.
> Drugstores—first aid, life-saving techniques.
> Bookstores—authors' meetings, speed reading.
> Camera shops—snaps of local teams in action.
> Building maintenance—free assessment of fuel saving.
> Knitting and sewing stores—free lessons on popular designs.
> Personal care salons—beauty pageant, advice clinics.
> Pet shops—free health checkups, free samples from suppliers, mutt parade.
> Flower and plant shops—care and handling clinic, free samples from supplier.

Sometimes merchandising instinct and ad timing combine to attain a satisfying step toward retail success. Sometimes it can be reached for little or no expense. A new junior executive in a large well-known department store was looking over some of his problems, especially one lot of 700 pairs of men's slacks from several years back. It was his responsibility to move a certain percentage of "prior stock" each month, and despite the obvious defect of this lot caused by the change in styling in that time, he felt that these slacks were a good value because of superior quality wool, especially at the price. A little timid about asking for advertising money from his superiors, he launched a personal letter to a "tip-off" column of the local newspaper that often received information that way, signing "constant reader." The paper checked, found the value as he had described, and printed a description, resulting in 700 pairs sold in less than two weeks—and a special commendation from the boss.

START BUILDING FRIENDSHIPS EARLY   You can publicize the store by contributing your time to career guidance at the high school. This will supply better young, interested part-timers for your store, as well as make future customers a reality. Work with them on fashion coordination, using some in fashion shows for good causes in town, with your name prominently displayed for families of these models to notice.

PUBLIC RELATIONS

P.R. is the different way to excite people about your store through stories of interest about you. Professionals in this field are trained to find the interesting facts as a reporter does, mold them into an acceptable form, and try to place them with the media to make you the talk of the town. When you are preparing your opening advertising, most of the media that carries the ads will cooperate by sending a reporter (and photographer) to develop a story. The more you involve local V.I.P.s or political figures, the more space will be devoted to the story and, of course, the more the piece will attract attention.

Some stores spend as little as one-half of 1 percent of their sales yearly on advertising, while others spend up to 3 percent because they plan to build the volume with the extra exposure. If your only outlet to the public is through your ads, as in mail order, a budget of 17 to 20 percent is not unusual. Here are a few *don'ts*.

- Don't advertise without the merchandise to back it up.
- Don't shout "sale, sale, sale" until it becomes meaningless.
- Don't repeat claim after claim about your merchandise until customers resent it.

And, be consistent about the program. Don't cut it out the moment sales are off expectations—it could get worse! Find the more suitable items to promote and be most professional in your presentation, including something different.

THE RETAIL STORE'S IMAGE

Build and maintain your image. Image is the view of the public, the customer's belief about the store. It is an impression, not always factual, but it is vital to your customers' feeling which affects their shopping loyalty. It is sometimes affected by such facts and actions as:

- Advertising promises and keeping them.
- Reliable quality of merchandise and services.
- Employee handling of customers.
- Constant emphasis on themes—price, fashion, designer names, and the like.
- Publicity about operations, for example: bad—a Better Business Bureau suit to enforce a guarantee; good—V.I.P. shopping in your store, praise from consumer's research comparison.

Watch for a negative effect on your image. It may be affected by things you may not be aware of:

- Very fancy store fixtures or rugs may give the impression of high prices in a popular priced store.
- Constant emphasis on "low-low" prices de-emphasizes quality.
- Featuring a few better brands brings up quality image even in a popular priced store. Some designer brands have a snob appeal above their quality.
- Emphasis of heavy dark printing in ads puts quality down.
- Light personal touch in ads (humor, poetry) gives a softer, less commercial image.
- Employee's social origin, if obvious, can have snob appeal or a negative effect.
- Store promoting irregulars or seconds often downgrades image.

Stores who are conscious of the effect study their image for changes, then seek to reinforce or correct it. Restudy your image with outside objective help from:

- Customer's questionnaires.
- Visiting market research students in a case study.
- Other retailers—you study their stores, they study yours.

Public relations events and stories can vitally affect your image. Always be on the lookout for P.R. *plus* items to help your image.

7

PERSONNEL MANAGEMENT

The smallest retail store will usually grow to need full- or part-time employees to help the owner. Most stores use peak-season extra employees their first year. Prepare your way by interviewing as people are sent to you, or drop in. Code your estimates of their capabilities and keep the information handy for future need. When someone applies unexpectedly, make a friend, not an enemy by having a "too busy" curt attitude. Be pleasant and hopeful to those interviewed because this meeting may influence their shopping habits or their friends.

General considerations:

- Interview many. You will acquire an instinct to select employees with talent, interest, and motivation; they are the very few from a large group of applicants.
- Spend the necessary time to take written applications, interview thoroughly, and check references . . . then select.
- Train and inform new employees what is expected, the rules, how to do it, motivate. Discuss discounts, holidays, payday.

Choose employees for help in these areas: sales, stock, management aid.

Selling and watching the floor are the most important performances in any store. Interview with an eye for an agreeable salesperson who will represent you, with a good memory to find things for the customer, and enough motivation to learn how to handle the trade your way, plus do suggestive selling.

Receiving, gift wrapping, packing, price marking, and counting and stocking goods to be ready for sale (plus maintenance of premises) are skills requiring your method and routine. They help to tie together the complete store performance when properly executed.

Register preparation and taking cash for sales, making bank deposits, taking note of stock needs, reordering, handling customer adjustments, entering figures, interviewing and training new employees, preparing displays, correcting customer lists, and preparing payroll are all semimanagement functions that are sometimes delegated to experienced personnel to share some of your burden.

Selecting, planning, and buying merchandise, choosing goods, media, and space for ads, handling bank transactions, payroll, and bonus decisions, markup and markdown strategy, sales and inventory forecasting, and store policy are management decisions that employees can only guide. The "buck stops here" at the owner, whose success depends on the employee choices made and the team performance of all.

Sources

How and where do you find employees? In addition to family, friends, and customers who will send candidates, you may need to seek a pool of people from these sources to make your selection:

- Classified ads in daily and weekly newspapers provide numbers of all types of full-time and part-time people whose best recommendation is that they are serious about seeking work when they answer your ad. You will be interviewing many who will be less desirable, inexperienced, or otherwise unqualified for your position. All of them, however, will *believe* they are qualified, and some will be looking for any slight note of prejudice in your manner. Federal and state laws are very strict against employer prejudice, and any official hearing of this kind is a terrible blow to your reputation, so be very careful that your interview does not turn antagonistic for any reason. A friendly manner and hints of future possibilities dissuades thoughts of prejudice and retains a neighborly feeling about the store.
- Employment agencies usually supply experienced retail personnel at a fee of one month's salary or more. Many of these people, unfortunately, will resist the difficult retraining to "your way" when they are set in retail habit patterns.
- Temporary agencies should be used as a last resort in emergency situations because their people rarely match up with your needed skills.

Part-Time Workers

For most small shops, working with part-time help offers the advantage of the lowest cost of labor because there are fewer unproductive moments paid for, if you plan their work schedule efficiently. It also promises a lower per hour cost because of the greater supply available. The many good part-time people include some who need the work financially and others who work to escape a "time-on-my-hands" problem. A great many men or women at home, people who work while children are in school, senior citizens, and the partially handicapped have excellent experience and good motivation. Students who are available generally have good physical capacity and are eager for the learning experience.

Notice of job availability for part-timers can be less expensive (or free) than for full-time workers. These sources will cooperate:

- Social, religious, and school mailings and bulletin boards.
- Senior Citizen Centers and their mailings.
- Supermarket bulletin boards.
- High school and college placement counselors.

For full- or part-time help:

- Federal and state employment service offices will send you applicants without charge. Many applicants, however, will not want to accept the job if their unemployment eligibility for checks is still valid.

CETA Workers

Under the Federal Comprehensive Employment Training Act, you may hire inexperienced workers and train them for a three-month period during which you pay the minimum wage and receive a federal grant of part of the wages paid. At the end of this period you are expected to retain these workers at regular wages. CETA, however, does not have a record of successful operation, and 1981 cutbacks by President Reagan mean even fewer people available in the future.

For special professional skilled workers, best sources are the placement offices of training schools and bulletins or trade association journals (drugs, cosmetics, eyeglasses, and such).

You may avoid carrying employees on your payroll by using agencies that bill you at about a 35% higher rate than you would pay. It is estimated that when you figure all the payroll taxes and bookkeeping entries for employees, you add up to 25% or more, so the cost of an independent billed supply does not amount to too much more.

Duke's Smoke and Book Shop is a small store, but its entire location occupies 10 front feet of Main Street center with good downtown walking traffic. Duke does an excellent volume (over $200,000) very profitably selling bound and paperback books, magazines, tobacco products, candy, and state lottery tickets. He employs two high school students and two or more senior citizens on a part-time basis all year long on very short schedules (10 to 13 hours weekly) until the busy holiday season. He employs one full-time (40-hour) employee and one for 30 hours weekly, in addition to himself. The students do the heavy stock work in books (unpacking, stocking, supplying the floor), the general cleaning and window changes, and the older part-timers do more of the selling, cash, and reordering. All of the part-timers work for the federal minimum wage, which seems to satisfy the students, and it keeps the total for the year for those on social security well below the allowable maximum, even with the heavier hourly schedule for holidays. Duke says that he has an inexhaustible supply of these excellent people, and it helps him to be very selective and keep his budget in control.

THE APPLICATION AND INTERVIEW

Application forms have spaces for name, address, phone, previous address, bank, last three jobs, time periods, duties, social security number, family status including children, and sometimes reasons for having left employments, charge accounts, and more. Federal Equal Opportunity regulations limit your right to ask many questions. Charge account information can be very helpful in tracing at a later time.

INTERVIEW FOR TRAITS   Your interview with the applicants concerning their work references and skills is intended to disclose emotional steadiness, motivation, and ambition, and it may tell you how well they will get along with you and the other employees. Always tell the applicant that you are going to check references to confirm the facts. A past history of few long-term jobs is preferable to many short-term changes. Gaps in time should always be questioned. After you explain some of the tasks to be performed, the applicant will be more relaxed if given a chance to discuss some interests or talents that may be applied, or that were utilized in some past experience. At this point if you feel favorably inclined, you can explain more about the hour schedule and the salary. You can postpone a decision by explaining that you still have others to interview and will make a decision at a later time, but at all times be hopeful and pleasant.

New employees should receive a printed paper with the work schedule of days and hours, store rules about employee purchases, discounts, and storage of personal property. It should designate one employee to guide and teach work methods and should note the names and number of someone to call in case of illness. Lunch and break time should be stated, as well as payday, holidays, and any fringe benefits enjoyed by employees. In this way, the first day nervousness partly caused by future unknowns is reduced.

New salespeople should be reminded that *every* customer is a V.I.P. and should always get their first attention. Guide them into the technique of smooth customer approach, sales persuasion without debate, smooth suggestive additions to purchases, "selling the store" without being obvious, and observing shoppers without making the clientele nervous.

No small store can afford to have specialists who work on one kind of duty, so on the first day delegate some added responsibility in addition to the primary one of selling. Any stock work details can be the automatic assignment in slower moments, so that no managerial direction is needed. It is much more difficult to break up employees' conversation to direct attention to patron traffic; and the older merchants say "keep 'em busy, keep 'em happy!"

Emergency Training

Instructions for action in the event of shoplifters, robbery, customer illness, or fire should be explicit and rehearsed.

Employee Budget

It is not always possible to assess an amount of your total expense to assign to employee cost, or not always logical to plan a percentage of your sales forecast. At first, the cost is planned as a lowest possible cost of floor coverage, with the sales forecast in mind, however. You are working the costs of part-time and full-time schedules to get that result. The budget, then, is more a result than a plan.

PRIDE, MOTIVATION, AND COMPENSATION

In your own way, you can best motivate your employees to superior performance with your own pride and example. They enjoy their work more in an attractive place alongside pleasant coworkers, especially if they are proud of the values offered to their neighbors. They admire a successful business and feel happier for a recognized contribution to the team effort toward that success Publicly admire and commend a job well done very promptly, and you may soon find another to admire by the same participant. Mention *corrections* only in private. Be sympathetic to the personal and family needs of your workers and show respect for the individual even when differing in opinion or philosophy. Intimate relationships with employees are self-defeating and should be avoided. Alcoholic celebrations may blow apart your team camaraderie.

Salary and Other Incentives

Salaries must be competitive with similar business in the area, whether it is the older employee on your staff or a new one you hope to attract. Pay increases or bonuses do not really move an unmotivated worker. Money rewards as bonuses always seem to set a pattern for future expectations, which have a strong negative effect when not repeated. Rewards geared to the pride of the receiver, becoming part of the decision makers, a title, or perhaps time off or additional vacation may be more effective. Older employees who have lost enthusiasm are often revived to surprising heights of effort when assigned to train new people in their special expertise. Perhaps the fresh motivation of the new employee rubs off on the old.

Federal and state minimum wage hourly rates are usually fairly close to each another, with time and one-half rate over 40 hours. Many very small stores do not qualify to come under the federal regulations, but that does not mean they can pay the lower of the two rates. Other stores near you will be paying at least the federal rate, and you must be competitive. Consider the difference between the full-time and part-time workers, the experienced and the novice, and the need for real expertise, as in the case of shoe stores, corset fitting, furniture and home decorating, better women's fashions and men's clothing, fine jewelry, and others where a real pro can often justify payment of twice the salary. For most of these, payment is made by base salary and commission (a percentage of the sales over a base amount), and the commission keeps motivation high. Some doubt exists where commissions are pooled (shared) to avoid controversy. There are many items requiring no selling technique, many stores whose very operations are so basic that within a small break-in period any willing person can fill the need. Try to match the skillful where needed and use the inexperienced in extra tasks to save the time of the others, including you.

WAGE LAWS AND FRINGE BENEFITS   Federal and state wage laws do not require payment or granting of fringe benefits, always so costly in union contract settlements, but as a fair person who wants good relations with workers, you should grant at least the more common ones, like paid holidays, paid vacations in relation to time employed, discounts on purchases, and perhaps pay on jury days. Larger firms who have labor union contract settlements (see below) pay hospitalization, accident, health, and life insurance, plus pension, retirement, and severance, and that information is known in town. You will have to judge what to offer depending on the competition for labor.

In some stores selling difficult items, where there is often a problem of leftover unsaleable odd sizes (shoes, for example), a system of P.M. (push money) or "stims," are added at "so much a pair" to keep older stock moving.

Being realistic in your offering salary scale and fringe does not always mean that offering more than the other stores will attract all the top talent. The other factors—a good place to work with reasonable, human management—attracts more talent than a small difference in wages. Your own employees will "sell" your store.

Unions

Small shops are rarely the organizing target of local unions, and more than likely you will not encounter any activity among your employees if your wages and conditions are comparable. If you do notice workers meeting to organize and join a union, you must accept their right to do so and refrain from any threat or action calculated to prevent it. To prevent workers' rights to organize is considered unfair labor practice under federal labor laws and will be strictly enforced against a store owner with considerable cost.

Internal Revenue Service and Taxes

When you have been given your I.R.S. registered number for identification, you will be sent many documents instructing you how to handle your payroll of employees and register them. Register all new employees on form W4, with information about married status, dependents, and social security number so that your payroll deductions of social security and all taxes can be verified. It is practical to keep all application information with a copy of this document in a permanent employee book because very often information of this kind is needed long after the employee has departed. Further history of employees on the job is added as time goes on. A payroll book with all employee deductions is required.

The Federal Fair Labor Standards Act applies to stores receiving or shipping goods in interstate commerce or that have yearly sales in excess of $325,000. These stores must pay the federal minimum per hour (others must pay what their state labor laws order). Federal law—the 1970 OSHA (Occupational Safety and Health Act) sets standards for working conditions, under the Labor Department—also requires that your premises be safe to work in; many states have similar laws. If you have 10 or more employees, you must make regular reports and keep routine safety records. (OSHA regulations were attacked by the Reagan Administration in 1981 as "fumbling" and "antibusiness," so cutbacks in its operating expenses can be expected.)

FICA is the Federal Insurance Contributions Act, which covers the requirements of employers to withhold a certain percentage of worker's pay (and company's contribution) toward the fund to pay the many types of benefits, Old Age (retirement), Worker's Disability, widows or survivors, and so on, all roughly described as *social security*. From the I.R.S. you will receive complicated detailed instructions about the employee-related regulations under this act that you must follow. These are the most urgent:

- Keep good employee registration and payroll records.
- You must withhold social security and federal taxes from every employee according to the latest table and guide. Guide 334 is sent to you with forms with your identification number. Use them filled out when you deposit these funds at your bank to receive proper credit. Some states and cities require withholdings, too.

DEDUCTIONS FROM WAGES   You are expected to deduct the federal taxes due from each employee on every payday according to the chart given you, the amounts depending on each employee's dependants. Many states and some cities have income taxes that must be deducted as well by employers, and this is complicated by a different tax for residents and non-residents, and disability deductions. To avoid the necessity of checking each chart, local stationery stores make available for payroll preparation one chart in color denoting social security and taxes to be deducted on behalf of each taxing authority. These charts save a lot of time and they are changed as taxes change. These deductions are deposited to your special account at your bank and forwarded.

Keep these points in mind:

- Your company owes a matching payment of the total of all social security payments of all employees.
- You are advised to separate these funds from your regular account until due to be paid. (Every owner or corporate officer is personally liable for these funds withheld, in addition, of course, to seizing all other company assets.)
- Self-employed noncorporate owners are charged with a self-employed tax of over 9 percent in lieu of the worker's and the matching company amount. This is charged to you on your ready tax return and an "estimated" should be prepaid quarterly.

EMPLOYEE–NONEMPLOYEE STATUS   Generally, if you can hire and fire and direct the work methods, the I.R.S. says you are referring to an "employee" even if the person is not in your place physically. Submit the facts on form SS8 for I.R.S. answer. If a nonemployee is earning more than $600 per year from your firm, you must file 1099 NEC with your tax forms.

Tips are income on which tax and FICA must be reported by you as the employer.

WORKER'S COMPENSATION INSURANCE AND DISABILITY   Firms with one or more employees must carry these policies in most states. If you are incorporated, even you alone must be covered for compensation covering injury on the job and disability for illness or injury not job-related.

CASH/CHECK PAYROLL   In most states, *you* may choose to pay by cash or check. List the deductions, the gross amount, and net on the side of the check (and the stub in the book), or on a slip in your pay envelope for the employee's own record. Your payroll book is your accurate record from which you figure FICA and taxes owed.

Many employers have turned to issuing checks because of the security risk with cash, and checks are good pay records. In some areas the banks have automatic deposits for employees on the payroll similar to automated deposits of social security or dividend checks. Check-cashing time is reduced if you issue payroll checks early in the week. Employers favor a lag of a day or two at the end of a pay week for payroll to eliminate the rush and to influence attendance on a day following a day off (usually a poorly attended day), for example, payday Tuesday for the week ending Saturday.

Payroll check-cashing for customers represents a source of good regular business traffic. It has inherent dangers requiring good identification, checking the worth of the check-issuing firm, and the ever-present robbery possibilities.

SELF-EMPLOYED SOCIAL SECURITY   "Every person for livelihood or profit who engages in a business, trade, or profession individually as a sole proprietor or as a partner is liable for self-employed (S.E.) social security tax" (see I.R.S. Income 1040 S.E.). This includes the total net income from all personal working, income-producing endeavors except rents, interest (not part of working business), dividends, capital gains or losses, or income to a limited (nonworking) partner.

The social security tax is charged on the same maximum as the employee salary maximum (above). If you have wages and individual self-employed income, the wages are first and the balance up the maximum is then assessed at the self-employed tax percentage.

In family partnerships, if proved a *true* partnership with all employed, each can be charged with a portion of the income and the corresponding tax, and the social security S.E. tax.

MANAGEMENT TRAINING

You have a most potent incentive to offer your bright, eager, most-satisfying employees, whom you know must eventually go on to a higher salary level (which you may not be able to afford), or go on to their own business. Offer management training by consulting in the tactics of everyday decisions together, explaining why you feel strongly about your way, the historical experience behind it, or admitting to an instinctive "hunch" or a guess, even a mistaken one.

Take more than an occasional suggestion from good employees, reviewing results and analyzing decisions. Allow them to select merchandise of particular categories as their special own, reviewing cost, markups, markdowns, additions of likely beneficial nature, and rewards to meet success. This will lighten your burden as well as develop a rewarding relationship. Discuss expenses.

Encourage learning to interview, train, and supervise other employees and especially to assume store responsibility in your absence. Teach making the immediate markdown on items, in your absence, by learning the cost code and your philosophy on goods that should be moved.

Consider and discuss the possibility that a joint involvement in another store in the future may be a successful well-founded investment for both. Suggest that the assembling of capital as well as the merchandising fundamentals should begin as early as possible to be ready for entrepreneurship.

MANAGEMENT SKILL REWARD   If you will choose your employees carefully, communicate the goals promptly, have concern for them personally, and encourage their collaboration in a team effort, your store will be the beneficiary of loyal, motivated helpers who will serve your store's clientele as you would have them served.

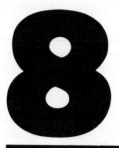

MERCHANDISING AND
INVENTORY CONTROL

It is said:

> Storekeepers operate a store, but good merchants MERCHANDISE it.

The difference, then, is *merchandising,* the process of planning the strategy of operating to satisfy the trade while making good profits and achieving healthy growth. Good merchandising requires controls to monitor financial developments.

Merchandising efforts, of course, include other decisions: the selections of lines and assortments, pricing strategy, presentation, and other judgments, all specially calculated to attract and satisfy the clientele. But profits demand *controls* that effectively result in the cash remainder necessary to grow. To do this, the owner plans and projects these controls:

- Logical buying quantities of merchandise to match projected sales of a period.

- Budget limits on variable expenses under control.
- Guarding the flow of running money, enough to handle retail problems.
- Attaining a goal of a minimum inventory residue to end a season, and cash profits.

The tools you need are a combination of good records and logical projections based on knowledge of the traditional sales in similar stores. You work primarily with inventory at retail value, as with sales and markdowns.

Planning merchandise buying for both replacement and in anticipation of the season starts with the basic preplanned inventory assortment discussed in Chapter 5. The budget limit on spending is sensibly proportioned to the sales expected, a forecast, and it is known as your "open to buy." Where staples are involved, stock fill-ins are based mostly on the quantity needed. Where style goods are needed, a more careful study of changing directions and your store goals must be considered. In both, the open to buy limits the total to matching your projected sales.

PLANNING THE SALES FORECAST

You already estimated a total year's sales goal when you discussed the investment in the store stock assortment, considered the stock turnover per year for your kind of store, and the estimated profit possible. Where several kinds of goods were involved, it was the sum total of all the stock considered. The merchandise involved affects the rate of sale at different times of year, but the general method of a sales projection is much the same whether it is a discount store or features expensive designer fashions. All goods have seasonal highs and lows in their own selling; and this is traditional and pretty much the same in all geographical areas. It can, of course, be slightly altered by your own promotional input.

The orders for your opening assortment have the total cost and retail value to give you the markon percentage to use in each category of the opening stock. This is the profit percentage you will be using.

First Year's Sales Forecast

Study the traditional percentage of sales in each period of the year by category of merchandise. Retailers and manufacturers are familiar with these sales peaks, the very busiest periods, and the estimates can be accurate for the months, as well as the quarterly periods you use to break up the sales year. In most items the peak periods for small retailers produces such a large percentage of the year's sales that there is no problem dividing up what is left.

Traditional trade experience is your guide. For example, your knowledge of the ladies' handbag trade, with its holiday gift-buying influence, might project 50% of the year's sales in the quarter November, December, and January. The Handbag Association or the National Retail Merchants Association can assist in confirming the figure. It is estimated also that the pre-Easter four-week period will often produce 25% of the year's sales, and Mother's Day in May about 8% leaving only about 17% of the estimate of the year to be allocated elsewhere on the sales calendar.

SALES CALENDAR   Most retailers prefer a fiscal year ending on January 31 (or July 31) because it is convenient to carry a low inventory at that time. This is the way it has been presented here, but it is your choice. Using the calendar (Table 8.1) in quarters, work with the information you have to insert the percentages and the dollar amounts. Next year, you will have the additional guide of last year's figures, which influence the plan, and an accurate feeling about sales trends in general. The end of the fiscal year is the lowest inventory, your busiest months the highest plan, and the months throughout the year vary up and down with your need for a balanced assortment enough to handle the planned sales, and ending the month with the inventory planned for that time.

TABLE 8.1. Year Planning: Sales and Advertising Calendar (in fiscal quarters)

Sales Volume Percent Projection	$ Sales	Holidays	Advertising $ Budget
1st Quarter		Ground Hog Day	
_____%	Feb. _____	Lincoln-Wash. B'day	_____
_____$		Valentines Day	
		St. Patricks	
	Mar. _____	Pre-Easter Fashions	_____
		Palm and Easter	
	Apr. _____	Dressup	_____
		Home Fixup	
	Total 1st Q. _____	Total	_____
2nd Quarter		Mother's Day	
_____%	May _____	Pre-Summer Fashion	_____
_____$		Summer Furn.	
		Memorial Day	
	June _____	Brides and Weddings	_____
		Father's Day	
		Summer Hot Promo.	
	July _____	July 4 Sales	_____
		Clearances	
		White Sales	
	Total 2nd Q. _____	Total	_____

TABLE 8.1. Year Planning: Sales and Advertising Calendar (in fiscal quarters) **(continued)**

Sales Volume Percent Projection	$ Sales	Holidays	Advertising $ Budget
3rd Quarter		Pre-Campus Events	
_____%	Aug. _____	Fall Fashions	_____
_____$		Back to School	
		Stationery Needs	
	Sept. _____	Labor Day	_____
		School Days	
		Jewish Holidays	
		Columbus Day	
	Oct. _____	Coat Sales	_____
		Fall Fashions	
		Home Furnishings	
		Halloween	
	Total 3rd Q. _____	Total	_____
4th Quarter		Area Promotions	
_____%	Nov. _____	Pre-Holiday Gifts	_____
_____$		Veterans Day	
		Thanksgiving Home Dressup	
	Dec. _____	Policy Ads-Gift Wrap	_____
		Gift Ads	
		Last Minute Pickups	
		Post Christmas Sale	
	Jan. _____	New Years Event	_____
		Jan. Clearance	
		Pre-Inventory	
		Crazy Clearance	
		Giveaways	_____
	Total 4th Q. _____	Total	_____
	Total Year Sales _____	Year Ad Budget	_____

In going into busier months, therefore, requires that additional goods be ordered in your open to buy; into slower periods, less goods.

THE PLAN FIGURE IS A STANDARD   Even if you consider these first year figures of sales and inventory rough and uncertain, they are a standard against which you contrast your actual figures to make any necessary operational adjustments. The contrast of plan inventory figures to (perpetual inventory) book figures as you proceed helps to predict whether you will have a cash profit or leftover merchandise that you may have to mark down in price.

Order Placement of Open to Buy

Using the estimated sales for the period ahead, the profit percentage, and subtracting the profit, you have the amount of dollars for your open to buy. Do you go right out and place orders for the entire amount at once? Not usually. It is generally preferable to leave yourself a little "hungry," depending on market availability of goods, lead time necessary for delivery, your access to the market, staple characteristics, or high-style timeliness of the goods.

Don't overbuy, especially your first year. Before you know demand or before you attain traffic, overbuying can be fatal. You have not yet built up a following of loyal customers, a traffic of lookers to feast on the promoted, lowered-price goods you need to unload that is authentically a real bargain. Don't buy beyond your open-to-buy figures because the over-stock uses up valuable cash you need for items that the trade is calling for. The extra goods diminish in value and eat up valuable turnover and profits. If your sales are below expectations, you know it from the comparisons and get the same "overbought" feeling. In both cases, summon your own merchandising ingenuity to scheme ways of promoting more sales to replenish running money supply. Without controls, you would not have the vivid bleak picture until the day you actually run out of cash., when it is too late to do anything about it. So, your controls keep you informed.

What about the loss of running money, the operating cash that disappears during security mistakes involving theft or natural disasters not covered by insurance? Or the insurance settlement that takes time to arrive? Control information is part of the loan application your bank requires for the *tideover* funds to get you rolling again.

MARKDOWN

Seasonal and Spot (or Individual) Markdowns

Revising downward the estimated value of goods you own is a normal functional procedure of retail operations, not an indication of mistakes. There will always be markdowns.

SEASONAL MARKDOWNS   Remember, in seasonal operations you always hope to sell 80 to 90 percent of your stock at the regular markup, and then you expect to mark down the balance 25 percent of so, to "clean house," to sell out. This seasonally planned markdown has a downward effect of about 5 percent on your overall maintained mark-on, not unusual where style is involved. Merchants expect it and plan an original mark-on with this in mind. They will confirm that selective buying perfection for complete sell outs is rare and some markdowns are inevitable. One old-time, self-taught merchant friend used to say, "If you haven't bought some goods which are marked down, you must be losing sales with a very dull assortment!" Even turtles must stick their necks out to get somewhere!

      INDIVIDUAL OR SPOT MARKDOWNS   There are always some mistakes and some promotions from stock.

      Recognizing that the real value of your goods is *saleability,* you re-mark to a lower price anything in stock that will sell more readily at that lowered price. There are times that you will not sell more pieces of a particular item if you mark it down. It may need the assistance of advertising or a special display. Heavy floor traffic and signs with comparative prices can do it. It is of greater benefit to use your markdowns in conjunction with helpful tactics to benefit the whole store, to bring people in who will buy other goods as well.

      Wyler's fine men's store in a large eastern city had an interesting incident with one of its best English raincoat brands. When the delivery of Burberry coats was held up during one period, several open orders were suddenly filled and Wyler found himself with double his usual stock. Needing a promotional ad for this period, he decided to sell half of these coats at a sale price, $69, advertising "an exact copy of the famous English raincoat," but not mentioning the name, and removing the labels inside the coats. For his inventory record he took a stock markdown of 100 coats from $125 to $69 in his markdown book to equal $5,600. Wyler's reputation for quality brought an excellent response and in a few days he had sold 44 of the sale coats, but surprising to him, he had also sold 81 of the Burberry coats in stock with labels and $125 price tag. (In better stores, "snob appeal" of brands is natural.) The next few days saw the alteration hands resewing Burberry labels back into the "reduced" garments and re-marking (a book markup of $2,800) 50 coats back up to $125 to meet the demand for the Burberry Brand.

Perpetual Inventory Book

Many stores record markdowns in a perpetual inventory book, which records the progress of the inventory value, starting from year-end physical inventory, throughout the year. Starting with this actual dollar amount, you add the retail value of every invoice each month, subtract the sales, and deduct the markdowns as taken, to give you a realistic estimate of the dollars in sales this inventory will bring. A realistic view of the value of your stock will aid your forecasting and help to maintain a well-rounded assortment. When you see items on your shelves that are not saleable as marked, because they are damaged, shopworn, no longer fashionable, or what ever, drop the price to the more saleable figure and record the markdown in the book. Goods brought in for a promotional sale and marked to the sale price on the invoice do not then require any markdown; but later they may require a markup in your book if later re-marked to a higher price for regular stock selling.

Perpetual inventory records are very valuable to you, but they are not required by law (I.R.S.). Many retailers keep this running record in the sales receipts book (daily), (which *is* I.R.S. required), and they enlist the aid of any competent employee to record the figures. Accuracy is a *must,* and the mishandling of entries will nullify the pertinent value of your confirmation of mark-on percentage for the season (maintained mark-on) and the markdowns. The most significant value to you may be the comparison of its book value inventory figure to the actual count at year end. Here, a great difference may indicate an inventory loss due to employee theft, shoplifting, or inventory counting. It can indicate sloppy bookkeeping, too, and it serves as a warning to investigate!

Many retail failures were over-bought and under-enlightened. The inventory and the open-to-buy controls are considered a retailer's most important and necessary tools to keep abreast of financial limitations on market spending for stock, because the experts say that most retail failures are a result of overbuying. But these tools do not project the variable and fixed expenses that need to be contrasted to actual spending to reveal the existence of possible profits.

THE Q CONTROL   One very useful tool is a quarterly analysis chart of sales, expenses, and projected profits, called a Q Sheet (see Table 8.2). This comprehensive illuminating report of 13 weeks of operations has columns of plan and actual sales with cumulative difference, receipt of goods at cost, retail, and inventory cumulative, plan and actual markdowns, overhead and other fixed expenses, variable expenses including advertising, display, salaries, and taxes— enough information to be able to estimate profit. It is a traditional department executive control. This kind of analysis of properly documented cumulative operating figures has been the basis of executive planning between management employees and supervisory top executives in stores for more than 75 years. Now, of course, most of these figures are entered and processed by electronic data processing (E.D.P.) with weekly up-to-date printouts.

CONTROLS BY COMPUTER   Computers are very valuable information storage and computing facilities where the special requirements of stock handling can sometimes justify the investment. The development of new technology into the 1980s, with smaller, less expensive hardware, has a promise of more practical future equipment, and priced lower than the computers available now, which are not easily programmed without training. There is more and more software programming available in cassettes and discs for some of the easier

TABLE 8.2. Thirteen-Week Quarterly Controls (Q Sheet)

Week	Last Year and Planned Sales (A)	Actual Sales (B)	Cumulative Percent (+ or −) (C)	Starting Inventory (D)	Minus Markdowns (E)	Buying Plan (F)	Invoices for Merchandise In (G)	+ or − Plan (H)	Overhead (I)	Salaries, FICA (J)	Advertising, Insurance, Audit (K)	Supplies and Misc. Maintenance (L)	Total Running Expenses for Columns I,J,K,L (M)	Gross Profit (B − G) (N)	Net Profit (N − M) Tax, Net Net (O)	+ or − Inventory Change Effect (P)*	Minus depreciation on Net Tax Profits (Q)**
1.																	
2.																	
3.																	
4.																	
5.																	
6.																	
7.																	
8.																	
9.																	
10.																	
11.																	
12.																	
13.																	

*Inventory difference from last year affects profit tax.
**Depreciation of capital assets affects profit tax.

functions of payroll, inventory, and such in standard programs, but this alone hardly justifies the investment (see Chapter 11, Books and Records).

POINT OF SALE TERMINALS

Point of sale (P.O.S.) terminals are the new cash registers seen in major stores. They perform many of the information functions on the sale of different classes of goods, keeping track of the inventory in stock, with automatic entry into storage computers to which they are connected. Their use is valuable for credit checking and check cashing when connected to other facilities.

Because of swiftly advancing technology, making much of today's equipment obsolete in a few years, most new store owners are advised to rent equipment that they feel is practical for their special needs. After the time necessary to get the "feel" of their store merchandise needs and the customers, they can better evaluate the benefits of computer technology's latest software applications to control stock and reorder, to do payroll functions, and to help with Q controls and cash flow projection.

OPERATING SUCCESSFULLY

WATCHING THE STORE: SECURITY

Among the varied backgrounds of those who have held the office of President of the United States (peanut farmer, university president, army general and movie actor, to name a few) one background that produced an outstanding president was the retailing career of President Harry Truman. Just after inauguration, Truman invited his men's store ex-partner, Eddie Jacobson, to visit him at the White House and similingly offered his friend the traditional query as he entered:

Who's watching the store?

Truman's humorous remark relates to the ever-present and very serious problem of safeguarding the assets of your business—your stock and your money.

Watching is necessary and worthwhile.

Novices and insurance brokers may discuss the viability of loss-covering policies, but retailers know that insurance does not protect against many losses, and it reimburses only partially. It is much more logical and protective to the security of your store to study and analyze your vulnerability to outside and inside losses, and the helpful ways to lessen the risk or prevent them.

Outside losses are caused by those strangers who prey on the more vulnerable, and inside losses result from employees who study your ways to find methods of adding to their salaries without your knowledge, sometimes referred to, only partially in jest, as becoming your "partner." Both inside and outside losses are a serious threat to profitability and, really, to your very existence. What you don't know about your vulnerability to crime can, indeed, hurt you!

LOSSES FROM OUTSIDE

- Shoplifters and switchers
- Sneak thieves
- Con-artists
- Robbery
- Burglary

Shoplifters and Switchers

You and your employees protect your store best against shoplifters and switchers with trained store surveillance methods. Watching eliminates the temptation for the greatest bulk of shoplifters, the unprofessional, opportunist "amateur" thief. You constantly place before all your customers the open displays of attractive goods to tempt them to buy. Most shoppers will not steal under any circumstances, but they will be annoyed if your careless watching tempts them, especially when they see others taking things. By showing customers that you are alert to their presence, and reminding them that you are there to help them make a selection if needed, you eliminate temptation and focus all the attention on the selection of goods to buy. The same alert attention prevents switcher thieves from changing price tickets, to buy it for less. The alert cashier should recognize a switch, or at least suspect enough to check a price list or call the manager. If the cashier knows the seasonal (time of arrival) letter and the classification on the garment ticket, a switch cannot be made.

Both the physical layout and your training help to frustrate shoplifters. Plan your premises with certain safeguards.

- Locate the register where you obtain the best view of most aisles. Add convex mirrors and television monitors, if needed, to assist employees and to warn shoplifters.
- Make the primary approach to all shoppers even when busy, reminding them of your interest and awareness.

- For expensive items, you can attach "wafer" tags that activate a buzzer at exit doors if the tags are not removed at the register by the special device. Other telltale devices to frustrate thieves are tiny, hidden, plastic-like sensitive strips that buzz if not deactivated at the register. (The strips cost about 7 cents each, the deactivating machine more than $1,000.)
- On busy days post an alert guard enforcer at the door to discourage all stealing (a uniform helps).
- Where some uncertainty exists, employees should approach suspected shoplifters suggesting firmly, "Can I wrap that for you; will it be charge card or cash?" Open accusations on the selling floor, without proof, can bring on a suit for false arrest. Better a stock loss than a suit. Professionals have been known to fake a shoplifting to induce false accusation, later agreeing to a substantial settlement in place of a suit.

A FIRST EASY SCORE ENCOURAGES   An easy first score by an amateur shoplifter gives encouragement for greater and greater challenges. Most shoplifters do not "feel" like criminals and resent being classified as such when caught. The more difficult shoplifters are people on drugs, kleptomaniacs with uncontrollable impulses, and, of course, the professionals who use partners (two or more) and props to perform the crime more adroitly. The partners separate, make a commotion, pack up whatever is left unwatched in the confusion, and leave quickly.

WATCH FOR INDICATORS   Store security professionals teach observation for certain traits. Be alert to certain indicators, such as an amateur's nervous eye movements, a startled look when approached, circling one area for a time while looking around for possible observers. The pro shoplifters usually work in pairs or a large group; one may divert attention by pretending to be ill or upsetting a display, while the other gathers in the booty. Watch for their large double boxes, huge shopping bags, coats slung over the arm to hide items, or oversized clothing to be stuffed as they go along. Many thieves, both amateur and pro, will leave an old garment on the rack as they walk out with the new, unless prevented from doing so by some kind of "buzzing" tag at the exit door.

In small stores when you hear the cry of "two-ten," it refers to your two eyes that should observe the 10 fingers of a suspected shoplifter who has been spotted on the selling floor. A friend, Sy Miller, in his management of a chain of small sportswear shops, always insisted on a limit (three) to the number of garments brought into try-on rooms at one time, and most large department stores have long had such a policy. Miller was suspicious one day when a shopper took an unusually long time in the dressing room with expensive bathing suits. He sent in one of his most experienced girls, who popped open the curtain asking, "Is the size all right, dear?" . . . just as the customer was putting on her dress over the three bathing suits she was wearing one on top of the other. The police said she had a long record and had once been caught wearing four suits!

When you observe shoplifters in action, don't stop them until they are outside your doors. (Some states, New York for example, now allow capture inside.) Then firmly bring the shoplifter into your office, call local police, promise leniency, and ask the suspect to sign a prepared statement. You will have to accompany police to the station house with the merchandise and sign a complaint at once. It takes time and trouble, but if you do not prosecute, the word will get around town to encourage others to share the bounty of an easy mark.

Logic and experience play a large part in the professional protection team's defenses of larger stores. Some years ago, the personnel of the sporting goods department at Macy's (New York) never looked up as two young men in gray stockmen's coats picked up a canoe on the floor and carried it into an unattended nearby receiving area. Some paper, tape, and an attached discarded sales check disguised it as a purchase, enough to pass the protection man at the exit. The embarrassed security people talked it over, and a team of "customer-looking" men were waiting several weeks later when two gray-clad young men were stopped as they tried to steal the paddles. The prosecution secured the return of the canoe, as the judge exacted a large fine and months of repentent charity service, in lieu of jail terms. This probably cut short their career in crime, which had started as a "lark."

DON'T MAKE IT EASY! Judges try all kinds of embarrassment to dissuade young amateurs from continuing a shoplifting career. They require family and clergy attendance in court to assure that someone is watching during a probationary period. Judges warn the stores to discourage shoplifting with signs, mirrors, television monitors, guards, and such; otherwise they feel that the store is encouraging theft. Oregon has an interesting controversial (1979) law that allows the store to bill the thief the price plus a penalty of $500 ($250 for a juvenile), which must be paid to the store in lieu of a jail term.

Sneak Thieves and Con-artists

Sneak thieves usually attack your register drawer money and the money or personal property of employees. Use your layout to help protect your store. The counter opening in front of the register should be equipped with a buzzer and not be easily accessible from the front door. Employee's property should be locked in drawers or lockers elsewhere in the store.

Con-artists use a great variety of tricks to get merchandise free—too much change from a purchase, donations for nonexistent charities, or sell you stolen goods or office equipment. Always insist on proper identification or authorization in writing from a charity, and follow strict rules of the store on register receipts. Warn cashiers never to allow a buyer to change bill denominations while completing the sale ring-up, and always keep the received bill on the register until the change is given. Con-artists usually operate when you are very busy.

RECEIVING   The merchandise becomes your property when someone signs a deliverer's receipt for a shipment. You must examine carton seals for pilferage enroute to you, note the weight, and make sure you have the complete shipment before signing. If the cartons seem to have been tampered with, open them and examine the contents before you sign; because your signature agrees to pay for the entire quantity of so many cartons, intact. Delivery people should not be allowed to remain alone in receiving or other unsecured stock areas.

Robbery and Burglary

Robbery is theft with force and arms (or the threat of) to the person. The ever-increasing threat of bodily harm during an armed robbery makes it imperative that store management anticipates this danger and plans to use procedures to minimize all risks. Keep these points in mind concerning robbery attempts:

- When confronted with a gun, store employees should give in to the demands calmly and quickly. Replace bravado with careful observation of physical traits or other characteristics of the robber, which may be helpful to police later. (Local police also may offer suggestions.)
- Cash in the register over a minimum amount should be periodically banded and locked up elsewhere, then deposited in your bank or outside night depository. Some stores have counter openings into a locked storage compartment below; others have a safe hidden from view.
- Professionals seem to favor robbing certain types of stores and those known to have large sums on hand to cash payroll checks—drugstores, liquor, fine jewelry (cash and stock), gold and silver buying shops, cigarette and lottery stores, and large supermarkets. Many of these provide a special bullet-proof barrier and an armed guard. Payroll days offer additional temptation to hold-up people, and many stores have started paying by check.
- Deposit visits to your bank should not be made on a predictable schedule.

Burglary is theft by breaking and entering your premises, usually after closing time. This unlawful entry may include employees who come back after hours using stolen keys.

Protective Devices

ALARM SYSTEMS   Store premises should be wired at all openings and an alarm set at closing so that a loud bell will ring inside and out if the door or window is opened without turning off the system with a proper key. This is the system most frequently used, and it is especially needed when merchandise is of high value and easily transported.

An alarm system can be installed and monitored by many companies who, for a monthly charge, will send guards to your place if there is a break. The guards have a key to enter, call the police to meet them there, and call you to give you an opportunity to get to the store, too. In some stores, there is only a silent alarm in the stores; it rings at the monitoring office (at police precinct, too). Some alarms notify local police by automatic telephone dialers with a taped message.

In addition to alarms activated by breaking in a wired opening, sensitive electronic monitors can be placed around the store, which detect movement, noise, foot pressure, or the breaking of an invisible light ray to set off an alarm. Store safes are a favored area.

LOCKS   Front and rear doors should be equipped with dead-bolt locks, made by many companies, whose "unpickable" locks have keys that are difficult to duplicate. (One good company is Medico.) To prevent thieves who remain secreted on the premises from escaping later, use two-sided door locks, which require a key on each side.

SAFES   Buy a safe with the fire security of the company's books in mind. In addition to locking up the cash funds overnight, you need room for checkbooks, inventory records, cash receipts book, accounts payable, receivables, or any record that might be needed in case of fire or destruction of the store, or for an I.R.S. audit. To prevent removal, it is wise to bolt the safe firmly into the floor.

OTHER CONSIDERATIONS   When the store is closed for the night, always leave the cash register drawer open so that it will not be destroyed by someone trying to force it open. Scratch identifying marks on machines, and make a separate list of the serial numbers of all office machines, especially valuable, easily sold IBM typewriters. (IBM has returned many such machines long after they were reported stolen because their repair department found the serial numbers on the "stolen" list, much later when sent in for repair.)

Use shutter screens. These rugged mesh steel gates across the front of your premises offer protection against penetration through your windows or vestibule, and at the same time they protect the glass in the show windows from vandalism or other damage. Gates help to keep intruders out during civil disorders, too. Imbedded steel bars as well as alarm screens are need over all skylight and ventilator opernings.

INSIDE LOSSES

It is a generally accepted fact that employees steal more from retail stores than all the ousiders, despite the more spectacular nature of robbery or burglary "takes." It is very difficult for owners, with their many details to perform, to watch for the warning signals of employees who are stealing. But you *must,* because experienced store employees can spot the owner's vulnerability immediately, and the new ones, who might be tempted, learn the defects in your routine when you choose to ignore what is missing.

INTERVIEW AND CHECK REFERENCES   The very best preventive defense against an experienced employee thief is the very thorough interview and check of applicants' references, which might indicate a choice not to hire them. Always ask references where the person has worked would they hire that person again. Any answer but "yes" should indicate a serious defect. Remember that very few references will say: "Don't hire Tom, he's a thief!" The question of slander is involved.

TEMPTATION AND GREED ARE ADDICTIVE   Employees are easily tempted to steal small amounts of cash or goods if store systems are not followed strictly to prevent it. They then grow more greedy as the ease of enriching themselves (tax free) at your expense upgrades their standard of living. Stealing is extremely difficult to stop when the employee has become addicted. It is much easier to enforce store systems strictly to prevent the first temptation. You must also know the kind of stock controls that keep you aware of substantial stock losses, so that you will investigate the leak. Train all employees your own or this safeguard system. Enforce it strictly *without exception.* If you don't follow it as an example, your employees won't either.

Safeguard Systems and Procedures

- All employee outside purchases should be stapled-closed, initialed, and stored in a separate area (safe from sneak thief loss and from an addition of your store goods), and checked out at closing.
- Employee's handbags should be locked away in an office, or in locked drawers or lockers safe from sneak thieves. Handbags near the register make it simple to add funds from unrecorded sales.
- Salespeople must call back aloud the price of the garment and the amount of money received. This helps to prevent any claim of error by the customer in price or change, insures proper ring-up as the cashier repeats it, and prevents error as the cashier calls back change given to the customer before putting the bill received into the register. Traditionally, before sales taxes created prices that require change from even dollar amounts, stores priced goods just below the even dollars ($2.98, $4.95, $6.99) so that salespeople had to ring the sale to get the change for the customer.
- A salesperson should staple the customer's merchandise bag with the sales ticket to close it. This prevents any customer's later claim of "no sales ticket" and also prevents adding other goods to the bag. It stops employees from using abandoned sales tickets as "proof of purchase," to void and replace cash in register, or to give friends to claim a refund as they pick up merchandise when entering the store. All refunds must be

entered in a book with name and address and must be periodically checked by management to see who made the refunds.

- Employees operating the register must close the drawer after each sale. Mistakes must be voided and signed by two, then rerung. Management must see that tapes are sufficient for the full day of register use No employee except the manager should have access to tapes in use. Questionable register cash integrity is sometimes indicated on the tape records.

- All discount sales must be entered into the book and approved by the manager in charge. These are markdowns, which must be entered into the perpetual inventory book.

- Daily register ring-off should be made by the owner or manager some time in the late afternoon. This eliminates the ring-off at closing time when you are busy with details of checkout as employees leave, and it adds to a more relaxed, unhurried closing.

- At ring-off, register tapes are removed from the register with totals ignored until later, and fresh tape settings are made for next sales. All change and bills are placed in a cash box without counting, and a new precounted "float" of small bills and change is placed in the drawer to use immediately after register ring-off. The total over the float amount is banded for deposit and checked against the tapes in the privacy of the office.

Receiving Department and Stockrooms

In your small store, at first you will be receiving shipments yourself, and the problems of theft are not as urgent as the efficient record often needed at some later date. To operate this function now and with employees later, you will probably do best with a system involving the receiving apron, a form in three parts (original and two copies, one in a permanent book), which is a helpful record. (See Figure 9.1.)

The original is attached to the vendor's invoice to the store (a packing slip temporarily, if invoice has not arrived); the second copy to the trucker (the form is signed by the person receiving and by the trucker if freight is paid, with names on all three copies); the third copy remains in the receiving department, or until

FIGURE 9.1.

Invoice #	VENDOR	Total Invoice $	Date _____ Time _____	Rec'y # Consecutive (123456)
Truck Co.	Truck Driver	Cartons	FREIGHT C.O.D. Ppd.	Rec'd by
Dept.	Merchandise	Weight	Inspected pcs. doz.	Rec'd on floor

the end-of-month audit. This copy in your office insures a record of merchandise received (for accounts payable) even if the original invoice is lost. It will be enough to remind you of the shipment, vendor, and total amount to be paid.

Aprons are serial numbered and have spaces for the date, vendor, (your) department number, invoice number and total invoice dollars, number of cartons, weight, freight COD amount or prepaid, number of dozens total, name of truck company, and space for trucker's signature, and person receiving. The store name is printed on top.

CASH FREIGHT AND SHIPPING FUNDS   The receiving function with freight paid and shipping money for returns (prepaid usually), as well as petty cash spent by this department for maintenance or building material supplies and other petty spending, seems to be an area subject to monetary or other loss. Some shipping and receiving clerks have shown great ingenuity in learning to outwit the system and divert cash to themselves with false invoicing, reworking truck receipts, and using old letterheads from supply jobbers "paid in cash" to steal funds. Some receiving clerks have worked with truckers and trash pickup workers to steal company cartons of goods, so the physical area (usually in the rear of the store) must be spotchecked regularly and merchandise should be checked in from receiving to selling floor.

The trash collection should be assembled at one point, near receiving, tied securely to reduce fire danger, and tightly covered in metal containers if they contain any food remains, to keep vermin contamination at a minimum. In most areas it is necessary to hire a local refuse contractor. Check with your neighbors.

STOCKROOMS   Open merchandise in stockrooms and easy entry sites invites stock losses, usually from employees. If the stock in the stockroom is in sealed cartons, an inventory should be kept handy to check in and out, and a key should be used with sign-up to reduce the amount of pilferage.

CASH SALE ALTERNATIVES

You are probably familiar with many of the alternatives to cash sales. These include checks, credit cards, charge accounts, and installment accounts. Each of these is detailed below.

Checks

The use of personal checks as payment for purchases has become very risky, and many stores in larger cities, who have suffered losses, now accept the cost of bank credit cards as a preference. Stores in small local payroll areas still cash known payroll checks from their regular customers as a means of keeping a continuous flow of store traffic on the days when these customers are most likely to be vulnerable to the store's tempting merchandise. Some insist on a purchase, others do not. Most keep a file with some description of the payee to check the identity of the person cashing the check. Some stores take simultaneous photos.

RISKS OF CHECK CASHING   Cashing checks does increase the risk of armed hold-up, and physical precautions and robbery insurance should be considered. Customers resent the delay in identification from your system, the photo taking, and the thumbprint form used occasionally, but the most resentful are the professional thieves, who do not want to be identified after they have successfully "proved" to you that their identification is OK. These pro check thieves know the regulations requiring permanent-type identification, driver's licenses, government cards with personal description, and so on, and they manage to forge what is necessary.

On all checks, use a rubber stamp with spaces requesting information most helpful when, at a much later time, your memory of the transaction has vanished. In many cities there are personal check guarantee services, a bureau you can call to verify before accepting the check, which for a 3 percent fee (plus a monthly amount) will underwrite the face value of it. This verification is similar to that used with bank cards, which have replaced most individual store charge cards because of the cost to stores of maintaining large staffs to operate.

Credit Cards

Bank charge cards are favored by consumers because there is no or little cost to them if paid regularly as a charge account, and they need to carry only one for most stores. The stores pay VISA, Master Card, and American Express a fee of 2 1/2 to 6 percent of the sale depending on their sale average and the total sales per month. (The charges paid by stores are negotiable.) These card companies charge a high rate of interest to the customer for late payments, which individual charge account stores generally found impossible to collect. Several of the card companies charge yearly fees (American Express, Diner's Club, Carte Blanche) to users, and some of the banks behind VISA and Master Card began to charge annual fees in 1981.

BANK DEBIT CARDS CHARGE YOUR ACCOUNT AT ONCE   Banks in some areas are working with "bank debit" cards connected to central system computers, which control the customer's bank account (but computer crime and multierrors have caused great anxiety to some at the prospect of a computer voucherless society). The store, using the customer's card and secret code, immediately debits the customer's bank account (or credit line) and credits the store's, in a similar way that the bank cash machines work. It saves bank bookkeeping and the necessity for monthly billing by credit card companies, plus a time delay *use* of the money; but consumers are deprived of this delay and have balked at accepting it.

Another card in use is the electronic "smart card," which contains secret data memory chips supplied by the bank with the latest credit allowance to the cardholder. The user can take it just about anywhere (soon worldwide), and with the proper secret code (eventually a matching of the person's signature code with that in the card), he or she can charge to his or her account until the card shows that the amount is used up. Card users return to their bank source to replenish the data and obtain a new credit limit. IBM, Philips Data Systems, and Honeywell are developing these systems further to integrate them with their present computer storage systems.

BANK CREDIT CARD CHARGES ARE LIKE CASH TO THE STORE
Stores enjoy the use of charges to bank credit cards because, after verifying the customer and the current limit of credit by phone (also verifying by point of sale terminal registers attached to central terminals), the store deposits the sale charge receipts as *cash* in the bank for immediate credit to the store. The percentage charge to stores seems to be negotiable, so be prepared with your best forecast estimates when signing the agreement.

Charge Accounts

Store charge accounts, with or without an identifying card, were the traditional "personal" relationship between the store and the customer, and many local merchants find that this relationship positively affects the loyalty of many of their regulars. These accounts require expertise in taking credit applications, time-consuming inquiry, office records work, and followup to keep collections current so that the use of funds (costly interest) is kept to a minimum. When the use of time cost of funds, and possibility of loss of goodwill (delinquent follow-up) are considered, a strong argument can be made against these accounts today.

Credit Installment Accounts

Installment credit accounts in stores involve regular payments weekly (or other) by the customer coming into the store and a credit percentage charge included in the payments. The advantage of customers coming into the store, to be tempted further by merchandise offerings as they make payments, is obvious, and many of them never quite get back to a zero balance. Traditionally, the stores who used time installment payments were big-ticket sellers, furniture, home decorating, fine jewelry and gift stores, and the department stores (joined small purchases). Expertise in credit application taking, checking credits, place of business, credit bureaus, and previous credit accounts is required along with the office record-keeping and followup ability. Payment traffic is a compensating factor.

COMPUTER CREDIT PROFILES   Banks and credit bureaus now evaluate the credit worthiness of potential debtors with an "instant profile" application, which is put into the computer as a punched card and develops fast answers. The federal government since 1974 has tried to limit its use because it seems to operate unfairly against minorities and women. Small stores without credit evaluation expertise should favor credit cards or other methods where the customer worthiness burden is on others, and they should be willing to pay for the service.

Layaways

Stores have always allowed customers to make an original deposit and later payments of cash on merchandise they planned to take home later when the total price was paid up. This enabled customers to buy on installments without the credit applications and pay installments at their own convenience, planning for the future take home. The extended confusing period of time requires stores to keep excellent records, which should have verified register-receipted payments and a duplicate record filed close to the register. Layaway seems to be a temptation to employee theft of goods stored and of part payments made, and it must be carefully supervised.

SECURITY SHOPPING SERVICES

Wilmark and Merit are two national companies who will shop in your store for a monthly service fee to check your systems or your employees for service or integrity. Their routine purchases offer the employee an opportunity to pocket an even dollar amount from a sale. New employees may be tempted; but experienced employees usually recognize the kind of transaction and make certain that the shopper reports how courteous, helpful, and honest they were. These services, however, do catch some employee thieves, and they work with the store to extract an immediate confession while the employee is still ashamed and sorry. This is a wise procedure to follow to obviate the possibility that the employee in the future can come back against you when you no longer have the proof at hand. (Insurance policies to cover security losses of your store are covered in the next Chapter 10.)

REMOVE TEMPTATIONS FROM YOUR OPERATION   Remember that most store losses are increased by the temptations offered to shoplifters, employees, suppliers, and even robbers and burglars, who will always select the least protected premises. Train your employees to act sensibly in an emergency and follow your store rules strictly.

Use a fireproof safe for all funds and store records and keep a duplicate set of critical inventory totals, monthly balances, and I.R.S. information in another place so that the loss of originals will not be fatal to your operation in the event of disaster. No safe is completely fireproof.

Work with your accountant to perceive any area of money handling, payroll or petty, that might be subject to employee theft. Bookkeepers who handle the checkbook have opportunities that offer temptations if the owners "sign" without verifying.

Remember that intimate information concerning profits, sales, petty cash details, or I.R.S. returns for your business are better unshared with employees. These details may be the basis for an I.R.S. vigorous examination at some future time if a disgruntled ex-employee is bent on causing you hardship.

10

INSURANCE FOR RETAIL STORES

PREMIUMS

For a sum of money called a premium, you agree to take a policy, a contract with an insurance company, which will repay you in the event that you suffer certain specified losses. For this fee, you transfer the risk to the insurance company.

Anyone, even the most careful and hard-working store operator who does everything "right," may suffer losses. You can buy insurance to cover *any* loss imaginable. You insure to protect against the vital loss, the one you can't afford.

Insurance experts say:

> . . . stores are extremely susceptible to liability claims. Their stocks of merchandise, fluctuating seasonally, represent a considerable investment and require careful insuring both against fire and similar hazards and losses through dishonesty. Because stores are on lease arrangements, special attention should be given to cover insured's extensive improvements of the building. . . .

No one can predict the health of the individual, the possibility of injury to employees or others, the casualty losses of a fire or natural disaster, or the calamity of crime losses, which can wipe out your capital and ruin your business future. You need insurance protection, but how much? You should have a carefully planned program based on an understanding of what the policies protect, and a helpful, interested insurance broker who can discuss your particular needs with you and get the best for your store for this invested premium. The broker should also be available on a continuing basis as your needs change, and should be helpful in pursuing your claim should a loss occur. The responsibility for the correct policy to cover losses is *still yours*!

INSURANCE SELLERS: BROKERS AND DIRECT WRITERS

Insurance is sold by direct writers, representatives who work exclusively for one company (Allstate, Nationwide, Liberty Mutual, State Farm, and others) and by brokers, who sell policies for many companies, which can cover every conceivable insurable risk. Dealing with either a direct writer or a broker has no built-in money saving, but most of the larger individual companies feature a countrywide network of their own people to handle loss claims. Individual brokers can give you a personal consultation service and offer a choice of several companies who write similar coverage. This can provide an advantage by choosing those companies with more favorable contract clauses for your needs or *can be* just a money saving.

Shop around for insurance because the price varies. Brokers and insurance companies can vary the premium charges as they wish for similar specifications of risk. Therefore, you should shop and compare what you are getting for your money as you do when you buy other services and supplies. Set a program for your store with a premium price you can afford, then get competitive quotes for the same coverage.

All companies and brokers who are licensed by your state are examined by your state insurance department for solvency and operating integrity. Despite this, you will have to choose carefully yourself when selecting a representative to work with. A state license to do business is no guarantee of a seller's insurance expertise or his or her devotion to your interest. Choose an agent you know from a past relationship, if possible, or ask friends in business or your attorney for the name of a knowledgeable person to help set up the program.

INSURANCE PACKAGES   There are "multiperil" programs that are separate risks, separate contracts for each, joined together. Or you may choose an "all-risk" package policy with the benefit of some cost saving over the premiums required for each separate insurance coverage when totalled. In this package, with all these separate insurance coverages, you want to cover the risks and threats to your store, but you do not want to cover more than you need or spend more than you can afford.

What are the store insurance policies you should consider in planning a program with your broker?

THE ESSENTIALS   The law says you must protect your employees from job-related injury and illness, so each state requires Workmen's ("Worker's in some states) Compensation and Disability Benefits Insurance. Most states have specific compensation for stated injury on the job, payments for loss of limb, and such, and policies cover these payments. The injury or illness on the job is *not* related to the business owner's fault or negligence, but the premium depends on the employment risks. Many states, such as New York and California, have set up their own State Insurance Funds to control compensation more closely and to offer a saving over the cost of similar policies from public companies. Policies cover job-related suits against the employer even if not specifically covered in the state law.

Many states also require a policy covering disability benefits to compensate employees for loss of work and injury when the happening was unrelated to the job. Some states allow employers to prove financial responsibility for these compensations and to post a bond instead of a policy.

LIABILITY INSURANCE

A large liability insurance policy always guarantees a legal defense of your store by the insurance company.

General liability insurance covers your liability to others for damages due to your negligence (or your employees') in operating your business. It includes happenings on your premises, sidewalks, machinery, elevators, and the like. Suits against store owners are not unusual, and you need an excellent professional defense against a suit because one accident, one verdict against you, one loss could be large enough to wipe out a business financially. A liability policy may also cover damage caused by the use of your products. Product liability usually involves a suit because of the illness (or death) of a food consumer or user of cosmetics, but it can include any product. Other than in a restaurant, the primary responsibility for most products is with the *maker* (or manufacturer), and retailers need only make certain that the maker is insured. If you pack some of your store products in your own store label, indicating that the product is made to your own specifications, you will need to be insured.

The insurance company will provide a legal defense against a suit and pay whatever verdict is rendered up to the limit of the amount of your policy for medical, surgical, hospital, disability, loss of earnings, funeral expenses, and death benefits. Jury verdicts for negligence-caused injuries are very large, and since the premium cost of a $1,000,000 policy is not excessively more than much smaller coverage, it seems worth taking the larger coverage. Anyone can sue you for damages; customers, passersby, messengers, delivery personnel, and even trespassers have succeeded in winning suits.

FIRE AND NATURAL DISASTER POLICIES

Fires and other disasters pose a threat to instant loss of all of your property, stock, money, securities, fixtures, expensively redecorated premises, and your building, if you own it. It is wise to account for newly purchased expensive equipment, sizeable additions to your inventory, and money spent on your physical store by increasing the face amount of your policy accordingly. To save on the premium, most store policies are written with a "coinsurance" clause, which is usually in the amount of 80 percent—meaning that if the face value of your policy is 80 percent or more of the actual value of all your property insured, you will be covered for the entire loss beyond the policy amount. You are solely responsible to see that your insurance policy keeps pace with the increase in value of your property.

POLICY TERMS   Policies call for payments of "actual cash value." This amounts to a payment by the insurance company of a loss equal to the (before fire) value of the property, less depreciation, the loss of value that time exacts, and "wear and tear." This can reduce your award substantially. The alternative clause for policies is payment of "replacement cost," full payment of the repair necessary or actual physical replacement without deduction for depreciation, a more complete coverage for loss, especially during an inflationary period.

FIRMAN FIRE DISASTER   Joseph Firman operated his Just Kids store for 28 years, so successfully that he would proudly point to his standing in the community after very humble beginnings, and the fact that he was able to support three of his four children through graduate schools. Firman also pointed with pride to his youngest son, Philip, who replaced his wife in the business after the young man graduated from business school and spent a few years working in department stores. The father was planning a period of lesser involvement in the business before retiring and turning over the store to his son.

Then disaster struck! A fire in the frame building next door ate its way into Firman's store, from across the alley, destroying everything. All the merchandise and fixtures and most of the building (not owned by Firman) were gone. Even the store delivery van in back was burned.

Firman retrieved the blackened contents of his (only partially fireproof) safe and called Charlie Chasalow, his insurance agent, to see what he could expect from the company who had carried his fire insurance policy for 12 years. Chasalow suggested that Firman might benefit from the help of a *public* adjuster, a professional who helps store owners get the best fire claim adjustments (for a fee of about 15 percent). This would get the maximum from the claim and secure enough of an award to justify the commission, while taking the details of settlement out of the hands of the Firman family, all of whom were terribly upset.

The completeness of the tragedy unfolded as a settlement was being discussed. the $20,000 fire policy covering the entire store, contents of merchandise and fixtures, was *underinsured* by 50 percent; Firman's January 28 inventory showed $39,000 (at cost) and his furniture-fixture ledger depreciation schedule showed $11,000 value, including the new $2,800 POS-register bought last year. (Firman said privately that he had actually "marked down" his inventory to this figure to reduce taxes in the fiscal year that ended January 31, that it was worth over $46,000, and the replacement cost of fixtures alone would be over $18,000.

The coinsurance 80 percent clause in Firman's policy required him to insure to 80 percent of his $50,000 actual "book" total, or a policy for $40,000. Since he only carried one-half of that (20,000 over 40,000), this fraction is multiplied by his loss, $50,000 to a total of $25,000; but *since* he *carried only a $20,000 policy*, that is the *limit* he *could collect!* His delivery van was covered by a separate fire policy that called for actual cash value payment for the complete loss. He was paid the original price of $7,000 less two years depreciation, or $4,600. This total settlement of $24,600 was a financial disaster that Firman blamed on his insurance broker. But they share the blame because Firman himself should have realized how underinsured he was. For another $450 per year, he could have been fully covered for his losses by carrying a $50,000 policy.

Firman was also compensated for his loss of profits because of the "business interruption" policy he carried as an extension of his fire coverage. It also pays for the full 90 days of expenses (or for a shorter period if the store reopens sooner). Fortunately, the building owner was fully covered for fire damage so the building itself could be restored.

FLUCTUATING VALUE FIRE POLICIES MAKE SENSE   Many stores have large variations of inventory from the slowest to the busiest sales time of year, and they plan their fire insurance coverage to increase and decrease by sending monthly reports. This has the effect of saving in not overinsuring when the inventory is lowest and provides the full coverage needed at all times.

INSURABLE INTEREST AND SUBROGATION   You can insure property that you do not own as long as you have an insurable interest. For instance, a tailor or repair shop can insure a customer's property because the shop owner will have to replace the loss. If you have several policies that total up to more than the value of the loss, you can only collect up to the total loss suffered, no more. Each policy will pay that proportion of the loss as their policy is to the total amount of insurance on the property. You will not be covered under ordinary fire policies for currency, bonds, deeds, mortgages, and such. Most policies call for subrogation of your rights to your insurer who has paid your loss. That means that if someone has negligently caused your loss, which would give you a right to sue for damages, the insurance company by paying your loss inherits this right to sue, by subrogation.

FIRE RATES   Company fire rates are based on the neighborhood fire loss experience, the construction of the building and its maintenance, and the very important factor of your neighbor's vulnerability to fire. A restaurant or a drycleaning plant in your building can cost you dearly in the rate. Automatic sprinklers can lower your rate, but you must be certain to cover for any "sprinkler water damage" losses. Remember that fire rates vary and can be rechecked and revised.

EXTENDED COVERAGE   An extended coverage added to your basic fire policy at a small extra charge is recommended to cover losses due to windstorm, hail, riots, civil disturbances, strikes, explosions, and damage from aircraft or automobiles.

Not long ago, a designer fashions and gift store, preparing for the "grand opening," was crashed into by a car that mounted the sidewalk, driven by a juvenile car thief, who was "unaccountable" for the damage. Although an extended "legal hassle" developed over the crash car's legal responsibility, under the extended coverage of the owner's fire policy, he was fully compensated at once to rebuild the front. His blanket fire policy covering "all perils" also added the business interruption insurance, which paid for six weeks of expenses and the loss of profits until he could reopen. The full insurance coverage resulted in a vital quick settlement.

AREAS OF HIGH RISK, THE FAIR PLAN   In certain rundown areas with very bad arson records, fire policies and extended coverage are impossible to obtain from regular companies. Many states, including New York and California, have created a pool of companies to write these policies under the Fair Plan, obtainable through your regular broker. In these same areas of high risk, policies normally unobtainable for robbery or burglary coverage have become available through your broker under the Federal Crime Insurance Act. These policies are administered through the Federal Housing and Urban Development Department, 451 7th Street, Washington, D.C. 20410.

Insurance coverage against burglary (theft by breaking and entering your premises to steal cash or property) is one of the optional policies not always considered necessary. But, properly wired for alarms, the average retail store is relatively inexpensive to insure for burglary, except where the stock is of a high unit value and easily carried (fine jewelry, stamps, coins, antiques). For proof of burglary, you must prove that the premises were entered "by force," showing visible marks. You are not covered for jewels or furs left in show windows, or for account books or manuscripts.

Robbery insurance protects you for loss of property, money, and securities by force, trickery, or threat of violence *on* or *off* your premises. It is relatively inexpensive because very little property is threatened at any one time. It is a good investment for the peace of mind it affords store personnel to know that they need not feel obligated to try to frustrate hold-up attempts, and for store owners to know that their *employees will not be tempted to be foolhardy* on such occasions and be injured.

3-D POLICIES   Comprehensive crime policies, known as "3-D," cover all losses of employee dishonesty, destruction of property, and disappearance, in addition to burglary and robbery, the loss of money and securities. Counterfeit and forgery can be included.

BUSINESS LIFE INSURANCE:
ACCIDENT AND HEALTH

If you cover all employees with a group life insurance policy, the cost is less than individual policies and the premium is a deductible expense for the firm. Employees are not taxed with the cost as income, and most plans permit withdrawal from the plan and conversion to a personal policy within 30 days after leaving the job.

Group health plans are also beneficial to employees, who pay less than they would as individuals. These plans help to reduce employee turnover because they are good for morale.

On most of these health and other policies, the I.R.S. restricts the use of company money as an expense unless *all* personnel, both executive and staff, are included in these plans.

Key Man insurance is obtainable to cover the loss or disablement of the essential person whose absence would be a hardship to the business. The premium is a deductible expense.

Discuss any of these policies with your tax consultants for the latest information on regulations on whether a policy is deductible.

PARTNERSHIP AND STOCKHOLDER AGREEMENTS

These agreements, detailing the obligations and responsibilities of partners and the obligations of the firm to pay out any withdrawing partner under certain circumstances, also usually include the buying of life (and health) insurance, the proceeds of which are to be used to buy out the interest of the deceased partner, in full or part. It is much simpler for the remaining partner to carry on the business without this obligation to pay the deceased partner's estate, and the cost is approved as an expense. In a corporation, the stock owned by the deceased is usually returned to the corporate treasury. (See Agreements, Appendix M.)

FIDELITY BONDS

Stores may buy fidelity bonds to cover losses caused by dishonest employees who handle company funds, or other valuable property. Bonding companies have access to more personal data on which to base a hiring decision and the very fact that an employee is to be scrutinized by them will discourage those with unsavory records from applying.

Many insurance policy premiums can be reduced considerably if a *deductible* amount is specified in the policy.

Because the building owner's coverage affects you, when leasing your store make certain that the owner of the property is fully insured for fire and extended coverage. Also be sure that there is some restriction on the owner to lease space in the building to high-risk tenants, who can increase your fire policy cost.

Your liability policy can include coverage against the store's vulnerability from suits for false arrest, detention, and slander when someone is accused of shoplifting or the like without proper proof.

Plate glass insurance covers your store front, the doors, and the glass in your inside fixtures against breakage. The replacement includes the cost of lettering and ornamentation as well as installation. Front structural protective gates seem a better investment than this very high priced coverage.

Make certain that two or more of your policies do not overlap, covering the same risk. One good example is the liability store policy that also will cover use of a delivery car. A separate car policy will duplicate the coverage; you pay additional premium with no more coverage. Have the store policies re-examined by an independant broker periodically for their effective coverage of your risks, and shop other brokers' prices to be sure you are not overpaying.

11

BOOKS
AND RECORDS

To keep a record of income and expenses of any business, you "post" the figures, enter the information of everyday financial transactions (sales, expenses, and the like), into a set of prepared pages of journals and ledgers. This posting of information is bookkeeping, the basis of accounting. The journals record day-to-day transactions for a given time period; perhaps all kinds of sales and income in one journal, and miscellaneous transactions showing all the money expended by the business in another.

Ledgers take the assortment of transactions from a journal and break them down into columns or pages so that, for example, you will know how much you spend on a particular cost of doing business (overhead, advertising, salaries or other) during this period and for the year.

You will soon realize that even though the government tax authorities require only a very basic set of information totals of your money, *you* need more details to run your business effectively. The I.R.S. requires only single-entry journals, entries for income and expenses that will show a net taxable profit at year end. You will, of course, also need year-ending inventory figures and a payroll book for employees.

REASONS FOR GOOD BOOKS

Good Books Keep You Informed

Money is the lifeblood circulating in your business. The control of this lifeblood requires your constant monitoring of the circulation flow—too little, or too much, in any one area at any time. You can work very hard, faithfully creating and observing the excitement of the daily turnover of goods on your selling floor, and still not be aware of future critical problems such as a cash shortage or the cash flow problem, which will arise shortly thereafter. Only the bookkeeping summaries can detail your trends of sales or expenses in one particular area. Only your ledgers can compare your various costs of doing business with other like stores, other time periods, or a ratio with store sales figures deemed unusual and needing correction. The information is, therefore, the basis of all your executive decisions of management to expand, change modes of operation, or run to the bank for needed cash.

UNDERSTANDING THE MOVEMENT OF CASH   This insight will make you a stronger, more confident manager as you enjoy watching, knowing your business is growing. You will appreciate the worthiness of your extra bookkeeping efforts more as you enjoy the luxury of seeing your successful strategic management decisions, which are based on them, create a winner.

BOOK SUMMARIES NEEDED FOR TAX RETURNS AND TAX SAVINGS   The preparation of tax returns to get the most savings out of depreciation, inventory valuation, and special tax credits requires skillfully recorded transactions for a basis.

NEEDED FINANCIAL STATEMENTS AND ACCOUNTING REPORTS   The summaries of the bookkeeping totals of the business into professional informational reports for interested outsiders are based on the accounting principle of "balancing the books," assets against liabilities. Most business owners prefer to leave the preparation of these reports, proft and loss statements or balance sheets, to a C.P.A., for a more professional presentation. For your very first books, too, unless you have a well-trained background, use the expertise of an accounting professional so that your bookkeeping will be better able to give you the information you will need later.

Others require information. Financial statements offer a glimpse into the financial well-being of any business, and all prospective creditors, whether lenders or merchandise suppliers, require a well-prepared professional document. These figures depend on your well-kept books and totals, and a good understanding prepares more favorable reports.

BOOKKEEPING

You can buy a basic set of record books in a stationery store, but one set up by a pro for *your* business is advised.

MAKE BOOKKEEPING AS EASY AS POSSIBLE   You can post the entries yourself, hire an agency, or use an accountant's employee to do the chore most people consider the least satisfying activity a store owner faces. But it is an absolutely necessary part of your store work, which is *worthless unless perfectly* done. You can make it easier on yourself by working in a pleasant, well-lighted work space, with helpful equipment, and schedule the work regularly and conveniently. If you prefer, you can pay an accountant to enter figures for you monthly or quarterly at roughly $100 per day or more. You need to enter some figures yourself, and after some time you should be able to guide an employee to relieve you of part or all of it.

Perhaps it would be more satisfying to get some expertise in bookkeeping and learn the relationship of the figures you will need to use in discussions with creditors. Evening courses are available at local colleges, as well as adult classes in local high schools. You may learn the relationship of certain of your totals to one another in ratios that are comparable with other stores, or other periods of your operation, in assessing how well you are doing. (Specific ratios are discussed later in this chapter.)

Journals

Typical of journals, recording all money coming in on a daily basis, is the sales and income journal. It keeps a "diary," a record of daily sales (perhaps matching your register tapes) with columns for sales tax received, credit sales, cash payments from previous sales, cash refunds, and so on, ending in a net column for the day, a cash figure that should match your deposit in the bank. Even the barest minimum set of books requires more than a journal record of your expenses because you will want to know how much you spend on certain groups of expenses that affect your profit so critically. Separate ledger pages or just columns for separation will do.

Business Bank Account

Your bank checkbook provides a convenient first entry for many of the financial transactions happening every day. These include deposits from sales or other income, payments made in cash where specific checks are cashed for the payment (and notations made), payments for salaries and wages, for invoices for merchandise or services, and other expenses. Bank statements and cancelled checks corroborate your recorded totals to taxing authorities.

DON'T MIX PERSONAL AND STORE FUNDS   It is unwise for you to pay personal bills directly from your business checking account. Because of the confusing mixing of personal and business funds, it is wiser to draw a check to yourself, deposit it to your personal account, and pay the bill from that personal account. Banks charge more service fees for business checking accounts and often requires a larger balance.

Store records affecting tax obligations should normally be preserved for six years, and your lease, insurance policies, and books and records should be carefully stored safe from fire destruction. Especially vital working inventories and the like may be duplicated for safekeeping in another place.

Expenditure Ledger Headings

The suggested list of headings below to break down store expenses into useable totals is not intended to replace one that is suggested by your accounting professional, but only to discuss the relationship and reasons for these entries in numbered columns:

1. Merchandise purchases for sales stock.
2. Miscellaneous nonselling supplies, packing, office, maintenance, petty.
3. Rent, utilities, regular overhead costs.
4. Employees salary and wages.
5. Nonemployee labor, advertising, insurance, legal, audit, loan interest, other expenses.
6. Nondeductible payments, loan principals, loans to others, payments of invoices from previous year.
7. Capital assets to be depreciated, fixtures, registers, cars, and others.
8. Payroll taxes.

PETTY CASH   A petty cash fund is established by drawing a check for a given amount, $25 to $50, to hold aside of those small everyday cash expenses not readily chargeable to special expense headings. When nearly exhausted, a new check is drawn to bring the fund back to the original sum. Many stores keep a one-line description of petty cash uses showing depletion and replacement in a running record.

There is a good reason to charge freight receiving costs on each invoice and the total in your column *one* (merchandise purchases) above. It is a more honest evaluation of the cost of your merchandise and of your markup. It is deeply affected by distant buying sources, especially imports or basic factory sources, and "freight" may aid your evaluation of its use against the cost of local sources delivered to your store. You may use the petty cash fund temporarily to pay truckers receiving funds, but their signed slips should periodically be replaced in the petty fund with a check drawn and charged to merchandise (column 1).

START RIGHT, DO REGULARLY   The best advice from store pros about bookkeeping is that you keep it up-to-date and not allow "catch-up" rushing of entries to breed the mistakes that take twice as long to discover. Start with a good setup by your C.P.A., post regularly, and use good equipment with a paper tape for rechecking.

There are some very inexpensive older adding machines that may be suitable if you make certain of their condition and the availability of paper tapes. Any machine can be used to multiply out for inventory totals, but the newer calculators save time in giving you markup percentages and ratios as well. Some of these calculators have memory capacity that may be helpful. Make certain if you invest in such equipment that you take the time to learn to use it for its fullest applications. Soon most store owners will be investing in computers.

COMPUTERS

Hardware refers to the computer machine itself. *Software* is the set of instructions designed to perform certain functions when you insert the data in the proper form, the language the computer understands. Over a period of time, the cost of software to get maximum benefit from your computer can cost more than the hardware itself. Without excellent instructions the hardware is useless.

COMPUTER COSTS   A computer can be of great service to a growing business by giving speedy summaries of data, perpetual inventories, ratios, and projections. But this alone cannot justify the investment in hardware or even the renting of off-premises "time." It will not save the cost of employees' wages for bookkeeping applications because the insertion of data is time-consuming. Thus, only in relation to myriad stock variety reordering, as in bookstores, drug and food supermarkets, can computer use be considered practical (used with point of sale electronic registers) for a small store.

Before considering the purchase or lease of computers, read about their application to your particular needs. One book on the subject is *How to Computerize Your Small Business,* by Jules Cohen (Prentice-Hall, 1980).

OFFICE WORK

In addition to bookkeeping itself, a store owner must establish office procedures of filing, correspondence, order checking, preparing payroll, entering invoices for payment, and writing checks. You will often hear that "store space is expensive and should be reserved for producing sales, not storing office trash—when in doubt, throw it out." Use three-part communication letters printed for you to impart information quickly, with a copy for your files. Select a time of the week when your floor is covered so you relax and concentrate on the size of the figures to make comparisons and to feel confident that you have the control to keep the progress of the store on a normal upward course. A trained part-timer should be able to ease much of the burden of posting and filing. Good posting and totals as outlined by your C.P.A. should provide the basis for a summary audit one day every three months (normal for a small store) keeping that cost to a minimum.

PERIODIC ACCOUNTING

There is no substitute for a professional advisor to guide you in financial management decisions after your books are balanced every quarter. The balancing of debits (what you owe) against credits (due you), accounting for all your cash, inventory, and other assets, gives a picture of what is happening financially since the last statement.

ACCRUAL OR CASH SYSTEMS   Your system of accounting for a retail store with inventory is called *accrual,* where financial transactions are deemed to occur in the period when they "happen," not when the cash changes hands, as it would be in a *cash* system. The cash system is allowed if you have no inventory, perhaps a complete service business. At the time of your year-ending (for example, January 31) inventory, merchandise invoiced to you in January is part of your stock, even though its invoice is not due to be paid until much later in the next fiscal year. The expense is charged against January, and when the invoice is paid later it is entered in the nondeductible column.

INVENTORY

Inventory counting (see Appendix R) at the end of your fiscal or calendar year is very much easier if done as professionally advised. You will have an opportunity to mark down goods before the counting, and another general opportunity for markdown before you hand over the total to your accountant for year-end summaries and tax return preparation. The inventory at cost value as compared with last year's raises or lowers your taxable income by the difference in value, and so is a critical figure. You control it as you make the translation from total retail to *cost* for that figure. You will note that accounting firms do not take responsibility for these figures, and they mark an audit "inventory submitted by management." Despite the appearance of a very simple figure, the valuations of inventory are the subject of much I.R.S. controversy and of changing theoretical philosophy. You may value your inventory:

FIFO—First In, First Out, or
LIFO—Last In, First Out.

LIFO creates a lower net profit in times of inflation and is now in favor. This is the assumption that the higher cost (bought later) of this inventory governs, leaving less profit made by the rise in the value of inventory (by inflation) itself, therefore less taxes due on less profit and more cash left in the company for capital investment. There is pending legislation that would give small business the opportunity to use the most favorable inventory valuation for tax purposes, but Congress cannot yet agree on a definition of "small business."

FIXED ASSETS ARE DEPRECIATED   *Depreciation* is the normal wear and tear of time that causes a loss of valuation of (fixed) physical assets of a business. "Normal life" is the period used on each asset as you depreciate yearly business. If it is possible to depreciate an asset in a shorter period of time for tax purposes, that enlarged depreciation can have the effect of lessening taxable income for that year, and so companies seek permission to do so. Recent regulations have allowed large corporations to use an "asset depreciation range system," an accelerated, complicated formula that is very difficult to apply to small retail stores. There is some activity in Congress to correct this inequity.

TAXES

Short-Term Profits, Long-Term Capital Gains

Income taxes, federal, state, and city, are based on the net profit earned by your company for the year, except that in some states there is a minimum, state, and local tax on corporations, whether a profit is made or not. (State income taxes apply to *profits made within the state* regardless of where corporation was formed and registered.) Over this amount, a corporation pays tax percentages on earnings, usually less than the federal tax brackets. These were reduced in 1978 to 17 percent for the first $25,000 of profit and this will be reduced to 16 and 15 percent. As discussed in Chapter 4, your tax liability for profits made in a Subchapter "S" corporation, a partnership, or an individual proprietorship is an individual responsibility based on the owner's total income from business and other outside income, and no profits tax is due from the sub-chapter "S" Corp.

itself. A long term gain or loss likewise accrues its tax benefits to the owner personally.

Tax law revisions changed the period of "long term" vs. "short term" to one year from a six-month period. When an asset is sold, after holding for more than one year, for an amount larger than the cost (for example, a store you sell after building up the business), the profit on the sale is a long-term gain, which is taxed at a lower rate than the store profit for the year, or any other short-term profit. In your firm's other than corporate form, these apply to your personal tax obligations, even though it is your "store" that had the long-term gain (or loss). (See Table 11.1)

TABLE 11.1. Federal Income Tax
for Corporations in 1982.

tax	first	1983
16%	$25,000	15%
19%	next $25,000 up to $50,000	18%
30%	next $25,000 up to $75,000	
40%	next $25,000 up to $100,000	
46%	profits over $100,000	

Employee Taxes, FICA, Payroll Book

Every business, in any form of ownership, is required to deduct from every employee's pay the prepayment income tax and social security payments, according to a schedule supplied by federal, state, and local tax authorities. Under the FICA federal requirements, employers must match employees' social security payments up to a specified total for each employee, paying the money into the fund with the employees' withheld taxes. All salary and deductions must be entered in a payroll book. A self-employed business owner who takes no regular salary as such must pay a sum of 9.35 percent of his yearly draw, or profit, in lieu of a regular social security payment. The firm then owes no payment. A simple tax chart easier to use for social security, federal, state and city tax deduction is available at business stationery stores.

In all states with sales taxes, stores are required to register at their local office of the state sales tax bureau, and in some states they must make a substantial deposit against future sales tax collections they make from customers. States vary on the required frequency of payments, but most allow payments to be made to the store's local bank.

Pending or new federal legislation that may be helpful includes:

- Tax regulations may allow smaller stores to deposit FICA payments and others on a less frequent schedule.

- Stores are able to get special tax allowances when they purchase energy saving equipment.
- The proposed tax reduction plan allows an accelerated "10, 5, 3" depreciation formula for stores. To encourage a store's investment in downtown real estate in inner cities, it reduces the depreciation term to 10 years (from 50). Any other capital store equipment may be depreciated (fixtures and registers in three years, vehicles in five years). In some cases, 80 percent of the depreciation on buildings may be taken in the first six years. For specialty stores who lease property, all refixturing and the like can be depreciated in the five-year period, at most.
- FICA need not be paid on employee sick pay (saves 6.7 per cent for store).

Stores are responsible to follow any recent changes in tax laws for amounts to be withheld and social security. On changes in sales tax rates, stores must inform their cashiers with handy charts or when using the point of sale registers, reset with the new percentages to be charged customers. These registers may soon be considered as qualified for income tax credits because of their speedy obsolescence, and possibly any computer hardware as well.

RATIOS

There are many ratios that compare certain key operating figures that you may find very helpful in making managerial decisions for your store. When you match your ratios with stores in similar circumstances, or merely examine your own against other months or other years, you may receive some answers to the question of how you are progressing. In many cases where you wish to compare with other store operations, the other owner who may be reluctant to disclose actual figures may be willing to compare ratios.

OPERATING PROFIT PERCENTAGE   Sales and other income minus purchases minus expenses equals net profit.

$$\frac{\text{NET CASH PROFIT}}{\text{SALES}} = \text{PROFIT } \%$$

Profit is the fuel that spurs the entrepreneur into a capital expansion, and the profit percentage is the best known of all ratios, and certainly the most important to the store owner. The operating strategy toward building a greater volume at the expense of a high profit percentage, until all of the overhead and running expenses are easily borne by the new level, is only one of the ways to pursue a solid future. Most stores show very little profit over salaries and expenses in their first year, and most strangers to retailing have an inflated idea of the percentage of profit made by successful stores. An examination of the profit charts of Dun and Bradstreet and of the National Retail Merchants Association shows that most stores during the 1970s showed a profit percentage of 3 to 8 percent (the latter figure applies to less than 10 percent of the stores). The examination of the expense ratios and how to control them arises from a comparison against other stores, other periods, and other years of operation. Improving these ratios will increase your profit percentage.

A lowering of any expense ratio is caused by lowering costs of operation *without* lowering sales volume, indicating greater efficiency or productivity. It can also be the result of a greater sales volume with no increase in costs.

$$\frac{\text{EMPLOYEE COST}}{\text{SALES}} = \text{LABOR \% RATIO}$$

More efficient scheduling and management training and supervision can result in greater productivity for employee dollars spent and the lower percentage cost, which is vital to the profit percentage. We discussed in Chapter 7 the sources and methods of obtaining this lower labor percentage ratio. Naturally, you may expect to spend a higher percentage in stores featuring a one-to-one selling style as against the lower priced self-service stores. The stores that require very professionally trained, experienced selling, fitting, alterations, delivery, high-priced settings, and other unusual services must be certain of customer acceptance of the higher percentage markups to pay for them.

LET THE FORMULA FIT THE STORE   Discussing Dorinsons men's store, mentioned in Chapter 2, with some of their loyal customers illustrates the success formula of their higher employee cost ratio's contribution to their success. One customer said, "they are so darned accommodating, they fit and alter so well that neither Steve nor I ever discuss the price."

The rent ratio is:

$$\frac{\text{RENT}}{\text{SALES VOLUME}} = \text{RENT \%}$$

Sometimes stores include all overhead:

$$\frac{\text{RENT AND OTHER OVERHEAD}}{\text{SALES VOLUME}} = \text{OVERHEAD \%}$$

Traditionally, stores have aimed at a rent ratio of 5 percent or less. The sophisticated leases of today have added steadily increasing charges during the life of the tenancy, which keep the overhead costs rising, especially in view of the large increases demanded by all the utilities. Many leases today automatically add a percentage of any local land tax rise and any increase in the labor contracts of building service employees. Shopping centers usually contract for a percentage of increased sales volume as well. Favorable rent and lease clauses depend on your (or your attorney's) skill as a negotiator and perhaps being fortunate in your timing to find and be offered a valuable location reasonably priced when you need it.

When you first try to assess the "reasonableness" of a rental proposal offered, attempt to establish in your mind an approximate volume of sales probable within your investment plans, in this area, this kind of goods and services with an approximate markup to fit the scheme. This is all a part of your business plan, which we all know in the beginning is far from flawless, but nevertheless is a fundamental basis for planning. Remember that every markup planned for the season has an accompanying normal markdown percentage, which limits your year-end cash profit. When you consider a rental over 10 percent, which leaves you unprofitable, you are making your landlord a partner.

The advertising ratio is:

$$\frac{\text{ADVERTISING}}{\text{SALES}} = \text{ADVERTISING \%}$$

Many retail advertising specialists believe that the "regular" advertising budget should have a percentage relationship to the sales expected for the period. This does not include your opening barrage promotion to call attention to your presence, what you are featuring, your giveaways as incentives to visit you, prizes, and so on, all calculated as an investment. After the opening, the budget is based on a percentage. The "special" ad budgets to build a particular new image, launch a new direction in merchandising, or tell about changed location also have an investment "flavor" in the planning, and yet both involve the hope of some immediate return commensurate with the budget spending. In the regular budget with promotional items, you have an expectation of a percentage return, "plus over normal" business of 10 times the cost of the ad as a satisfactory goal. If advertising goals are not reached, the amateur reduces the expenditure and breaks the continuity; the professional merchant examines the items, the timing, the media, and the other elements of ad programs, filling the gap between unappealing and successful ones. Try harder; don't quit!

The insurance ratio is:

$$\frac{\text{INSURANCE BUDGET}}{\text{SALES}} = \text{INSURANCE \%}$$

Insurance budgets vary considerably by the risks in the area of the store location, the kind of merchandise carried, and the physical makeup of the store property itself. When you work with a knowledgeable broker who is serving you honestly in your best interest, you will be offered coverage for all the applicable risks of your store and perhaps a few others that appeal to the more worried store owners. Does your insurance coverage feel comfortable? When your policies have been included in your well-planned program, they become more of an overhead cost not usually reviewed in cost budget cutting operations.

The turnover ratio is:

$$\frac{\text{YEARLY SALES}}{\text{average monthly INVENTORY (retail value)}} = \text{TURNOVER}$$

Turnover charts are indicative of the normally expected number of times that a particular stock will be rebought and give rise to profit. They are rough guides to compare with your own retail operation. An increase in the times turnover in the store stock will be indicative of a more favorable use of store operating capital and a probable profit increase. Increase in volume of sales itself is not a forecast of increased turnover, even when accompanied by a new tactic of reduced markup, or other incentives of a promotional program aimed at increased units.

Turnover is affected by stock assortment, timing of style, and replenishment. When you compare turnover in your store and find it below the suggested average, examine the stock assortment, the timing for seasonal changes and the strategy in delivery dates of merchandise ordered for stock needs. Reexamine your customer market, their life-styles, and trends for subtle changes in demand for your products or services. Newspaper readership, the occupants of recent housing, or trends in political voting may indicate a change in your public that requires your attention. Alert reexamination produces better assortments, turnover, and profits.

UNIT SALES

With inflation in double figures, most stores have enjoyed a rise in sales volume, somewhat keeping pace with it. The ever-increasing cost of doing business, rents, utilities, help, services, supplies, and so on have conspired to narrow the net profit figures, and the largest of the American successful department store groups plan meeting-after-strategy-meeting to try to improve these fiscal end results. Fortunately for small store owners there is more control at their fingertips and more vital decisions of management that will make an immediate difference. Inflation-rising prices can easily cost a loss of unit sales if measures are not taken to maintain the earlier pace. Advertising multiple-pricing with savings, and attractive displays of multiples are some ways that stores can induce customer interest in that direction. Sales help training with incentives is also helpful, and the small store owner has an advantage over large stores that have less-present supervision. Working to maintain the pace of unit sales is an important contribution toward the profit goal.

STORE CAPITAL BUDGETS

Your first capital budget was a total of your plans in the comprehensive operating plan, the money set aside for building the store, fixtures and physical needs, original stock of merchandise in categories and the planned replacement goods for the first few months of operations, all deposits and costs of licenses as you developed the form of business best suited for you, and the costs of general expenses, audits, advertising, insurance, and so on. Now you are operating, turning over your inventory, and controlling your expenses so well that profits are the logical result!

PLANNED PROFIT IS PART OF THE BUDGET   The capital operating budget is the logical use of all of the funds available to management, including the developing overage, the profit to be reinvested for growth. Put to work, there are logical investments in other merchandise that will bring in more volume, in advertising programs of special nature to improve appeal, in machinery for improved efficiency savings, and possibly physical changes needed. But remember that, with all of these operating uses of the funds, some amount must always be set aside for the major expansion of the future. The everyday operating decisions of how to squeeze expenses, incite more interest in your store, infuse higher profit margin goods into the assortment without slowing sales, and thinking out your future direction are challenges that offer you the most enjoyment "in the big boss seat" you have taken with your own money. *Don't* expect *all* your efforts to reward you handsomely!

You may regret some decisions made, but you should understand why they were made and learn from the mistakes. You may make moves that help you, or sometimes you may do nothing and benefit through good fortune. You may make decisions that will not seem noticeable, but think out where you want to be and spend to achieve the results. Don't gamble the last dollar, and try to keep the cost of mistaken decisions below the "life and death" level.

MONEY COST IS HIGH, SO USE IT WISELY   The very high cost of borrowed money must always be an ingredient in the decision to invest in an operating change, even if you have set aside the capital from the operating budget to cover it. If a delay in the return on this investment will squeeze your cash flow, consider ahead the moves necessary. Consider whether the capital needed for this decision would be better invested in a high interest temporary investment outside. What would be the result of this inactivity? Good cash management makes full use of every dollar you have, to spend it wisely in your business to make more profits, or invest it outside for interest income.

CASH LIQUIDITY IS A REAL ASSET   Cash liquidity in your business allows you to take advantage of discounts in your payments, as well as tempting off-price merchandise, for cash, that is often offered to aggressive credit-worthy merchants.

THE BALANCE SHEET

Understanding the elements of the balance sheet will help you to understand your financial progress and help to evaluate any other business. While operating your "net worth" is your present "capital."

The balance sheet is a still picture of a company's finances at the very moment, usually taken at the end of the firm's fiscal year. It lists for comparison and evaluation the assets of all kinds (what you own) and the liabilities (what you owe), calculating the difference, which is the net worth, or capital, of the business.

FIXED AND CURRENT ASSETS

Assets are of two kinds: Fixed assets help you run the business and depreciate in time, with only that depreciation portion of their life chargeable as an expense this year (buildings, fixtures, vehicles); current assets are cash in any form or able to be converted into it during the current year. Inventory, cash or store funds, paid supplies, receivables, prepaid insurance, or rent are all current assets. Fixed assets are listed with gross value, the amount already depreciated, and the net, theoretically the portion "still of value" to the business.

Liabilities are all outstanding accounts to be paid, whether for merchandise, supplies, or for fixed assets, loans outstanding, interest owed, and so on, and for the corporation, corporation stock outstanding.

NET WORTH   The difference between the total assets and total of the liabilities is your net worth, or capital. It is your original capital of the business plus or minus your profit, losses of operations, or additions or withdrawal of capital amounts during the period since then.

The capital stock of a corporation is listed by the total outstanding share ownership, and in a partnership is the relative equity of each partner. Any profits left in the corporation are listed under *surplus*. None in a subchapter "S" corporation.

The study of a balance sheet tells you:

• The difference in net worth of a business since the last report.
• Any dissipation of capital, or addition to it since the last statement.
• A large asset figure that may be impressive in potential, despite a high liability figure possibly amassed in a recent bad period.
• Relative liquidity of the business. If liabilities alone exceed assets, the firm is insolvent.

LIQUIDITY   An important ratio is:

$$\frac{\text{CURRENT ASSETS}}{\text{CURRENT LIABILITIES}} = \text{the current LIQUIDITY RATIO}$$

If this is poor, there is not enough working capital to operate efficiently, pay bills currently, and so on.

YEAR-END INVENTORY AND TAXES

Most retailers have a strong aversion to paying income taxes on the "book" inventory value, especially during an inflationary period. Declaring an inventory figure total larger than the previous year, of course, increases the current asset figure and agreeably enlarges the totals the store would like to present to the credit agencies in the year-end reports. This higher inventory figure also increases the income tax liability for the year, and you will be deciding whether to pay the increased tax or to mark down the total inventory value to avoid doing so for this period. The "cost" value is in your control, and you will be, in effect, postponing the tax liability until the future when these goods are turned into cash.

Keep in mind that when you have recorded a cost inventory figure at year end, you will be bound by this total should an insurable loss occur in the near future (see Chapter 10 under the Firman "Just Kids" store loss).

AMERICAN UNDERGROUND BUSINESS: TAX EVASION

Tax evasion by underreporting sales and profits is a crime, which when detected, is punishable by a jail sentence, plus a fine, the full payment of tax due plus high interest. Overcharging expenses to stores, even when personally benefiting the owner, is not "fraud" treated with the same severity. Many store owners play games in figures on tax returns to save taxes, and this had led to electronic surveillance of returns to try to detect it. The I.R.S. uses software programs in computers to indicate that the return doesn't "jibe!"

TABLE 11.2 The Year: Final Taxable Profits

Year's Net Sales		$000*		
Other Income		000		
TOTAL INCOME		000	$000	
	Merchandise			
Inventory	Purchases	000		
Last year	$000			
This year	000			
Difference (+ or −)	000	000		
Cost of Good Sold		000	000	
			000 (Gross Profit)	
Expenses				
Overhead	000			
Salaries	000			
Supplies	000			
Running	000			
Misc.	000			
TOTAL EXPENSES	000		000	
Net Profit			000	$000
Depreciation of Fixed Assets			000	
Special Tax Allowances			000	
Total Tax Red. Items			000	000
YEAR'S NET TAXABLE INCOME				$000

*All zeros represent the dollar amounts you will be inserting into this table.

In a *New York Times* article and other periodicals, concerning the "underground economy," discussing ways that smaller businesses cheat on taxes due the government, one East Side (New York) tavern-restaurant owner claimed that he only reported 75 percent of his sales by using two registers ("one is for show"), reporting the sales on just one. This is only one of the growing list of methods of tax cheating. Some firms do get caught, however, and the result can be devasting.

In the 1960s, the owner of one of New York's finest, most profitable chains of restaurants (Longchamps) was called in for an audit when one disgruntled hat check girl claimed that the owner kept all the large tips for himself, paying the check girls only a salary. The audit proved that, indeed, this six-figure income for the chain was unreported both by corporation and the owner who got the cash. A further delving into the financial operations, with the help of other pressured personnel, proved "skimming," reporting less than all sales, retaining funds and sales taxes collected by the restaurant. The owner served time for income tax evasion and, in the settlement, lost all his interest in the restaurant chain and the income, said to be close to a million a year.

Current articles that deal with tax evasion by keeping two sets of books (fraud), pocketing tips (unreported income, also fraud), or dealing in cash (unreported income, fraud) make it obvious that the I.R.S. has difficulty keeping control of all of this untaxed underground business. There is occasional help, however, from disgruntled employees, who enjoy blowing the whistle on the boss who fired them (perhaps for good reason). Once started, the I.R.S. investigators go deeply into property ownership of the storekeeper to find the source of funds employed. As a deterrent, the I.R.S. often makes a headline case of jailing owners and taking all of their assets (for example. Studio 54 in New York).

Many small business owners exchange goods, services, or charges with one another in a sort of barter system almost impossible to detect. Many owners charge personal or living expenses, vacations, entertainment, and such to their businesses, in the knowledge that some may be disallowed, but some may be overlooked, and that no severe penalties worse than interest are involved. Of course, the I.R.S. will be looking at this return again next year. Many accountants refuse to allow clients the luxury of over-indulging in personal "expenses" because of the reflection on *their* reputations (and extra time required for audits).

There is a professional barter agency in New York, Pfeister, which arranges barter deals. Professionals, stores, restaurants, and other producers work with Pfeister credit cards to interpay for services with no money changing hands (no secret to the I.R.S.).

Albert Einstein once was quoted as saying, "If I had my life to live over again, I would elect to be a trader of goods rather than a student of science. I think barter is a noble thing." Imagine the impact he might have made on the world of commerce. Take a tip from Einstein and enjoy your small store. Happy Retailing!

APPENDICES

A. STORES . . . THE STORY

Stores seem to be born, grow, and multiply. Others seem to be afflicted with fatal policies of operation, wither and die. Many are influenced by outside factors; but the most important factor is still the *guiding driving* force of the operator, usually the owner.

Customers feel very personal about stores, become "addicted" to shopping regularly, and have emotional attachments carried on from their earliest buying days. Many stores capitalize on their involvement in the lives of local residents with nonmerchandise promotions that build customer acceptance and loyalty. For example, when Macy's took over an old-time store in San Francisco and brought in typical New York merchandising and price promotions, it failed to attract the expected portion of local trade. After years of struggle and a change to emphasize "make shopping fun," Macy's began to establish teenage clubs, flower shows, a Thanksgiving Day parade, and other nonselling community activities . . . which *sold* the store.

Despite public offerings of company stock and corporation takeovers, many famous stores still involve third and fourth generations of the founders in command. Strawbridge and Clothier in Philadelphia, Macy's in New York, and Sakowitz in Houston are among some of the successful descendents.

This succession does not always guarantee continued success, and some owners do as Marshall Field did. He turned over management to his brilliant merchandiser John Shedd, who rebuilt the store and its image to become one of the greatest stores in the world. Some of the descendants built on the volume with their own way of merchandising as conditions demanded, some with their personal hobbies. Hinks of Berkeley, California, offers the "homey" touch with surprises, jingles, holiday poetry, and jokes along with their merchandise offerings. Lester Hink said, "You can find what you are looking for there, and that's what Berkeley ladies like."

Stores such as Gumps in San Francisco have hardly changed over 100 years from their museumlike facade of the world collection of art treasures, porcelains, jade, lacquered boxes, and carved animals. Like Tiffany's in New York, they offer superb value because of uniqueness and style, a quality worth a higher price. Another San Francisco store, City of Paris, although considered a physical landmark, died out in 1972 after losing money for several years. San Francisco citizens have resisted a rebuilding effort to replace it with Neiman-Marcus. (It is now a Carter-Hale store.) Its first presentation of goods arrived on the ship *La Ville de Paris* from France after the goods were carried across Panama. It sold from the ship's deck, fearing loss by brigand or fire in the then rough shanty town full of gold rush money. Later, stocks of fine wines and luxury goods were sold in regular store locations and were supplied from France by the same dangerous route across Panama. Its style and home furnishing decor had such a profound influence on the tastes of San Francisco that sentiment for the 130-year-old survivor of earthquakes, fires, and floods supported petitions for the city to preserve the famed dome and Christmas tree as a downtown landmark.

My First Entrepreneurs

In early 1905, Grandma Cantor and her daughter Clarice left my Dad to manage their women's millinery and clothing store while they entrained south to avoid the wintry New York weather. Shortly thereafter, a strong epidemic flu bug struck down Dad, and he left the shop in the hands of a recently hired saleslady, Myriam. This shop had prospered under Grandma's equisite millinery workmanship, Clarice's style merchandising, and my father's management talents, and it drew fine clientele from far away to its 6th Avenue near 28th Street location.

Dad was very pleased by Myriam's shop operations in his absence and was especially impressed by a Florence Nightingale quality as she made regular visits to his bedside with therapeutic homemade chicken soup.

A short time later, Dad married Myriam, and with typical youthful bravado they left Grandma's shop to open their own women's apparel store in Jersey City, New Jersey. Mother's selling and merchandising ability, Dad's excellent figure management, and some old-fashioned bootstrap financing developed a tiny store into a department store as I grew up.

It is the same kind of opportunity that many ambitious entrepreneurs are offered today. Of course, more start-up capital is needed, but the sales volume expected is that much greater and the same planning and hard work are required.

Mom knew how to buy just enough for their weekly needs and how to fill in stock. Their weeks were six and one-half days, ending at 5 p.m. on Sunday, so it is a wonder there was time for four children. Mom loved working until she was 80. She said a good retailer has the ability to "buy what the customer wants or sell her what he has."

She did both very well.

B. STORES AND THEIR HUMBLE BEGINNINGS

Most of today's major stores had very humble beginnings. I. Magnin (San Francisco) started when Mary Magnin preferred to send her husband Isaac out with a pack of her handmade children's garments, rather than have him fall off a ladder decorating gold ceilings for Gump's in San Francisco. They settled the line down into a store location, then more stores and more lines added. Always top quality, and growth came.

Most of what became the big department stores were started by peddlers—Gimbels, Macy's, Goldwaters. Strawbridge and Clothier's huge (Federated store) Philadelphia store was at first a tiny mama-papa operation. In 1872, the brothers Bloomingdale (two unsuccessful manufacturers) opened a ribbon and lace store, with a total $3.68 of first day's receipts. One hundred years later, their (publicity seeking) promotion of India goods was reported to cost $5 million to produce the extravaganza.

By contrast, John Bullock was a $12-a-week men's wear buyer at the Broadway Company in Los Angeles when rich Mr. Winnett took Bullock's expertise into a partnership in 1907 and opened a beautiful store with "bands playing, birds singing, and flowers" as gifts; luxury and beauty in the setting for the finest goods with the world's best personal service. Later he built Bullock's Wilshire, a monumental "world's most beautiful store," after merging his memories of a trip to France with local Spanish architecture. His salespeople each personally called customers when new styles arrived at the store. The front door attendants parked and returned patron's cars with the merchandise they bought in the store. Bullock wanted you to know he sought *you* as a customer and that you would be treated *royally* when you came in.

Some of our most famous American stores are the large department stores. There is some doubt as to where the *first* department store was established, the English claiming that Kandel Milnes in Manchester predated the French by 20 years. In Paris in 1852, the Boucicants small piece goods shop on the Left Bank was expanded to include some clothing, shoes, millinery, and underwear, bringing the open-air stalls under one roof called Bon Marche. American store owners visited and noted customers were welcome to "look around" (Americans shopkeepers were wary and rude to "lookers") and noted that all prices were marked— no price bargaining allowed. (There is still bargaining throughout much of the world.) Also, Bon Marche allowed exchanges of merchandise. Visitors there later noted sale prices to induce extra buying for fast turnover and a good final profit on the greater volume. Cutting prices was first observed as "sheer folly"; but Le Printemps (in Paris) and others copied it as they recognized the benefits, and American stores followed suit. American merchants learned these new operating principles:

- Shoppers allowed
- Exchanges
- One price as marked
- Sale prices

As stores welcomed "shoppers," they also began to use interior and store window displays to captivate the customer's appetite for beauty on the figure. Stores in New York stopped using street "pullers" to actually force passersby into the store (In 1826 Lord and Taylor on Catherine Street, N.Y., was one of the first to stop). Later, store advertising of values, sale goods sold off regular price, loss leaders, and such became builders of store traffic. But stores also built up service, beautiful surroundings, theaterlike settings, charge accounts, delivery, parking for cars, and the like to make it easier for customers to buy. (Personal service was a mark of Oklahoma City's Ballietts, where shoppers were served in elegance.) Stores have huge theatrical and cultural events, parades, and community programs to create a loyalty.

The Industrial Revolution provided the piece goods supply and many new classes of customers for the growth of stores of the nineteenth century. England's Hargreave's invention of the "spinning jenny" for thread and Cartwright's cloth weaver, powered by Watt's steam engine, produced the raw material for making clothes in quantity. Retail stores were able to secure a volume of supplies. After Eli Whitney's cotton gin tripled the supply of cotton, and Elias Howe and Isaac Singer improved the sewing machine, the requirements of steel for machinery to make the new mechanized industries (and railroads) brought many farm workers into industry. New jobs made new consumers. Factory owners suddenly took the power from the landowners, and a new wealthy class was born, needing servants and they, in turn, needed uniforms. Also, they could buy more of their own clothing.

Free trade policy developed, and workers were producing goods and earning money needed for buying what stores offered. Coal was mined to run the industrial machines, and these workers shared in the new circulation of money in the economy. Workers and servants imitated the new moneyed classes to dress up for their important life events, and dry goods stores supplied the needs of thread, trimmings, and piece goods to sew on the home treadle sewing machine (still in worldwide use).

Entrepreneurs gathered a few good home sewers and began to supply parts of outer garments that could be made by machine, leaving hand work to a few very skilled sewers. In the United States (I. Magnin, for one) and Europe, many stores started with these workrooms to make garments to suit particular customers. Some American makers split off to become ready-to-wear manufacturers. But garment shaping was difficult because of the tiny waist, hourglass shape, and most better customers went to "coutouriers" to be personally fitted if they did not have someone at home to do it. Paris taste, so admired, became the center of this world of fashion garments and remains a style mecca today.

Of America's three largest retail stores, R. H. Macy, New York, J. L. Hudson, Detroit, and Marshall Field, Chicago, Marshall Field has the greatest physical area (2.2 million sq. feet). It started as a tiny dry goods store named Field, Palmer and Leiter, the name changing after being rebuilt in 1879. In bawdy, elegant, jazzy Chicago, the store advertises in a "whisper." It has been described as an "exposition, a school of courtesy, a museum." It lives by the retailer's most famous motto, "the customer is always right."

Rebuilt in 1907 when Marshall Field died, the store developed additional appeals and the huge acreage was built over merchandise-supplying railroad tracks. Finest fashions in a glamorous setting with a private elevator from the street gave the Number 28 Shop snob appeal. The men's store label is accepted in Chicago as the very top quality, and the restaurants and take-out foods are imitated in stores throughout the country. The basement store is a quarter mile long and is "less expensive but reliable."

The presentation and advertising of Marshall Field are always low key, never using "sale," comparative prices, or free gifts with purchases. When the world-famous antique department with globewide sources says "special selling" or another department says "box sales" (special price for box multiples), Chicagoans react with confidence as to a "fire sale."

Dayton's in the Minneapolis-St. Paul area is known especially for participation in all community (noncommercial) activities, from cultural music and art to the sports programs in schools. These events involve all ages—from teens who are wooed as "beginner" customers to senior citizens—and the de-emphasis on commercialism only makes the store that much more important to potential customers of the area.

J. L. Hudson's main store in Detroit (once second in sales to Macy's, New York) is going down with the central city decay so prevalent among American cities. Like Abraham and Straus (a Federated store) in Brooklyn, New York, it found salvation from crime and decay in the area around the main store by branching out into suburbs, which account for an ever-increasing share of the total volume. Detroit central shopping has moved to the fabulous new urban development called Renaissance Center, spurred on by Henry Ford II and an auto manufacturer's fund and designed by John Portman, famous for Atlanta's Peach Tree Center. These hotel, office building, and shop centers attract customers for the joy of shopping in glamorous comfortable settings.

Neiman-Marcus, so famous worldwide for their offerings in the exotic Christmas gift catalogue for multimillionaires (gifts as high as $1 million each), has a more reasonable selection of finest quality down-to-earth ready-made clothing in their expanding chain of stores (now owned by Carter-Hale stores). Like Hightowers and Connolly men's stores of Oklahoma City, price is never influential, only quality and service to a "must be satisfied" customer.

Macy's and Gimbels in New York City have (through publicity) long capitalized on their semifriendly store rivalry, which has in recent years disappeared as the West Side of Manhattan lost retail popularity to the East Side, Bloomingdale's, and the suburban stores. Macy's has made great strides to recapture their number-one New York image by rebuilding many sagging departments, relocating some in favor of the a-la-mode "today's" goods, and replacing a useless budget basement with a "now visitors'-place-to-go"—the Cellar. This home appliance superfood and drug center is divided into attractive shops and has a popular (P.J. Clarke's) restaurant.

Gimbels, New York, was losing volume and profits despite management changed by the Gimbel descendants, and sold out to English company Brown and Williamson in 1973. Their efforts so far have not succeeded in reversing the trend.

Both Adam Gimbel and Lazarus Straus (of the Macy's family) were immigrant peddlers, Adam Gimbel opening a first shop in Vincennes, Indiana. He was known for an honest reputation, and he said "a good name is better than riches." His sons helped spread to the Philadelphia store and to Milwaukee before opening New York's 32nd and Broadway store near Macy's, at the hub of West Side transportation.

Rowland H. Macy (called "captain" because of one seafaring experience) and his family from Nantaucket had failed in stores in New England before trying a New York retail venture. He leased a glass and china department to the Straus family, who had just arrived from Georgia in 1866. In 1877, at his death, Macy disinherited a n'er-do-well son, leaving only his partner, Charles Webster, as owner. Webster took the Strauses in with him and they soon acquired a half-interest in a Brooklyn store (Abraham and Straus), which still retains the Straus name even though their interest in it was sold. Webster later retired and sold all his interest to the Staus family, who were then sole owners of the Chambers Street store. (The original Macy store was a tiny 14-foot shop at 6th Avenue near 14th Street.)

Rowland Macy's policy had been "cash only" and "one price" (no haggling), plus the refusal to be undersold, and this was a standard for the Straus family until the 1950s when the D.A. (customer prepaid Deposit Account) was replaced by a "converse" charge account status.

Macy's, under descendant Jack Straus, developed an executive training program reputed to be the first in retail on-the-job training to graduates of American business colleges. Bloomingdale's and Abraham and Straus training graduates have also become famous throughout the world of stores.

In New York, Bloomingdale's, under the guidance of Lawrence Lachman and Marvin Traub, has captivated the imagination and the loyalty of the city's "now" generation. The store's events, staged to coordinate the sale of specialized merchandise, have earned hundreds of editorial pages of comment far better than any paid advertising. Dubbed "Bloomie's" by its addicts, who adore the food departments, walking models, and fellow-shopping celebrities, the store is *the place* to shop.

The Italian influence on merchandise arrived in the United States with the entrance of Gucci on the scene in 1947. Father Guccio Gucci, harness maker deluxe in Florence, sent his son at age 21 to test the prospects. Before long, the original hotel location moved to its own store with a loyal following crying for Gucci styling regardless of price or arrogant treatment. Today the descendants of Gucci have spread shops (own or franchise) anywhere that potential clientele is a possibility, and the items, priced more outrageously than ever, have spread into scarfs and other nonleather gifts.

I am especially fond of Stanley Marcus's comment made in his book *Minding The Store* (Little, Brown, 1974)—"I have simple tastes, I am easily satisfied with the very best!"

C. STORE INNOVATION, DISCOUNT STORES

The *different* way . . . one of the ways.

Of all the ideas and concepts that have come into retailing since the 1930s, none had a more profound effect on the industry than the one word—*discount.*

No one person symbolizes the discount store concept more (according to

Fortune and *Time* magazines, 1962) than Eugene Ferkauf of E.J. Korvettes, who built a small store into a 44-store chain worth millions. Ferkauf's book, *Going into Business,* is fascinating reading on the subject.

With a background in luggage store merchandising and capitalized at $4,000, he opened a second-floor tiny luggage store and sold small household appliances at a very small profit to help draw traffic. He kept buying and replacing a small stock of jobber-obtained appliances, sent discount cards to nearby buildings (instead of paid advertising), and excited the crowd drawn by the discounts. Korvette's reputation started to grow.

Bringing customers in to buy "sale" priced goods at little or no markup (called "loss leaders" or "door busters") is a traditional bait to get valuable store traffic. Even more effective, therefore, was Ferkauf's use of branded appliances in his discount offerings, a proven value because he was cutting the Fair Trade (see Appendix O) list price. Other stores objected, and manufacturers made efforts to stop it, but the more they did, the more Ferkauf became a hero to the bargain hunters who flocked in to buy. Other stores (Buy Wise and Masters Mart) started to offer discounts on small appliances, too, but their efforts to build on the success were never consistent. Ferkauf and Korvette's discount retailing became a news story, and the public was interested in reading about this maverick retailer. These stories were extremely valuable in building a following, who bought $1 million worth the first year, at about a 20 percent profit.

The retail scene today does not offer a chance to open a store with $4,000, nor the special charm of the discount merchandising concept being as effective because there is no Fair Trade list price being enforced any longer. There are still stores using the discount idea, and where the public has confidence in the consistent effort there has been growth (example are K-Mart, with the second largest volume in the United States, Woolco of the Woolworth Co. and (Caldor Stores, which grew from a mama-papa store to a 50-store chain in 25 years now in the Associated Drygoods Co.)

Ferkauf agrees that he could not have done the same job today, but suggests the use of discounts in general merchandise stores of approximately 10,000 square feet.

Another interesting discount development has been the company store, where the goods of the many divisions of some of our largest conglomerates are offered on the company premises at prices slightly above wholesale (usually 15 percent to cover overhead). Many of these large companies have become disillusioned with their own efforts in maintaining an efficient operation and would be interested in an outsider taking over if the terms are reasonable. If a young, eager entrepreneur could arrange for a discount of 10 percent from the company wholesale price, he or she could sell all the company employees at about 15 percent above wholesale, own all the inventory, safeguard the receipts, and make a good profit.

One very successful company store for a conglomerate is the Kayser-Roth Company store in New York. This very large shop, resembling an army P.X., has a volume in excess of $1 million despite restocking problems and help turnover.

Many of the attempted conversions of the large variety store to the discount store format ended in the failure of the conversion and sometimes of the company itself (W.T. Grant, for example). Some major exceptions are conversion from a slumping Kresge to a successful K-Mart discount chain and the opening of many Woolco stores by Woolworth. At this time, although the probability of success in large chains is not great, there is feeling that a conversion of a small variety store independently managed into a part discount operation may be very successful for an aggressive merchandiser.

Korvette's managment, after Ferkauf took his $28 million and left, lost the thread of the concept, changed toward department store high overhead operations, and began to lose ground. They never were able to secure the best lines in soft goods or fashions, lost reputation with a shoddy furniture operation, and soon lost many vendors by not paying bills on time. In 1979 they were acquired by a French corporation, which replaced many top executives, and in 1980 were in the process of closing stores in the hope of effecting a turnaround to profitability. By 1981, most leases had been sold and other stores were in liquidation.

D. ART, HOBBY & CRAFTS STORES

These stores are recommended to experienced hobby-crafts people or artist professionals with a commercial flair. An analysis of art, hobby, crafts stores reveals the excellent retail opportunity for a reasonable sales goal in excess of $400,000 per year with a total investment of $60,000 to $70,000 with some trade experience. Some store experience, as well as hobby or art skills, is recommended. Small chains of these stores, like Craft-Showcase shops, are good examples of a successful operation you would do well to emulate. Despite needing local managers and problems of absentee ownership, they have produced excellent profits.

LOCATION   A location in one of the larger (over 100 store) shopping malls is recommended at a rental not over $8 per sq. foot. Many local areas with good pedestrian traffic and some parking, drawing from a 50,000 population, will support a large unit of 3,000 to 4,000 square feet if there is an indication of local interest in the merchandise (rental $2,000 to $2,400 per month is best).

CAPITAL BREAKDOWN   In a $60,000 to $70,000 capital budget:

- $10,000 for physical premises.
- $15,000 to $20,000 store fixup decoration, fixtures. Child Fixture Co. Pittsburgh, is recommended.
- $25,000 first basic stock.
- $10,000 to $15,000 operating cash.

MERCHANDISE ASSORTMENT   Art supplies, brushes, paints, paper, tables, matt board, frames, custom art frame source, hobby stitchery, crewel and needlepoint, macramé and other trims, books, yarns, sewing supplies, plant hangers and supplies, stained glass, seasonal decorations, and paper supplies for party should be included. Greeting cards and stationery items may be advantageous in some locations.

SOURCES   Many of the manufacturers of this stock are represented in offices in the trade buildings at 225 and 230 Fifth Avenue, New York City. Others have offices nearby and may be listed in the New York telephone classified directory under "Arts and Crafts, Wholesale," or in Fairchild publications or Directories.

PROFIT   The pressure of mounting expenses so commonplace in retailing today is somewhat less in stores featuring less competitive "blind" assortments of this kind.

ADVERTISING   The recommended advertising in mall locations is the joint efforts of the entire area stores promotions, plus mailed brochures (manufacturer co-op), and one or two yearly catalogues to your own store-cultivated mailing list. Contests involving customer-produced new patterns and samples create great interest and picture stories with public relations value. These stories perpetuate enthusiasm and create an interest in new hobbyists.

E. FINE JEWELRY STORES

A fine jewelry store is a good investment for experienced, knowledgeable people, a couple, or partners, preferably with specific store experience and some jewelry repair background, able to evaluate repairs, settings, watch repair cost, and possibly rebuy value of gold or silver. Knowledge of antique settings for purchase of estate jewelry is valuable.

CAPITAL   Minimum capital is estimated $100,000 to $110,000:

- $30,000 to $35,000 premises fix-up, front, deluxe setting, finest fixtures for display, backgrounds, showcases.
- $50,000 ($100,000 retail) stock assortment (break down below). Turnover expected 1.1 to 1.25. Volume $110,000 to $125,000.
- $25,000 operating capital.

After the first-year, profit range should be 5 to 8 percent in addition to salary for owners.

PREMISES   A 2,000-square-foot minimum store, shopping center, or local where a "need," paying a rental 6 to 8 percent. Store must have built in safe office and secure repair area, with television monitors and sneak thief safeguards. Steel folding front gates are suggested with a wired, monitored alarm system (ADT or Holmes) and internal sensors.

PERSONNEL   Part- or full-time male and female employees with a scheduled male on hand at all times. (Only females on hand is an invitation for strong-arm shoplifters who would hesitate when a male is present.) In some areas foreign language facility is urged. Training sales help is important to convey a feeling of reliability, confidence, and friendly service. "T.O. (takeover) training" is important where an expensive jewelry transaction seems to require the aid of a more skillful salesperson to close, and where the salesperson is able to smoothly transfer the customer to this more experienced person to effect the sale.

Stock Breakdown

Below you will find the breakdown of money by percentage in each category.

Watches 25%
    Digital (less and less) 8%
    Quartz Analog 50%
      Pulsar line, half of total
      Bulova, Caravelle, and others, balance
    Timex 10%
    Luxury Omega, Longines, Seiko 20%
    Very highest ($400 and up), Concord, etc. Swiss
      4 men's styles, 4 women's styles minimum selection
    Watch strap line 10%
Rings 25%
    Wedding rings 15-20% (25% of these with stones)
    "Stone" rings 85% (friendship, cocktail, costume, engagement, all metals)

Earrings 7-8% (gold, better quality silver)

Necklaces 5-6% (gold, better quality silver)

Bracelets (5-6%) (gold, better quality silver)

Plated Costume, branded jewelry 10-12% (Trifari, Krementz, Kramer, and others)

Men's tie tacs, pins, rings (stronger) 5%

Fine diamond jewelry 6-8%

Household gift assortment 12-15%
> Samples only of fine table silver or fine china (better lines, none carried by discounters)
> Table gifts, printed linens
> Glassware gifts
> Cocktail gifts
> Imported handmade gifts

Carry *no* electrical, kitchen gadget appliances that are featured in discount and hardware stores.

Fine jewelry stores gain a following through small no-charge accommodation repairs, reasonable and prompt repairs sent out to professionals, reliable watch maintenance, and well-handled complaints.

Leaflets to regular patrons of new styled novelties will often bring in trade for gift jewelry unrelated to it. A yearly holiday catalogue (with vendor-paid participation) usually pays.

F. HEALTH FOOD, NATURAL FOOD, VITAMIN STORES, AND OTHER FOOD SPECIALTIES

The ever-increasing popularity of health food, "natural" food, and vitamin stores, along with gourmet shops coupled with headlines to keep aware of the benefits of these panaceas, has opened a whole new industry valued by the Health Food Stores National Association in billions of dollars annually. Despite the lack of medical confirmation, many nutrition writers inflame the appetite of Americans for natural foods not wholly confirmed in their origin and for vitamin supplements not prescribed by doctors. The health food stores are here and doing a growing share of the food business, very profitably. Vitamin retailing is growing rapidly and professional franchises are offered.

STOCK   Health food retailers must know the claimed special attributes of the products and preferably should be "health nuts" themselves who can easily convey their enthusiasm. There are bulletins to the trade regularly available with the information necessary to keep owners and employees knowledgeable enough to retain customer confidence. The small store here again has the advantage over the supermarket, which carries many of these products at lower prices. The personal relationship instills confidence.

Many of these stores have added to their volume by carrying luxury priced coffees, teas, cheeses, flour, grains, herbs, spices, breads, and so on, and their traffic helps to sell biodegradable shampoos, vitamins, and philosophical literature. Health and diet-related books are sold in volume to many of these presold clients.

In some states special licenses are required after a course of study is completed. Some specialized store operations experience on the job is advised and research in the industry periodicals for countrywide sources of merchandise.

PREMISES   The premises should have adequate refrigeration units to protect freshness and a well-prepared repacking room to accommodate the reduction from bulk-buying quantities into saleable retail packages and mail order. This mail business is an excellent addition to volume, which utilizes employees during slower floor periods.

Some stores encourage walking traffic into the store with inviting health food lunch service, a profitable venture of its own. This traffic often picks up promoted and displayed items in volume. Lunch trade may be served well by part-time senior citizens whose limited earnings fit into the schedule and whose service becomes an asset.

CAPITAL   The Association of Health Food Stores suggests a $40,000 to $50,000 investment with about 60 percent for stock, and recommends a location in a busy shopping mall or a downtown area with traffic from professional, hospital, or industrial workers. Traffic is a must even at a higher overhead cost. A 5 percent advertising budget is recommended and a product liability policy to cover store name products packaging liability. Unprocessed foods require special care to preserve freshness and safety from vermin contamination. Plan a shop of 1,000 to 1,500 square feet at first, and use decoration themes like old posters or the old "natural look." Rental in shopping centers may be as much as $5 a square foot plus. Good turnover can be 12 times a year.

Gourmet Food and Specialties

Specialty food boutiques have become more of a viable opportunity for the well-prepared entrepreneur in America. Food prices have advanced so rapidly that paying that extra premium for a palate-pleasing specialty does not seem to seriously violate the food budget. Many women who are working full time don't have the preparation time to entertain at home and so depend on these already prepared gourmet foods to serve guests. Many family-treasured receipes induce couples to leave salaried jobs for a business of their own, a retail food boutique from which they hope to gain financial and personal rewards. Some even picture a chain of stores with a franchising concept. (Don't leave the job prematurely!)

Here are some thoughts to consider as you prepare your own recipes and other foods for retail:

- Original startup money should be your own. It is almost impossible to get banks interested in such a loan unless you have at least a matching sum and have a comprehensive plan that shows both established culinary expertise and management ability. S.B.A. loans are all but impossible.
- Some retail food experience is advised in at least one working partner.
- An investment in expensive equipment and premises will probably keep you poor and unsalaried for most of the first year.
- Your hours of work will be many more than any regular salaried job.
- Selling this retail food requires a license from the city health department. Preparing and selling food wholesale in several states requires Department of Agriculture approval and a huge investment in national distribution, advertising budget, large manufacturing processing plant, expensive packaging equipment, and so on.
- Problems of maintaining freshness, refrigeration, contamination from vermin and mice, and leftovers are natural to all food businesses and can negate profitability.

Some gourmet food operations have made out very well. An example is the very successful David's Cookies (originally working with wife, Susan, on recipes), where franchise buying includes the specially developed baking machine and controls that turn out the same chocolate chip cookies and others in all units throughout the country. The baking mix dough is sold to each store as needed and uniformity is achieved.

Young David started with a love for Lindt's bitter Dutch chocolate and the cookies his mother made until he and Susan improved the recipe, borrowed funds from his family, and opened the first shop to "muncher's" accolades. His home recipes had much more butter than his commercial ones. Many of his copiers have done well, too. David instructs that baking a full eight minutes makes them crisp; a shorter time leaves them chewy.

Other homemade delicacy shops include combinations:

- Caviar, smoked gourmet fish, salmon, sturgeon, pates, quiche, baked goods, stuffed artichoke, stuffed baked potato, strong aroma cheeses, poached fish in aspic.
- Fancy dessert shops including all special baked fruit open and deep dish pies, French pastries, cruellers, napoleons and the like, Danish crumb, and a variety of baked fruits (in wine), cream and yogurt treats with fresh sauces.
- Pasta shops with homemade varieties made in the window of the shop draws "sidewalk superintendents" who observe the noodle stretching with "drooling" interest. The signs call forth the latest information that "the

pasta is light in calories" and it is the heavy sauce that fattens. They offer low calorie "light" sauce, too.

- Full meals of low calorie salads with choices of "our own herb dressings and delicious spiced treats made fresh all day."
- Exotic coffee and tea blends featuring coffee tasting every day of different blends. The local aroma is free for the sniffing!
- Chinese exotic Mandarin specialties include flavorings, desserts, fortune cookies, and exotic soups "with spices to lift your spirits, food gifts to thrill your friends."
- All individual and original food specialties gift-wrapped to stay on as gifts in reusable trays and servers. Special coffee, tea blends, cookies, jams, and steak sauces are "gifty" as are chocolates and tempting cakes.
- Japanese Delicacies . . . sashimi, shrimp tempura, and other seafood, flavored rice balls, green beans with sesame seed sauce, Gyoza (dumplings), Yakitori (skewered chicken), and many other tempting exotic delights.

An excellent location is city stations where commuters leave for home.

Some small bake shops that became "big dough" do the volume dough handling and shaping by machine, but "touch it up" for that "handmade look." They do baking as a science with exact measuring, copy recipes of known success, use untrained people so they can teach own methods without "untraining" and do no advertising, but do go to sell restaurants at first for volume and other shops not nearby. Price must accommodate top fresh ingredients and off-hour labor (night preparation). Store names usually include words like *epicure, country kitchen, gourmet,* and boast "nothing artificial." Flavor and quality reign supreme as contrasted to fast food restaurants where gimmicks, promotion, and production with low price help add up to success.

G. HOMEWARES STORES' DEVELOPMENT

Life-style and economics have created changes in the traditional demand for furniture and home accessories, and a store owner in the field should be aware of the trend of this demand, note the reasons, and watch how some of the successful merchants are meeting the challenge. We are all well aware of the effect on home furnishing buying in the United States, where single-occupant dwellings are surpassing 30 percent, and where life-styles encourage short-term relationships that easily change. Many of the participants are reaching a stage in life that calls for a well-decorated home to entertain in rather than expensive entertainment spots. In this climate there have been changes.

The trend has been away from the large traditional "a little of everything" furniture, furnishings, floor coverings, lamps, and such, toward the smaller one kind of item specialty units. There are still a few national chians, like Levitz, still operating, who use decorator room concepts and their volume buying leverage to advantage. Others in like operations have had to merge to survive because of the competition from discounters in some of their items and the specialty stores who offer better depth and variety,

SPECIALITIES   Some of the more successful home furnishing specialties are:

- Scandinavian, modern, unpainted furniture shops including some franchises like Butcher Block.
- Recreational, terrace, patio, outdoor, and dinette.
- China and glassware emporiums (barns), some with other gifts; select from sawdust boxes.
- Bath and boudoir boutiques.
- Lamps and lighting shops; some feature "special effects" installation.
- Floor covering and carpet shops (there are several highly advertised franchises).
- Home entertainment centers, hi fi, TV, video recorders, video disc players, tape centers. The competition is strong among volume buying, highly advertised "price" promoters.
- Sleep shops, waterbed centers, glamour bedroom planners.
- Major appliance centers (most claim "discount priced," but match other's prices; few show real profits).
- Do-it-yourself shops, paint and paper, hardware-lumber and mortar, plumbing and hardware supply. Real growth because of soaring home repair labor. Leading chains are now owned by conglomerates who have management problems.
- Dry-cleaning and other equipment required for upholstery or carpet cleaning.
- Antique, slightly used furniture (special licenses needed).
- Furniture and appliance rental (based on the continuous moves of many large company employees).

It is undesirable to have a used or furniture rental business physically located with regular furniture selling since it is often suspected that the new being sold may have been rented or used previously.

SELLING POINTS   The higher priced furniture stores are most successful when broken into beautiful trimmed showcase rooms, and when a professional decorating service is offered. Delivery and installation services are normally expected with the sale, as well as credit payment service, be it installment or bank card.

The most effective furniture promotions involve the featuring of "price points" for your area and your trade. As an example, the strategy is to picture four to six upholstered sofas in an ad for medium-priced clientele, with several at the key price of $300 and others up to $500 or $600. Good salesmanship will affect 80 percent of sales in higher brackets despite the freedom to choose whatever the customer seeks. They invariably seek the "better" covering material, or higher priced "newer" shape when offered in floor comparison, for "long-term investment." Recliners promoted at $199 bring in people who usually buy one for $300, or even a few Barcolounger S model at $1,000. Bedding promotions are easier for stores to run because manufacturers offer special deals periodically to their regular stores and back them with warehouse stock in the event of great success in a sellout.

Furniture back-up stock is often unavailable to stores in a sellout, so larger stores counter this by buying lines of similar goods from different sources, hoping to fall back on at least one. Many furniture promotions depend on the store reduced markup for price. Stores are using this tactic—warehouse sales. The selling of furniture on the plain warehouse floor adds an atmosphere of bargains, especially when clientele is seeing samples, damaged pieces, and leftovers at lowered figures and reduced pieces of furniture they have come for. Warehouse sales achieve volume and turnover.

The higher priced furniture categories sold in sets with designer names do better in decorator roomette display on the regular selling floor. Stores buy these from fewer, most reliable quality sources, knowing that a customer waiting for goods will not be disappointed when the set arrives. It is a great advantage to a small furniture outlet to deal with a local manufacturer who can serve well to mutual advantage.

Several franchises are available in furniture—Ethan Allen is probably the best known. Manufacturers like Thomasville will promise regular users co-op ads and back-up stock if the retailer prominently displays the line on the selling floor.

The lack of security feeling in buying for less than permanent households brings up the question of whether your trade will buy the "romantic" bedroom for this present image or settle for a practical modular space-saver that is more practical in the event of a breakup.

For most of the variety of furniture, there are showrooms in major centers such as Chicago, Los Angeles, Dallas, New York, usually called a "Furniture Mart." The major upholstered furniture is exhibited twice a year (April and October) in special showrooms in the factory itself or special buildings near High Point, North Carolina, the manufacturing center for the country.

H. MEN'S WEAR RETAILING TODAY

The large traditional men's clothing stores have fallen in popularity in recent years and many chain retailers have failed. The larger department store men's departments have also suffered and are struggling to regain some of the lost volume from the promotional and special concept men's stores, whose ideas and local management seem more timely.

In the New York area, three companies with a unique approach seem to have made their mark.

Syms was started about 1959 by Sy Merns when he separated from his brother in the Mern's Men's Shops. His advertised "designer" names at low prices (never using the word *sale*) has built the business to seven large stores growing steadily, adding women's and children's items at low markup as well. Many of these designer names have never been associated with men's wear lines, and thus the image of discount against the department store's price is somewhat tarnished. The quality is good generally and the atmosphere, few services, no bank credit cards (personal checks are okay), basic alterations only, few salespeople, and such, bespeaks of discount operations, and business is good. The owner and his wife appear on television ads in a homey sincere explanation of their creed, which includes an automatic markdown system of women's clothing after time periods have transpired. This, of course, is the concept of Filene's Basement Store in Boston, Massachuetts.

Among the many factory outlet stores that have spread around the country in recent years, many who feature men's wear clothing have been successful. In the New York area, National Brands Outlet (N.B.O.), which uses television extensively, has grown to eight suburban locations despite the traditional competition of the clothing factory Fifth Avenue lofts, which have always done a cash business, after hours, supposedly at about 30 percent off the store prices. The claimed discount on national brands as a regular offering is not found, although some of the brands are known. There is a mixture of many prices and sources and the knowledgeable shopper may be able to find some gems among the stock offered on the bare racks.

Barney's in New York, which originally began operations as a "price cutter" with an out-of-the-way store location in central Manhattan with free parking, has changed its image toward the man who seeks designer clothing, continental styling, and the "very best." It is probably the largest single men's clothing store in the United States, carrying almost every fine brand name, American and European, of any note. Barney's does not hesitate to try a new designer if it has "flair." Price is only featured on rare occasions, one being the semiannual warehouse clearance, when the lines of waiting shoppers are pictured to show New York customers' commitment to Barney's value. The service and alterations departments are tops. Some boy's wear and a few items of tailored women's garments are also of the highest quality name brands. Here it was the second generation owner who changed when he saw demand change away from the original concept of his father, Barney.

In the early days of the great growth of Korvettes, the men's accessories and furnishings achieved the same success as the other departments, but the clothing department was an exception. None of the strong major brands would chance displeasing all their traditional shops or department stores by selling Korvettes.

Many small, no-frills discount stores of men's wear do well throughout the country, mostly in the larger population centers. They must have thorough men's clothing experience and ready access to the major men's market. The best chance for success is in aiming at one particular segment of their possible trade— natural shoulder, Ivy League, or any other appropriate trendy style with enough nearby following. Several shops have operated low key with little or no paid advertising. They get writeups in shopping columns and other free public relations stories because they do give genuine value. They do not accept credit cards, do not do alterations, and do not send a suit home without being paid for it. They buy very carefully, often closeouts, brands, or designers samples, returns, or late in season. They make a fair markup and yearly profit. Many have joined buying groups to secure better prices, closeouts, and values bought with the power of large orders.

WOMEN IN MEN'S CLOTHING   The growing list of successful women executives in big business has given birth to a new tailored market opportunity. Men's wear designer Stanley Blacker, Saint Laurie, and others have featured advertisements with men's and women's blazers together. They comment in interviews that the men's wear make is far superior to that made for women on Seventh Avenue and, therefore, will make sizeable gains. Even a traditional retailer like Brook's Brothers has been carrying a women's line since the middle 1970s. The most respected quality men's lines of Hickey Freeman and Oxxford Clothes ($500 suits) have entered the women's field, presenting the traditional all hand-tailored quality made with handstiched, canvas-backed lapels to be contrasted with women's maker fused collars. The Levi Company started to make garments for women many years ago.

THE STRETCH WEAR BOOM   In 1980 retailers were delighted to find some interest in the new Levi Action Wear texturized woven slacks. The possibilities of stretch seem to open up the men's wear world to items never before thought possible—washable suits and sport jackets that never need ironing and pincords and chinos with this same quality, light enough for summer wear.

Levi's David Hunter brand, Haggar's Body Motion line, and Farah use variations of the poly-spandex-stretch combinations with cottons, wools, nylons, and such to produce the traditional textures and patterns acceptable in slacks and jackets for men's clothing. Mature men find an attraction in the gentle comfort stretch around the middle, the slim younger men in the close show-off hung fit.

BOATING AND OUTDOOR WEAR   Boating and outdoor sports *apparel* has an appeal quite distinct from other men's wear and has its own opportunity for retail profit. Increased water recreation for many average families has brought about a demand for dress-up boating clothes and foul weather gear. New firms entering the field used special expertise and had the courage to try new fabrics and ideas to excite consumers. Despite the setback of gas shortages, the demand for this clothing and accessories has continued to rise.

Firms such as Sea Gear features a gore-tex fabric that "breathes" and yet keeps water spray from penetrating. Other companies use P.V.C. (polyvinyl chloride) coated nylon for foul weather suits despite the "sealed-in" factor. Other prominent producers are:

Peter Storm, Connecticut.

Neese, Louisiana.

Atlantis Weather gear, Long Island, New York. Known for natural oil wool sweaters, chamois shirts, and ultralightweight weather suits.

Mighty Mac, New York. Known for high quality outdoor and sea apparel, a tri-nyl light broadcloth, major exporter to Europe.

Gordon-Ferguson, Minneapolis. Established outdoor supplier for many years.

Sierra Design, California. "Thinsulate" lined lightweight garments.

Misty Harbor, Baltimore, Maryland.

Robert Lewis, New York.

London Towne (London Fog). Terry-lined nylon-coated slicker.

Fox-Knapp, New York. Traditional Navy peacoats.

Another class of outdoor goods that has succeeded in creating its own retail following is camping-outdoor clothing and equipment as shown in firms like Eastern Mountain Sports, Paragon, Kebbler, and others, who replaced a failing Abercrombie Company. Clothing, sleeping bags, tents, and other camping necessities for living in the wild are carefully chosen for high quality, regardless of price, as this young adult generation seeks an escape from the "plastic world" to nature—but always prepared and well equipped.

Section off your space if possible to have the look of departments for backpacks, sleeping bags, cross-country footwear, tents, life-saving equipment, lighting, cookware, tents, and such, with charts showing quality recommendations and reasons, prices, and so on. Offer repair services and seek available skilled repair people part or full time.

Ads are not always necessary in the commonplace manner. You will accomplish more with an affiliation to clubs and organizations that gather these people for weekend trips. Sponsor contests, celebrity appearances, demonstrations in store and out regularly to keep your store on their minds and these trips a tempting vacation.

WESTERN STYLE Revival of the Western interest by TV programs and President Reagan's well-publicized horsey costumes has led many retail stores into full assortments of western wear, some of it promoted cleverly and successfully. Without special promotional efforts, many firms found this investment costly and profitless.

Some areas of the country have retained an interest sufficient to support individual shops featuring boots, hats, fringed jackets, buckskins, vests, beaded Indian moccasins, belts, and the ever-present jeans. Cowboy boots of top quality and Stetson hats are a continuing interest for gifts in the finest shops, with price no problem. This interest, however, may not last.

I. SHOE STORES AND ATHLETIC FOOTWEAR

The great fashion interest in boots, including Western styles, and the return of high heel slender, appealing women's dress shoes, along with inflated leather prices, have added great dollar volume in footwear stores. Athletic footwear, both imported and domestic, has become an important profit maker for shoe stores and the activated athletic equipment stores are competing for the business. The shoe store should have an advantage because of the specialized experience in presentation, fitting expertise, and customer loyalty carried over from their satisfaction with the store's other lines. To build the athlete's following the shoe store must, however, become familiar with the latest selling talk related to jogging shoe fitting and comfort.

The very personal nature of fitting is a great advantage for the small shoe store owner over the shoe chains or department stores, especially in the children's and infant's ranges. The owner can overcome the advantage of the chain store lower prices by instilling confidence and giving personal service. Parents buy fit and comfort for a child's shoe as a priority over price, despite the expected short span of shoe life.

One key to shoe store success is organizing a fine eager sales force with good teamwork and keeping good records to avoid "outs" (of stock), or kept to a minimum. Cooperative stock work is a must to be able to find sizes and styles needed quickly at busy times. The remaining sizes of past season's styles must be grouped in back stock to be easily selected and sold, perhaps aided by push money per pair, so that the unsold remnants do not reduce turnover and cash profits. Some "family" shoe stores secure patron loyalty offering the special services like orthopedic shoes and made-to-mold "space" shoes, even including prescription shoes for child foot defects, after special training.

ATHLETIC SHOES   Not too long ago, shoe stores relegated sneakers to the "also have" status in their presentation. Now, the new pricing and intense, universal popularity of jogging has brought all athletic shoes into the forefront of promotional activity in shoe stores. Careful stocking of the many new names in athletic footwear can mean good profits, especially where the favorite sport heroes have endorsed some special construction. Child athletes will want to buy a different sole cleat for each sport and will soon return for additional pairs as they outgrow the size. Names like Nike, Adidas, Brooks, Converse, and Yamaha join Keds and Spaulding in the assortment.

Men's leather dress shoes prices have more than doubled in a few years, causing great concern in many fine shops as the number of pairs sold dropped dramatically. Some of this dollar volume is returning in the demand for "casual" styles, mostly using less expensive materials and these are being used for everyday wear. The professionals advise:

- Carry a smaller variety of styles in the leather higher priced dress shoes, but buy the styles that more or less match life-style clothing being sold in your area.
- Prepare your stock with a good supply of casual styles for well over 50 percent of the business expected, with the "loafer" look, and pull-ons, especially the Hush-Puppy line, some in high fashion colors. Some will be canvas-top boat shoes with crepe bottoms, others the preppy look of saddle shoes. Bass Weejuns penny loafers, Sperry Topsiders, Hush Puppies, Dexter, and Nunn-Bush lines are expected to be winners.

The number of women's pairs sold will likely decline in higher priced leathers. Style ingenuity by several new foreign crafts people, using lower cost materials, have crept into the area vacated by leathers and seem to be doing volume. Sandals are the outstanding style succeeding. Imports from Europe, which dominated American leather high-fashion footwear of the 1970s, are too high for the popular priced market. Some hand-sewn moccasin shoes are competing with these American styles. A re-acceptance of preppy styles in clothing for juniors will undoubtedly bring a return of the two-tone saddle shoes, the penny loafers, and the wing-tips in pumps so popular years ago.

Selling and merchandising shoes is a very specialized skill, and traditionally many department stores invited professionals to operate their departments as concessions. It is strongly advised that practical in-store experience be the basis for opening your own small shoe store.

J. VARIETY STORE POTENTIAL

In the 1930s, imitators of the F. W. Woolworth variety stores grew up everywhere, enticing customers on the premise that because they were a 5-and-10-cent store, the savings were there with the variety of small goods offered. Popularity waned as other stores copied the variety of notions, trimmings, and stationery and used competitive prices to undersell Woolworth and draw the traffic for 3-cent notions. Many of the established chains, H. L. Green, McCrory, McClellan, Kresge, Ben Franklin, W. T. Grant, and others, tried to become department stores or discount chains, but they failed to attain real success, except for Kresge (K-Mart) and Woolworth (Woolco), who started a whole new division, separately merchandising and managing. Grant tried several concepts in some of its losing, existing stores and managed to kill the entire firm.

Many of the smaller, locally run variety stores have survived, earning a living, usually without the promise of any real growth. Some have added personal expertise and specialties as management at the scene perceived a new opportunity to expand merchandise profitably, added to the notions, greeting cards, toys, and so on. Many of these stores have suffered loss of volume as the main shopping in town was decaying and the shopping mall on the highway offered free easy parking to car oriented Americans. With gas shortages and price hikes, downtown is making a comeback, and the federal government is encouraging investment in central cities with tax incentives (see Chapter 11). Cities are offering property tax and loan assistance in order to revive downtown, and the traffic is returning, helping the variety store that needs it.

Many of these independent variety stores are run by older, almost retired, or just uninspired owners whose children may have chosen not to follow their parents in the business. A number of these stores have thus become available at reasonable prices, possibly on easy terms.

Imagination and ingenuity can rekindle a spark in some of these locations and bring the charisma of modern assortments to attract today's sophisticated adults. Using traffic-garnering merchandise, promotions, and adding the owner's special expertise can draw attention to its new presence without heavy ad expenditure. Discount records, tape departments, kitchenware, small appliances selling at discounts a-la-Korvette's beginnings (see Appendix C), and auto-hardware home items with help offered to home owners are just a few of the many ways to interest local patrons. Sewing and knitting needs can be promoted with part-time senior instructors, or kitchenware appliances with cooking experts. You may even have the opportunity of taking over older, very favorable leases to get you started with less overhead.

K. HOW TO BUY A STORE

- The many sources are:
  - Newspaper ads, trade journal ads
  - Business brokers (note possible charge to you)
  - Realtors, bankers, lawyers, accountants
  - Merchandise sources and salespeople in the trade
  - S.B.A., Merchants' Associations, Chamber of Commerce

- Always be aware that even if they are very helpful, brokers are paid *commissions* by the seller and so are apt to be on the seller's side of the deal.

- Draw a Dun & Bradstreet report at your bank at once for general history of the business.

Analyze the Figures

Remember that some of the figures suggested will not be very meaningful as guides if the seller is very firm in his or her asking price. The facts and figures below are to be used as a guide in your calculation of price.

1. Four to five times the average yearly net profit.
2. Note owner's income from business in last four to five years. (If the owner won't show it to you, his or her accountant may show it to your accountant.)
3. Sales tax records of volume, as well as sales journal.
4. Note markup and markdowns to judge inventory value.
5. Note overhead and expense ratios.
6. If the business isn't profitable, see if there is potential. Could your methods improve it? Do you have a special idea or additional trade the owner wasn't taking advantage of?

Assess the Physical Assets

- Have the physical inventory taken by a pro, to know markdowns, saleability, and vintage.
- You should take it just as you take over (without lapse of time).
- Fixtures, furniture, and physical plant (estimated value and condition).
- Is all physical property free and clear (no liens or balance owed)?
- If there is customer credit, accounts receivable must be judged and sharply discounted for *age*. (What percent is old?)
- The lease—transfer rather than a sublease (see original lease and lessor).
- Customer lists, mailing lists, etc. Examine credits and refunds records.

Assess the Other Assets

- What business "name" is owned by the owner?
- Is there really "good will"? Is it transferable or personal?
- How is this business reputation with trade? What does Dun & Bradstreet say in report?
- Are any key personnel to leave when you take over? Will it be a big loss to you?

Remember

- If you are buying the *corporation* you need a lawyer and accountant to ferret out hidden liabilities, liens, unpaid bills, chattel mortgages, back taxes, back benefits of employees (including vacations owed), pending suits, creditors claims, judgements, etc.

- Always provide in contract the *unlisted liabilities remain* obligation of seller who executes a "bond" to guarantee payment.

- You must evaluate business trend in area with data given, project sales, and profits and cash budget to evaluate sufficiency of working capital.

- Need "running money" available (at least 25 percent of inventory value) for adequate payroll and overhead cash, money for unexpected expenses, unanticipated slack business, and needed special merchandise to round out inventory, etc.

- Arrange downpayment and installment payments which are not excessively burdensome to business (so that there will be adequate "cash flow").

- Before closing have *pros* check:

  1. Local health and other codes to know business conforms now.
  2. Must conform to Bulk Sales Act provisions (public notices required).
  3. Guarantee against outstanding liens.
  4. Insurance and taxes prorated as of transfer day.
  5. A bank holds funds in escrow account to fulfill all obligations.

- If the owner has been drawing an adequate salary and has had a + profit in 4 to 5 years equal to the asking price, it would seem to be priced within reason.

Looking to Buy
a Top Successful Business?

Michael Baseman suggests looking for potential and especially a store which is poorly managed. Where management is tired, uninspired, under-financed, or absentee you may have a good store to take over. Michael bought a business in 1976.

He was an aggressive home builder in suburban Rochester, N.Y. who unfortunately was squeezed into bankruptcy by the evaporation of mortgage money in the state when the rate ceiling diverted funds into the higher rates available elsewhere. At fifty-five, he was not optimistic about the job market and so he looked to buy a business.

"I saw this printing shop whose volume, profit, and price were small and affordable. I liked it because it was the number two shop in the area and the proprietor who wanted to retire did only enough to make a base living—no zest for new things, no new duplicating techniques."

Michael bought the store for $15,000, borrowed another $15,000 for new copying and typing equipment and went out looking for legal office and court printing work. He added mat services and arranged for freelance copywriting and artist work when needed, in an attempt to develop big company catalogue and manual work.

He found a good source of labor at the three colleges nearby, using each employee for the hours convenient to his or her class schedule. He hired part-time after-hours typists who used his latest rented super-typing equipment to produce perfect copies overnight and do briefs and catalogues.

His income in 1979 will be in excess of $60,000 on a volume close to $400,000 (original owner–$11,000 income). Michael says, "If you buy a top producer business you pay top price and have a tough time matching the excellent volume and profit. Find a business that's *number two* like mine was in a town where *number one* does a beautiful job and where there is potential. Buy this business and go after the *number one* . . . invest and try harder."

Buying a Franchise

A company grants a franchise, a right to operate a business using its product and name with its know how and methods. Franchises are offered by franchisors to francisees (you), for a down payment and regular payments of a percentage of sales volume.

The first known franchisor was the Singer Sewing Machine Company in the late 1800s. There are many in automobile and gasoline distribution; but most Americans think of McDonalds, Burger King, and other food franchises when franchise is mentioned.

Many eager franchisees expect so much and study the proposition so ineffectively that they lose sight of many important factors to confirm before they proceed, such as

1. Is the company a financially responsible firm offering a known opportunity for a profitable business?

   For the first inquiry see a Dun & Bradstreet Report and call the Better Business Bureau in the franchisor's operating area. A typical "loser" was sold by a slick (phone sales on commission) lady. When Brad answered a magazine ad "Part-time, make $10,000 to $12,000 profit a year with Vending Machine with 8-track tapes." "Invest $2100 for vending machine and $200 for first stock of fast-selling "Top of the Pop Chart" tapes which should sell out and return $400 per week at least." Brad said that the deal "clincher" was that his contract "guaranteed" they would take back the machine and return his money in 6 months if not satisfied.

   Brad said that he had called the Atlanta office trying to return the machine according to the guarantee. He couldn't get them on the phone and the store where the company had helped him place the vending machine wanted it out because they only sold ten tapes in five months and needed the space. A hasty check showed the franchisor to have more than twenty judgements against them, and only "some office furniture" as assets. Either D&B or the Atlanta Better Business Bureau would have discouraged the investment. Without checking, common sense could not prevail over eagerness.

2. The second inquiry to be made should always be to other operating franchisees for their estimate of the deal.
3. In general the fact that the franchisor's profit is mainly derived from the sale of equipment should be a tell-tale warning.
4. After gaining knowledge of the franchisor's background and length of time this product or service has been offered, a market survey should confirm its value and the profit potential, using our other advice.
5. Other franchisees will confirm the value of the franchisor's training and his cooperation toward franchisees' success.
6. An attorney can determine the territorial rights and general fairness of the contract.

The federal government offers a list of all franchises being offered (usually two years behind). Write to the Superintendent of Documents, U.S. Printing Office, Washington, D.C. 20402, and ask for the *Government Franchise Opportunities Handbook.*

Twenty-four states have passed franchise control legislation making the franchisor responsible for issued equipment even if the company isn't the actual manufacturer of it. These laws protect against unreasonable termination of contract and provides that state officials take action where multiple complaints of unfair actions such as territory "flooding" by franchisor (if franchisee does not operate maximum hours a day, etc.). The "Mikva" bill for national control has been introduced in Congress and would prevent franchisor from cancellation during term. Franchisor companies complain this threatens product image when product handling is less skillful than franchisor's prescribed routine.

In July '79 the "Truth in Franchising" Federal regulation was enacted into law by the Federal Trade Commission. Sometimes called the "Magna Carta of Franchise," it requires "fair information disclosures by franchisors, including proof of profit claims *only by past 'track records'* of other franchisees." It allows franchisees to bring lawsuits for fact misrepresentation and allows the FTC to act against companies who flaunt their new regulations.

You may *not* assume that contracts are therefore "fair" and that you are protected against the "small print" you didn't read. Evaluate products, locations and training with the same care we suggest for your own new store or when buying a store.

L. LEGAL REFERRAL AND ACCOUNTING HELP

The use of a competent attorney for the complicated legal aspects of leases and contracts should be well understood. A lawyer's assistance as counsel as you make this major investment should also be appreciated.

The time to plan for legal help is before trouble. The best plan is to avoid legal complication. These are some of the areas where a lawyer may be especially helpful:

- Explanation and decision on your legal form of business.
- Partnership and stockholder agreements.
- Corporate formation, certificate filling, stock issue, meetings, minute book requirements.
- Securing and approving the provisions of a lease; buying real estate.
- Acquiring a store, title to an inventory, liens, bulk sales, and so on.
- Local zoning, license, and permit requirements.
- Guidance on personal future plans, tax obligations, business expansion, or aid in judging a prospective co-owner.

Legal referral is an effective service of the local Bar organization to supply an attorney at a reasonable fee if you do not have a lawyer. There may be instances, also, when your personal friend who is an attorney, is too "busy" with large corporate clients to devote the personal attention you desire, or is too much of a specialist in another phase of law to be most helpful. For these times you may investigate this referral service with very little obligation unless you decide to use the lawyer and accept the stipulated fee.

Contact your local Bar Association directly and ask for the legal referral person in charge. If you have been working with any of the free business consulting groups (see Appendix Y), they will discuss the matter with you.

In many large cities in the United States, the local bar will arrange an appointment for you with an interested attorney for a very short period, perhaps half an hour, to discuss your needs and estimate the cost to you. You may then choose to obligate yourself for the lawyer's estimated fee for services to be performed or pay only for the referral time, a minimal amount (in New York City $25 for one-half hour).

You may not always get a perfect choice of counsel for you, but the service tries to provide an interested, capable attorney, whom the Bar Association believes is most likely able to fulfill your special needs as given to them.

A similar referral system is available in some cities for securing the services of a C.P.A. for your books, accounts, and tax preparation.

Forming Your Corporation
Without Legal Help

The corporation form of business is very popular, but its use should be evaluated carefully and balanced against the greater expense and added preparation of tax documents. After considering the merits of an attorney's services (see preceding section) for other reasons (so that the corporate formation would be only a small added fee), you may conclude that you want to form the corporation yourself. If so, follow these steps:

1. Commercial stationery stores carry Articles of Incorporation, which apply to your state (or province in Canada) and corporation kits (about $25-$35) with stamp and minute book, forms, and instructions.

2. Complete the forms, sending them to the corporate department of your state, accompanied by a certified check in the amount requested for filing and organizational tax.

3. Choose a name not being used by other companies. In your search, cover all possible phone books and make a list of about 10 choices in your order of preference. The state will honor your preference and select an available corporation name from the list. (You may also ask the state office to make a search for a particular name before you send your completed forms; one search is free.)

4. The filing fee is approximately $50, and the organization tax is a small minimum (often $10) or a larger amount based on par value (or no par value) and how many shares are to be issued (your own choice).

5. The critical item is "corporate purpose," which should be written to give your company the widest possible latitude in zones of operation; for advice use S.B.A. manual 223 or "Corporate Formation" at your library (this is the reason most people use attorneys). It will allow your company to change direction if a new business is advisable.

6. After the formation is completed and you have been notified, you hold a meeting, adopting by-laws, electing directors to hold office, and electing officers of the corporation. Shares are issued to stockholders according to their investment. At a meeting of stockholders, directors are elected annually and they in turn select the officers to run the company, decide salaries, and such. Minutes of these meetings are kept in the corporation book (in the kit). A decision to operate under Subchapter "S" status must be the unanimous vote of all stockholders at a meeting. Minute book should be kept-up-to-date and a meeting held at least once a year.

M. PARTNER AND STOCKHOLDER AGREEMENTS

Here are the major elements of partner and stockholder agreements:

- Names of participants, company name, address.
- General purpose of business.
- Officer's names and positions; checks to be signed by.
- Activities and responsibility of each (full time or part).
- Salaries, basis, and time, any other cash provision.
- Financial contribution of each (receive so many shares if a corporation).
- Detailed responsibility of each if desirable.

- Salary paid in case of sickness or accident above a period; insurance policy to cover, if any for accident and/or death.
- Death of either party, provision for payment to estate.
- Dissolution by either party, provision for payment time period as a buy out. (Notification period in writing.)
- Provision for failure of buy out, to advertise business sale.
- Major policy dispute, third party (lawyer or accountant) help, binding (or American Arbitration).

Stockholders Agreement (Example)

The stockholders of the Just Togs, Inc. Corporation (of New York) do hereby make the following agreement among themselves as sole owners of all the shares of the corporation. The stockholders are: Mr. Max Dawn, president, Mr. Irving Henry, vice-president, Ms. Lawrence, secretary, and Ms. Pearl, treasurer. Only the president and vice-president are actively working on a regular basis and drawing salaries, always on an equal basis with one another. In this agreement, they shall be referred to as "partners."

Responsibilities of president and vice-president have been adopted during 1967 and 1968 and will be roughly as follows, with changes made as need arises. The partners shall each contribute $15,000 in cash or physical assets at once to form the stated $30,000 capital of the corporation.

Mr. D. is responsible for the purchasing of all women's wear and other miscellaneous women's merchandise. Mr. H. will be responsible for children's wear and the miscellaneous buying. Mr. H. will buy all store supplies, equipment, and handle repair and store maintenance. Mr. D. will do all necessary office work and bookkeeping preparation for accountant's quarterly visit.

Each will do stocking and marking of merchandise bought by him. Each will work approximately 80 percent of the store hours each week, being covered in the store for the other remaining 20 percent. Hours are to be arranged before the 20th of the month preceding the one involved. Vacation periods shall be equal and arranged two months in advance.

Any active work performed by other officers is to be compensated at 50 percent above federal minimum wage rates.

Sickness or accident: If either party shall become sick or disabled the salary shall continue for four full weeks, not counting the last week in which the disablement occurred. The corporation shall take out an insurance policy covering such disability as soon as possible so that the corporation will be able to hire a replacement and the proceeds of the policy can then be applied to the disabled for the period covered in the policy. Permanent disability shall be handled at the end of one year under provisions later noted for dissolution or one partner leaving business.

Death of either president or vice-president: At the time of execution of this agreement an insurance policy on the lives of the above is to be taken by the corporation for the express purpose of covering the value of the stock held by either party or their respective families. The original face value of the policy is to be $20,000. It is hereby agreed that the shares owned by the deceased and family are to be tendered to the corporation for this amount, plus enough additional cash to equal one-half of the net worth as of the previous August 1, or January 1, whichever date is closer to the date of death. All stockholders agree that this shall be the stipulated value of the shares to be returned to the corporation at time of death. All amounts over the $20,000 shall be paid to the family of the deceased in equal monthly installments for 12 months following death. The amount of the policy ($20,000) is the least amount to be paid for the shares as a stipulated amount should the one-half net worth be less than this amount.

It is planned that the corporation will likewise take out a policy covering accident and health, which would enure to the benefit of the president, vice-president, and other essential participants in the business. This policy shall be taken by the corporation when funds are available and the most advantageous policy has been determined.

Dissolution or termination of the business: Should either partner wish to terminate and leave the business, he must notify the other in writing. The remaining partner may buy out the leaving partner's shares or acquire a third party to do so within 90 days of notice. The price to be paid shall be one-half of the net worth at the last fiscal statement and this amount shall be paid to the departing partner one-third in cash, two-third in equal monthly installments for the succeeding 24 months. These installments shall be secured by a chattel mortgage on the physical assets of the company, and the stock certificates of the departing partner shall be held in escrow until fully paid for.

Should the remaining partner choose not to, or cannot buy out this share, the firm should be liquidated as follows: All operations shall cease at the end of the 90-day period as noted above, and all salaries and payments likewise. During this time business should be advertisied and sold as a running business, if possible, and failing this, in auction or other sale. After all debts are paid, the final accounted assets under the direction of Mr. Ernest, accountant, shall be divided equally.

In the event of any dispute between the partners involving policy of the company of the greatest urgency, whether in this agreement or unrelated to these matters, the dispute shall be handled by submission in writing by each of the partners to Mr. Ernest, who shall discuss the matter with Mr. Gorman and Mr. Lester, our attorneys, and render a decision which shall be binding on both partners.

This agreement shall be drawn into final form, be executed by the partners, and become part of the minutes of the Corporation. Any changes and amendments shall be in writing, and likewise be incorporated.

_____

Max Dawn

_____

Irving Henry

Witness	_____
	L. Ernest

Witness	_____
	R. Lester

Dated_____

Sworn and
Subscribed   _____
Before me

_____

_____

                      Notary Public

Escape Clause

The needed "escape" clause. The prime mover [the person who starts and plans original project] in any new business should have a period during which he can judge the quality of personal relationship between himself and an associate who he takes on to complete both capitalization and/or expertise. Before the end of a given period either should be given the right to withdraw or break up the association on certain notice, repayment of investment, and any additional payment originally agreed upon.

A recent case in point will illustrate. Vera Crosnick is a talented cosmetologist whose skin treatments and her career in one of New York's fine skin treatment salons started when she and her husband, Martin, fled the Hungarian revolution of the 1950s. She had wisely collected many names of devoted clients over the years, saved some money, and was now ready to open a shop of her own.

We discussed corporate form for safety (malpractice), her planned capital, lease, fixtures, shop layout, and how to contact her past clients. Later she called to say she was taking in her husband's sister, Lee, not for the $7,000 she would add to the capital or for her manicuring experience, but mostly to have another responsible person to cover the shop.

"Make sure your lawyer writes an agreement with Lee in case things don't work out EXACTLY as you plan," I suggested.

A few months later Vera called to tell me that the shop opening was successful, but that she was upset about Lee's work, her poor relationship with clients, and of their growing personal open hostility. I asked what her agreement with Lee stated, suggesting that she see her attorney about terminating the association. She confessed that in her haste the agreement had been prepared at the office of Lee's lawyer and did not think there was any provision to cancel the agreement.

"Offer her a bonus and get your lawyer to settle it the best you can so that you will not allow this animosity to interfere with the smooth running of the salon," I suggested.

A conference was scheduled with Lee's lawyer's to settle the matter, and after some discussion about the family turmoil this was causing, they settled on a profit of $7,000 on top of the return of Lee's capital.

It was a costly lesson to Vera in addition to the personal agitation. We had suggested to her a simple escape clause such as:

> If within 120 days of the opening of the salon, Vera Crosnick shall determine that it is in the best interests of the business to terminate the relationship, Lee will return her stock for full immediate payment of the $7,000 plus her share of the profits from the salon for a period of 90 days thereafter payable at that time. Notice from Vera to Lee shall be in writing and her work at the salon shall cease on receipt of this notice.

N. A COMPREHENSIVE BUSINESS PLAN

Entrepreneurs should work up a plan to settle their own thoughts and goals and be able to project their optimism to potential creditors and lenders. This is the required information in such a plan:

I. Preplanning Study

When you have selected your kind of goods, shop the stores that are doing well in it, familiarize yourself with the outstanding brands, note unbranded price and quality for comparison, walk around your area for ideas of specific people needs, make notes of layouts, displays, advertisements, note business area merchants' ideas of future trends, see salespeople and showroom people, attend shows, check your total funds available, and assemble.

II. Story of Your Business
(as you would tell it to a friend)

a. Your merchandise, brands, and other kinds.
b. Where, the area, the size store—lease, rent, term, options.
c. Customers, their needs, your unique appeal, area competition.
d. Knowledge and experience you have; why it will succeed.
e. Rough idea of costs, fixup, opening stock, operating funds.
f. Company name, form, any coowners, and their expertise.
g. Pricing and strategy, promotional ideas.
h. Planned sales volume and profits for next few years; and longterm goals.

   i. Capital needs total, money on hand, money needed from lenders.
   j. Money for opening stock, three-month plan, and fill-in buying.
   k. Opening expenses, advertising, insurance, other budgets.
   l. Legal and audit plans and expenses, maintenance and supplies, deposits.

III. Loan Request for Additional Funds

   a. Letter outlining the need for funds and describing this data.
   b. Reference to all business facts of the "story" (above).
   c. Amount of the loan request, the period, and repayment plan.
   d. Total Capital Plan with personal input of management, balance needed, special use of funds and it's effect.
   e. Business goals, earnings projections, expected return on investment, sales volume projected period of loan.
   f. Any other co-owners, their management responsibilities, investment, and expertise.
   g. Past history of finances (if any), I.R.S. returns, balance statements.
   h. Projected financial data to predict return of loan:
      1. Profit and Loss Projection.
      2. Balance sheet end of year one.
      3. Cash Flow Chart Projection.
   i. Net profit ratio projection for the loan period, anticipated profits, and expansion goals.

O. FAIR TRADE LAWS

During the 1930s, Congress and some state legislators became convinced that the property rights of a manufacturer in his or her name brand merchandise should be protected against the "depreciation" effect of price cutting of the manufacturer's list prices. The agreement for all to maintain a price was contrary to the basic antimonopoly federal law, the Sherman Anti-Trust Act of some 20 years before, and so federal and state fair trade legislation was enacted to secure this price listing protection. Manufacturers could stop price cutting by injunction or sue for damages in any state where enacted.

More than 40 states passed similar bills, which required manufacturers to contract with one retailer in the state to maintain list prices and enforcing all others to follow. Consumer groups often rallied against this and later succeeded in defeating it in some states. Price enforcement was very costly and manufacturers more effectively resorted to delivery delays or curtailment to prevent price cutting by an individual store. In some courts the defense to a manufacturer's suit requesting injunctive ("stop price cutting or be in contempt of court!") relief was thwarted by the offending store's claims that the manufacturer had not pursued other small price cutters, had not been "diligent," and, therefore, was not entitled to this drastic relief. (Courts agreed with E.J. Korvettes on this point.)

Korvettes and other price cutters changed public opinion. The philosophy of price maintenance was defeated in the courts, and by 1976 Fair Trade was abolished.

P. RESIDENT BUYING OFFICES

Out-of-town specialty shops and smaller independent department stores have traditionally been served in market buying of their lines by resident buying offices. They provide a market city working office site as well as everyday in-the-market representation by professionals who keep store people abreast of the best available styles and prices.

Stores pay a monthly fee starting at $200., depending on their store volume, departments to be serviced, and so on. Additional services and expertise available are:

- Executive assistance in managerial problems and exchange of expense ratio experience.
- Promotion and advertising suggestions and assistance.
- Participation in private label and import programs.
- Consultation to assist management in merchandise direction, price lines, and so on.
- Assistance to management on plans to expand, relocate, or branch out.
- Aid to evaluate a store purchase, including inventory evaluation (at additional cost).

Felix Lilienthal, president of the buying office that bears his name (begun in 1907 by his father), said in an interview with *Women's Wear Daily:*

> Because of today's market conditions we have had to hire stronger department store executives including top notch promotional talent. We can assist the independent store to secure his share of the retail volume holding off the increased competition of the Federated Stores, Allied Stores, etc., Sears, Penneys, etc., and the discount chains. The edge our fast-moving independent has now over the chains is his ability to make quick decisions to change, where change of direction is indicated.

Q. SMALL BUSINESS ADMINISTRATION, TODAY'S LOANS, SBA FORMS

First go to your bank. If they want to participate with S.B.A., just send the papers to S.B.A. If they do not want the loan at all, you may still get an S.B.A. loan if S.B.A. has money, *if* you prove ability to repay, and if you have at least 50 percent of your own capital.

S.B.A. instruction sheets for companies applying for loans up to $500,000 call for submission of these facts to your bank:

- Brief history of business and need for the money, why it will help.
- What equipment and improvmeents will be bought with money.
- Personal resumes of owners (over 25 percent).
- Signed balance sheets, profit and loss statements, (current 90 days) and the last three years.
- Federal I.R.S. returns three years, and of the owners two years.
- Copy of lease or letter describing it by landlord.
- Business certificate or corporate stamp on papers.
- Projection of earnings, how sales volume will be achieved.
- List collateral as security.
- Personal financial statement.

If bank approves the loan with S.B.A. backing, three S.B.A. forms are required:

- S.B.A. Form 4   Application for loan.
- S.B.A. Form 912   Personal History each principal.
- S.B.A. Form 413   Banks form of personal financial statement each principal.

The S.B.A. officer will evaluate:

- Eligibility of small business for particular program.
- Availability of funds from other sources.
- Evaluation of balance sheet and working capital.
- If collateral is adequate for loan.
- Analysis of earnings and projection, repaying ability.
- If owner's equity is adequate.
- Management ability and expertise.
- Adequate lease, insurance, business practices.

If bank refuses loan, get the "letter of decline" and go to another bank. If second one refuses, you may apply directly to S.B.A.—amount limit is $150,000.

If direct S.B.A. loan application is made, use same general data, but availability of funds is so limited that the agency is highly selective (policy change on S.B.A. loans). All application forms are available without charge at local S.B.A. offices.

SBA Form 4
Loan Number

OMB # 100-R-0081

U.S. Small Business Administration

APPLICATION FOR LOAN

I. Applicant/Information About You

Name

Street Address

City, State, Zip Code

Telephone

II. Information About Your Business

Name of Business

Address of Business

City, State, Zip Code

County	Telephone
Type of Business	Date Established
Number of Employees	IRS Employer I.D. Number
Present: After Approval:	

Bank Where Your Business Has An Account

III. Information About Management:
List the name of all owners (having 20% or greater interest), officers, directors, and/or partners. Provide the percent of ownership and the annual compensation.

Name and Title	% of Ownership
Address	Annual Compensation
Name and Title	% of Ownership
Address	Annual Compensation
Name and Title	% of Ownership
Address	Annual Compensation
Name and Title	% of Ownership
Address	Annual Compensation

IV. How You Plan to Use the Loan Money

Building	Amount for Building	Amount for Land
☐ New ☐ Purchase ☐ Renovate	$	$
Amount for New Equipment	Amount for Notes Payable	
$	$	
Amount for Working Capital	Amount for Equipment Repair	
$	$	
Amount for Accounts Payable	Other (See Instructions)	
$		

Total Loan Requested ➡ $

Term of Loan ➡ Years: Months:

V. Summary of Collateral

	Present Market Value	Present Mortage Balance	Cost Less Depreciation
A. Land and Building			
B. Inventory			
C. Accounts Receivable			
D. Machinery and Equipment			
E. Furniture and Fixtures			
F. Other			
Total Collateral $			

SBA Form 4 (9-78) Previous Editions Are Obsolete

VI. Assistance

List the names of attorneys, accountants, appraisers, agents, or other persons rendering assistance in preparation of this form.

Name and Occupation	Total Fees Paid
Address	Fees Due
Name and Occupation	Total Fees Paid
Address	Fees Due

INSTRUCTIONS FOR APPLICATION FORM

Sections I, II, III. Please provide the information requested. "You" refers to the proprietor, general partner or corporate officer signing this form.

Section IV. Use of the loan money; if your use of the loan fits one of the categories listed on the application form, please fill out this section. If you use "other" submit a list on a separate sheet of paper and label the list Exhibit A.

Section V. Summary of collateral: if your collateral consists of (A) Land and Building, (B) Inventory, and/or (C) Accounts Receivable, fill in the appropriate blanks. If you are using (D) Machinery and Equipment, (E) Furniture and Fixtures, and/or (F) Other, please provide an itemized list (labeled Exhibit B) that contains serial and identification numbers for all articles that had an original value greater than $500.

Section VI. Provide the information requested for all professional services used while preparing the application. You will be asked to complete another form **after loan closing** that will itemize compensation actually paid for services rendered in connection with this application.

Yes	No	CHECKLIST FOR APPLICATION PACKAGE
		All Exhibits must be signed and dated by person signing this form.
☐	☐	1. Have you submitted **SBA Form 912** (Personal History Statement) for each person e.g. owners, partners, major stock holders, etc.; the instructions are on **SBA Form 912**?
☐	☐	2. Have you filled out a personal balance sheet (**SBA Form 413** may be used for this purpose) for each stockholder (with **20%** or greater ownership), partner, officer, and owner. Label this Exhibit C.
☐	☐	3. Have you included the statements listed below: 1,2,3 for the last three years; 1,2,3,4 dated within **90 days** of filing the application; and statement 5? This is Exhibit D. (Management Assistance has **Aids** that help in the preparation of financial Statements.) 1. Balance Sheet 2. Profit and Loss Statement 3. Reconciliation of Net Worth 4. Aging of Accounts Receivable and Payable 5. Earnings projections for at least one year (If Profit and Loss Statement is not available, explain why and substitute Federal Income Tax Forms.)
☐	☐	4. Have you completed a list which contains the original date and amount, present balance owed, interest rate, monthly payment, maturity and security for each loan or debt that your business currently has? Please indicate whether the loan is current or delinquent. An asterisk (*) should be placed by any of these debts that will be paid off with the **SBA** loan. This should be labeled Exhibit E. *(over)*

Yes	No	
☐	☐	**5.** Have you provided a brief history of your company and a paragraph describing the expected benefits it will receive from the loan? If not, you must do so. Label it Exhibit F.
☐	☐	**6.** Have you provided a brief description of the educational, technical and business background for all the people listed in **Section III** under management? If not, you must do so. Please mark it Exhibit G.
☐	☐	**7.** Do you have any co-signers and/or guarantors for this loan? If so, please submit their names, addresses and personal balance sheets as Exhibit H.
☐	☐	**8.** Are you buying machinery or equipment with your loan money? If so, you must include a list of the equipment and the cost. This is Exhibit J.
☐	☐	**9.** Have you or any officers of your company ever been involved in bankruptcy or insolvency proceedings? If so, please provide the details as Exhibit K.
☐	☐	**10.** Are you or your business involved in any pending lawsuits? If yes, provide the details as Exhibit L.
☐	☐	**11.** Do you or your spouse or any member of your household, or anyone who owns, manages, or directs your business or their spouses or members of their households work for the **Small Business Administration**, Small Business Advisory Council, SCORE or ACE? If so, please provide the name and address of the person and the office where employed. Label this Exhibit M.
☐	☐	**12.** Does your business have any subsidiaries or affiliates? If yes, please provide their names and the relationship with your company along with a current balance sheet and operating statement for each. This should be Exhibit N.
☐	☐	**13.** Do you buy from, sell to, or use the services of any concern in which someone in your company has a significant financial interest? If yes, provide details on a separate sheet of paper labeled Exhibit P.
☐	☐	**14.** If your business is a franchise, have you included a copy of the franchise agreement? Please include it as Exhibit R.
☐	☐	**15.** If you or any principals or affiliates have ever requested government financing, list the name of the agency (including **SBA**), the amount requested or approved, date of request or approval, present balance, and status (i.e. current, delinquent). This should be Exhibit S.

CONSTRUCTION LOANS ONLY

Yes	No	
☐	☐	**16.** Have you included in a separate exhibit (Exhibit T) the estimated cost of the project and a statement of the source of any additional funds? If not, please do so.
☐	☐	**17.** Have you filed all the necessary compliance documents (**SBA Form Series 601**)? If not, loan officer will advise which forms are necessary.
☐	☐	**18.** Have you provided copies of preliminary construction plans and specifications? If not, include them as Exhibit U. Final plans will be required prior to disbursement.

DIRECT LOANS ONLY

Yes	No	
☐	☐	**19.** Have you included two bank declination letters with your application? These letters should include the name and telephone number of the persons contacted at the banks, the dates and terms of the loan, the reason for decline and whether or not the bank will participate with **SBA**. In towns with 200,000 people or less, one letter will be sufficient.

SBA Form 4 (9-78) Previous Editions Are Obsolete

AGREEMENTS AND CERTIFICATIONS

Agreement of Nonemployment of SBA Personnel: I/We agree that if **SBA** approves this loan application **I/We** will not, for at least two years, hire as an employee or consultant anyone that was employed by the **SBA** during the one year period prior to the disbursement of the loan.

Certification: I/We certify: (a) I/We have not paid anyone connected with the Federal Government for help in getting this loan. I/We also agree to report to the **SBA Office of Security and Investigations, 1441 L Street N.W., Washington, D.C., 20416** any Federal Government employee who offers, in return for any type of compensation, to help get this loan approved.
(b) All information in this application and the Exhibits is true and complete to the best of my/our knowledge and is submitted to **SBA** so **SBA** can decide whether to grant a loan or participate with a lending institution in a loan to me/us. I/We agree to pay for or reimburse **SBA** for the cost of any surveys, title or mortage examinations, appraisals etc., performed by non-**SBA** personnel provided I/We have given my/our consent.
(c) I/We give the assurance that we will comply with sections 112 and 113 of volume 13 of the Code of Federal Regulations. These Code sections prohibit discrimination on the grounds of race, color, sex, religion, martial status, handicap, age, or national origin by recipients of Federal financial assistance and require appropriate reports and access to books and records. These requirements are applicable to anyone who buys or takes control of the business. I/We realize that if I/We do not comply with these non-discrimination requirements **SBA** can, call, terminate, or accelerate repayment or my/our loan.

Authority to Collect Personal Information: This information is provided pursuant to Public Law 93-579 (Privacy Act of 1974). **Effects of Nondisclosure:** Omission of an item means your application might not receive full consideration.

I/We authorize disclosure of all information sumitted in connection with this application to the financial institution agreeing to participate in the loan.

As consideration for any Management and Technical Assistance that may be provided, I/We waive all claims against **SBA** and its consultants.

I/We understand that I/We need not pay anybody to deal with **SBA**. I/We have read and understand Form 394 which explains **SBA** policy on representatives and their fees.

For Guaranty Loans please provide an original and one copy (Photocopy is Acceptable) of the Application Form, and all Exhibits to the participating lender. For Direct Loans submit one original copy of application and Exhibits to **SBA**.

It is against SBA regulations to charge the applicant a percent-age of the loan proceeds as a fee for preparing this application.

If you make a statement that you know to be false or if you over value a security in order to help obtain a loan under the provi-sions of the Small Business Act you can be fined up to $5,000 or be put in jail for up to two years, or both.

Signature of Preparer if Other Than Applicant

Print or Type Name of Preparer

Address of Preparer

If Applicant is a proprietor or general partner, sign below:

By: _____ Date

If Applicant is a corporation, sign below:

Corporate Seal _____ Date

By: _____
Signature of President

Attested by: _____
Signature of Corporate Secretary

☆ U.S. GOVERNMENT PRINTING OFFICE: 1979--293-442/5294

Section 3. Other Stocks and Bonds: Give listed and unlisted Stocks and Bonds *(Use separate sheet if necessary)*

No. of Shares	Names of Securities	Cost	Market Value Statement Date	
			Quotation	Amount

Section 4. Real Estate Owned. *(List each parcel separately. Use supplemental sheets if necessary. Each sheet must be identified as a supplement to this statement and signed). (Also advises whether property is covered by title insurance, abstract of title, or both).*

Title is in name of	Type of property

Address of property (City and State)	
	Original Cost to (me) (us) $ _____
	Date Purchased _____
	Present Market Value $ _____
	Tax Assessment Value $ _____

Name and Address of Holder of Mortgage (City and State)	
	Date of Mortgage _____
	Original Amount $ _____
	Balance $ _____
	Maturity _____
	Terms of Payment _____

Status of Mortgage, i.e., current or delinquent. If delinquent describe delinquencies

Section 5. Other Personal Property. *(Describe and if any is mortgaged, state name and address of mortgage holder and amount of mortgage, terms of payment and If delinquent, describe delinquency.)*

Section 6. Other Assets. *(Describe)*

Section 7. Unpaid Taxes. *(Describe in detail, as to type, to whom payable, when due, amount, and what, if any, property a tax lien, if any, attaches)*

Section 8. Other Liabilities. *(Describe in detail)*

(I) or (We) certify the above and the statements contained in the schedules herein is a true and accurate statement of (my) or (our) financial condition as of the date stated herein. This statement is given for the purpose of: *(Check one of the following)*

☐ Inducing S.B.A. to grant a loan as requested in application, of the individual or firm whose name appears herein, in connection with which this statement is submitted.

☐ Furnishing a statement of (my) or (our) financial condition, pursuant to the terms of the guaranty executed by (me) or (us) at the time S.B.A. granted a loan to the individual or firm, whose name appears herein.

Signature	Signature	Date

Form Approved
OMB No. 100-R-0081

PERSONAL FINANCIAL STATEMENT

As of _____ , 19 ___.

Return to:

Small Business Administration

For SBA Use Only
SBA Loan No.

Complete this form if 1) a sole proprietorship by the proprietor; 2) a partnership by each partner; 3) a corporation by each officer and each stockholder with 20% or more ownership; 4) any other person or entity providing a guaranty on the loan.

Name and Address. Including ZIP Code *(of person and spouse submitting Statement)*

SOCIAL SECURITY NO. _____

Business *(of person submitting Statement)*

This statement is submitted in connection with S.B.A. loan requested or granted to the individual or firm, whose name appears below:

Name and Address of Applicant or Borrower, Including ZIP Code

---

Please answer all questions using "No" or "None" where necessary

ASSETS		LIABILITIES	
Cash on Hand & In Banks . . . . $ _____		Accounts Payable . . . . $ _____	
Savings Account in Banks . . . . _____		Notes Payable to Banks . . . . _____	
U. S. Government Bonds . . . . _____		*(Describe below - Section 2)*	
Accounts & Notes Receivable . . . . _____		Notes Payable to Others . . . . _____	
Life Insurance-Cash Surrender Value Only . . _____		*(Describe below - Section 2)*	
Other Stocks and Bonds . . . . _____		Installment Account (Auto) . . . . _____	
(Describe - reverse side - Section 3)		Monthly Payments $ _____	
Real Estate . . . . _____		Installment Accounts (Other) . . . . _____	
(Describe - reverse side - Section 4)		Monthly Payments $ _____	
Automobile - Present Value . . . . _____		Loans on Life Insurance . . . . _____	
Other Personal Property . . . . _____		Mortgages on Real Estate . . . . _____	
(Describe - reverse side - Section 5)		*(Describe - reverse side - Section 4)*	
Other Assets . . . . _____		Unpaid Taxes . . . . _____	
(Describe - reverse side - Section 6)		*(Describe - reverse side - Section 7)*	
		Other Liabilities . . . . _____	
		(Describe - reverse side - Section 8)	
		Total Liabilities . . . . _____	
		Net Worth . . . . $ _____	
Total. . . . . $ _____		Total . . . . $ _____	

Section 1. Source of Income

(Describe below all items listed in this Section)

CONTINGENT LIABILITIES

Salary . . . . $ _____		As Endorser or Co-Maker . . . . $ _____	
Net Investment Income . . . . _____		Legal Claims and Judgments . . . . _____	
Real Estate Income . . . . _____		Provision for Federal Income Tax . . . . _____	
Other Income *(Describe)* . . . . _____		Other Special Debt . . . . _____	

Description of items listed in Section 1 _____

_____

_____

_____

_____

_____

* Not necessary to disclose alimony or child support payments in "Other Income" unless it is desired to have such payments counted toward total income.

Life Insurance Held *(Give face amount of policies - name of company and beneficiaries)* _____

_____

_____

_____

_____

_____

_____

_____

SUPPLEMENTARY SCHEDULES

Section 2. Notes Payable to Banks and Others

Name and Address of Holder of Note	Amount of Loan		Terms of Repayments	Maturity of Loan	How Endorsed, Guaranteed, or Secured
	Original Bal.	Present Bal.			
	$	$	$		

SBA FORM 413 (12-78) REF: SOP 50 50   Edition of 8-67 May Be Used Until Stock Is Exhausted

United States of America

SMALL BUSINESS ADMINISTRATION

STATEMENT OF PERSONAL HISTORY

Please Read Carefully - Print or Type

Each member of the small business concern requesting assistance or the development company must submit this form in TRIPLICATE for filing with the SBA application. This form must be filled out and submitted:

1. If a sole proprietorship, by the proprietor;
2. If a partnership, by each partner;
3. If a corporation or a development company, by each officer, director, and additionally, by each holder of 20% or more of the voting stock;
4. Any other person, including a hired manager, who has authority to speak for and commit the borrower in the management of the business.

Name and Address of Applicant (Firm Name)(Street, City, State and ZIP Code)	SBA District Office and City
	Amount Applied for:

1. Personal Statement of: (State name in full, if no middle name, state (NMN), or if initial only, indicate initial). List all former names used, and dates each name was used. Use separate sheet if necessary.

First   Middle   Last

2. Date of Birth: (Month, day and year)

3. Place of Birth: (City & State or Foreign Country)

U.S. Citizen? ☐ yes   ☐ no

If no, give alien registration number:

4. Give the percentage of ownership or stock owned or to be owned in the small business concern or the Development Company.

Social Security No.

5. Present residence address

From   To   Address

City   State

Home Telephone No. (Include A/C)

Business Telephone No. (Include A/C)

Immediate past residence address

From   To   Address

BE SURE TO ANSWER THE NEXT 3 QUESTIONS CORRECTLY BECAUSE THEY ARE IMPORTANT.

THE FACT THAT YOU HAVE AN ARREST OR CONVICTION RECORD WILL NOT NECESSARILY DISQUALIFY YOU. BUT AN INCORRECT ANSWER WILL PROBABLY CAUSE YOUR APPLICATION TO BE TURNED DOWN.

6. Are you presently under indictment, on parole or probation?

☐ Yes   ☐ No   If yes, furnish details in a separate exhibit. List name(s) under which held, if applicable.

7. Have you ever been charged with or arrested for any criminal offense other than a minor motor vehicle violation?

☐ Yes   ☐ No   If yes, furnish details in a separate exhibit. List name(s) under which charged, if applicable.

8. Have you ever been convicted of any criminal offense other than a minor motor vehicle violation?

☐ Yes   ☐ No   If yes, furnish details in a separate exhibit. List name(s) under which convicted, if applicable.

9. Name and address of participating bank

The information on this form will be used in connection with an investigation of your character. Any information you wish to submit, that you feel will expedite this investigation should be set forth.

Whoever makes any statement knowing it to be false, for the purpose of obtaining for himself or for any applicant, any loan, or loan extension by renewal, deferment or otherwise, or for the purpose of obtaining, or influencing SBA toward, anything of value under the Small Business Act, as amended, shall be punished under Section 16(a) of that Act, by a fine of not more than $5000, or by imprisonment for not more than 2 years, or both.

Signature	Title	Date

SBA FORM 912 (3-79) SOP 50 10 1 EDITION OF 6-78 WILL BE USED UNTIL STOCK IS EXHAUSTED

1. SBA FILE COPY

The S.B.A. Scandal of the 1970s changed the operation methods by Congressional and President Carter's directives. Losses of almost $500 million from unpaid S.B.A. loans caused an investigation which uncovered fraudulent dealings involving the agency. Funds for direct loans were cut off and the agency became a guarantor (90 percent of the loan) of small business loans made to special classes of citizens by banks working with S.B.A.

Here is a check list of required papers (please submit only the checked items).

_____ 1. Application for Loan: SBA Form 4 (copy of form that follows).

_____ 2. Statement of Personal History: SBA Form 912.

_____ 3. Personal Financial Statement: SBA Form 413.

_____ 4. Detailed, signed balance sheet and profit and loss statement *current* (within 90 days of application) and *last two (2) fiscal years.*

_____ 5. Detailed one (1) year projection of income and expenses (attach written explanation as to how you expect to achieve same).

_____ 6. Certificate of doing business (if a corporation, stamp corporate seal on SBA Form 4 section 12).

_____ 7. Written vendor's estimates for all equipment and leasehold improvements to be purchased with the required loan. These should include sales tax, delivery and installation changes, if applicable.

_____ 8. Every effort should be made to obtain direct financing from a lending institution. If not available, ask for an SBA guaranty or participation loan. If this is not available, obtain written proof of refusal from two (2) banks. This proof of refusal must contain the date, amount, and terms requested and the reason for decline.

_____ 9. *Signed* business federal income tax returns for previous two (2) years.

Washington (AP)—Small businesses face "tough sledding" in coming months, and many may be forced to default on loans or go bankrupt, the head of the Small Business Administration says.

"Small firms face more difficulty than usual in getting long-term financing and continuing difficulty in even short-term funds," said A. Vernon Weaver.

"Small entrepreneurs have to pay higher interest rates than large companies. Small businesses are squeezed by cash flow problems," he continued. "They face possible dropoffs in sales and may be forced to reduce their work forces."

Weaver announced a series of steps by his agency that he said would speed up the processing of SBA loans to encourage banks to help small businesses.

However, he stopped short of asking banks to offer businesses lower interest rates than they provide larger clients.

Banks' best customers are charged the prime rate. Small business—because they are greater credit risks—often must pay 2 to 3 percent higher interest. often must pay 2 to 3 percent higher interest.

"We're not encouraging banks to go to a two-tier system," Weaver said. "We're not going to be big brother."

Weaver said he hopes the administrative changes will encourage more private banks to make loans, guaranteed by the SBA, to small businesses.

The SBA had authority in fiscal 1982 to guarantee up to much less in private loans to small businesses. The agency can guarantee up to 90 percent of an individual loan.

Weaver acknowledged that small businesses are hard-pressed to borrow because of record-high interest rates.

"It's a dubious proposition," he said.

"I won't be surprised to see default and bankruptcy rates among small businesses rise in coming months," he said.

Currently, however, the SBA reports no increase in loan defaults or bankruptcies.

The economy, after a surprisingly strong spurt in the third quarter, is expected to slow down significantly in the fourth quarter, many economists predict.

"I would advise small businesses to be very prudent, to take every measure they can to get their cash flow in good shape, to be tough with accounts receivable and keep inventories manageable," Weaver said.

A summary of SBA information leads us back to the negative encouragement for Retail Capital Loans as expressed in Chapter 3.

R. TAKING INVENTORY

Taking inventory is required by the Internal Revenue Service at the end of your year, calendar or fiscal, because the variation from your last year-end figure raises or lowers your taxable income for tax purposes by that amount. It is not difficult to count your stock to get an accurate value, and the figure is a most important bit of information to keep you informed. This method is used by several of the largest accounting firms with their clients, retail stores, and is recommended for its simplicity and accuracy.

1. Store layout map is drawn (see Figure R.1).
2. All fixtures, windows, and other areas are marked and numbered, one sheet numbered to match each of them.

FIGURE R.1.

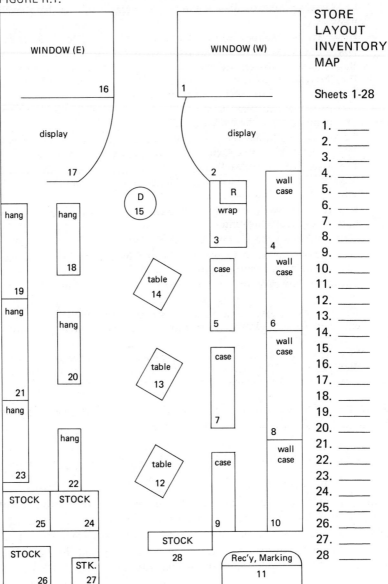

3. Numbered sheets are distributed on each area as on the map.
4. Inventory counters, the personnel, are instructed how to call item, manufacturer number, number of pieces, and the retail price to be recorded by partner in the team.

5. Example of sheet headings and listing of stock:

Item Description	MFG#	Pieces	Retail Each	Cost Each	Total Cost	Total Retail
Silk blouses	17a	10	$59.00	30—	300—	$590.00
″ ″	11b	5	75.00	35—	175—	375.00

Cost figures and totals are to be written on sheets by management after sheets are collected.

6. Owner or manager spotchecks sheets on several tables or other areas to verify the accuracy of the counting. Any area without saleable merchandise is marked "NO RETAIL" on the sheet.

7. Owner team picks up all sheets in order when completed verifying: all are properly detailed as instructed, and all sheets are accounted for as listed on the side of the map.

8. Totals are made at retail, the cost of each item noted, and this total extended as well; and each sheet is totalled at the bottom. Proper markdowns may be taken if not taken before this. (Notation for pertinent buying information are valuable to management during this time of calculation.)

9. One summary sheet should contain the inventory total value, cost and retail for accounting purposes, and for the planning of the new seasons open-to-buy figures (retail total) and the figures for perpetual inventory start of the new year.

S. OPENING INVENTORY AND QUARTERLY STOCK BUYING PLAN

Week	Holidays	Last Year Sales	Plan Sales	Actual Sales	+ or – Plan	Opening Inventory
1.						
2						
3						
4						
tot. mo.						
5						
6						
7						
8						
9						
tot. mo.						
10						
11						
12						
13					End inv.	
tot. 3 mo.						

Open Inv. _____
End Inv. _____
\+
or
–
\+ sales _____
=
At retail open-to-buy
_____
open buy cost.

Money Plans: Needs, Estimates

USE	DEPOSITS cash now	est. month	est. year
Rent			
Telephone			
Power, electricity, heat			
Petty cash: travel, entertainment			
Stationery, supplies			
Licenses, registrations			
Owner draw			
Other payroll			
Taxes, soc. sec.			
Operatg cash			
Audit & legal			
Maintenance, misc.			
Advertising, PR.			
Insurance			
Interest and Installments			
Other professional fees:			
Contractors (realty)			
Architects (display)			

TOTALS   month _____ year _____

cash now   . . . .

Opening Plan
Merchandise   cost _____ retail _____

Wrapping, bags, hangers, selling supplies _____

USE	CASH NEEDS		
Store prep			
FIXTURES	estimate $		final
Shelves, cabs, wall cases			
Showcases, counters			
Hang racks, tables, etc.			
Wrap, cash counter			
Register, safe			
Floor			
walls			
lights			
internal signs			
carpenter			
plumber			
electrician			
paint, paper			
toilet			
fitting room			
clean-up labor			
Machinery, carts			
delivery equipment			
FRONT: sign			
glass			
walls			
lights			
floor			
display: Manneq.			
stands			
decor			

. . . . cash now . .

total
now: _____

U. ADVERTISING AS PRACTICED BY SELECTED SMALL BUSINESSES

Type of Business	Average Ad Budget (% of Sales)*	Favorite Media	Other Media Used	Special Considerations	Promotion Opportunities and Warnings
BICYCLE SHOPS	1.5-2.0%	Newspapers (sports section)	Flyers, Yellow Pages, cycling magazines, direct mail		
BOOKSTORES	1.5-1.6%	Newspapers shopper Yellow Pages	Direct mail	Cooperative advertising from publisher	Autograph parties
DRUG STORES (INDEPENDENT)	1.0-3.0%	Local newspapers, shoppers	Direct mail (list from prescription files)		
DRY CLEANING PLANTS	0.9-2.0%	Local newspapers, shoppers, Yellow Pages	Store front, ads, pamphlets on clothes care		Specials on seasonal cleaning (sleeping bags, parkas)
EQUIPMENT RENTAL SERVICES	1.7-4.7%	Yellow Pages			
GIFT STORES	2.2%	Weekly newspapers	Yellow Pages, radio, direct mail, magazines		Open houses, demonstrations of product lines like cookware
HAIR-DRESSING SHOPS	2.0-5.0%	Yellow Pages	Newspapers (for special events), word-of-mouth		Styling for community fashion, beauty shows, conducting free beauty clinics at local high schools

Store Type	Percent				
HOME FURNISHING STORES	1.9-3.2%	Newspapers	Direct mail, radio	Cooperative advertising available from manufacturer	
LIQUOR STORES (INDEPENDENT)	0.5-0.6%	Point-of-purchase displays	Newspapers, Yellow Pages	Manufacturers do all product advertising; coop funds available	Caution: see Alcoholic Beverage Control's advertising and promotion regulations
MAIL ORDER FIRMS	15.0-25.0%	Newspapers, magazines	Direct mail	Displays ads, not classified, in publications	Firms spend up to 40% of sales on advertising some promotions
PET SHOPS	2.0-5.0%	Yellow Pages	Window displays, shopper newspapers, direct mail		Talk on pet care to schools, community groups.
PLANT SHOPS	1.3-1.5%	Local newspapers, word-of-mouth			Plant care clinics, courses in plant care, plant sitting, repotting
REPAIR SERVICES	0.8-1.6%	Yellow Pages	Signs on vehicles direct mail, shoppers		
RESTAURANTS AND FOOD SERVICES	0-3.2%	Newspapers, radio, Yellow Pages, transit, outdoor	Television for chain or franchise restaurants	Word-of-mouth relied on heavily by independent restaurants	"Free" advertising in restaurant critics' columns, specialty advertising, birthday cakes or parties for customers
SHOE STORES	0.5-0.8%	Newspapers, direct mail, radio	Yellow Pages (especially for specialty items)	Cooperative advertising available from manufacturers	Collecting outgrown (but not worn out) childrens' shoes for donation to local charity

*Slightly higher in new establishments; Statistics compiled by Small Business Reporter Bank of America.

V. PROJECTED CASH-FLOW CHART

CASH (beg. mo.)	FEB.	MAR.	APR.	MAY	JUN.	JUL.	AUG.	SEP.	OCT.	NOV.	DEC.	JAN.	TOT.
On Hand													
In Bank													
Other													
INCOME (month)													
Sales													
Other income													
Credit sales													
TOTAL													
Purchases due													
Expenses													
Salary													
Wages													
FICA													
Taxes													
Overhead													
Maint. etc													
Ins./Prof.													
Transp./Petty													
Interest													
Other Cash													
TOTAL													
End month													
Cash Flow excess.													
Months cumulative													

W. YEAR PROJECTED PROFIT AND LOSS

	Jan	Feb	Mar	Apr	May	Jun	Jul	Aug	Sep	Oct	Nov	Dec	tot
SALES PLAN													
(minus)	…	…	…	…	…	…	…	…	…	…	…	…	…
Purchases goods—													
incl. frt.	…	…	…	…	…	…	…	…	…	…	…	…	…
GROSS PROFIT													
PLAN													
Var. expenses													
Wages, salaries	…	…	…	…	…	…	…	…	…	…	…	…	…
Payroll taxes	…	…	…	…	…	…	…	…	…	…	…	…	…
Tel., elec., heat	…	…	…	…	…	…	…	…	…	…	…	…	…
Car and del'y	…	…	…	…	…	…	…	…	…	…	…	…	…
Adver. & P.R.	…	…	…	…	…	…	…	…	…	…	…	…	…
Maint., pack'g	…	…	…	…	…	…	…	…	…	…	…	…	…
Prof, legal	…	…	…	…	…	…	…	…	…	…	…	…	…
Miscel.	…	…	…	…	…	…	…	…	…	…	…	…	…
TOTAL VAR. EXP.													
Fixed expenses													
Rent & security	…	…	…	…	…	…	…	…	…	…	…	…	…
Insurance	…	…	…	…	…	…	…	…	…	…	…	…	…
Audit C.P.A.	…	…	…	…	…	…	…	…	…	…	…	…	…
Interest pay	…	…	…	…	…	…	…	…	…	…	…	…	…
Taxes, license	…	…	…	…	…	…	…	…	…	…	…	…	…
Depreciation	…	…	…	…	…	…	…	…	…	…	…	…	…
Total Fixed													
TOTAL EXPENSES													
NET PROFIT (LOSS)													

197

Personal Living Budget

Monthly Payments

Rent (or house)	_____	Invested	
Car cost paymt.	_____	other income	_____
Car, other insur.	_____		
Appliance furn. pay	_____	Part-time work	_____
Home impv., loan pay	_____		
Health, life ins.	_____	Int.	_____
Misc. payments	_____	Misc.	_____
Total	_____	Other Income	_____

Household:

Food	_____	Minimum monthly	
Clean, supply	_____	NEEDED	_____
Telephone	_____		
Power, gas, water	_____	Savings	
Maint., repair	_____	estimated	_____
Drugs, clothing clean	_____		
Aver. Dr. and dentist	_____		
Travel, auto upkeep	_____		
Mags., papers, dues, personal petty	_____		
Dining out	_____		
Fed., state taxes	_____		
Other taxes	_____		
Clothing or house purchases	_____		
TOTAL EXPENSES	_____		

Y. FREE CONSULTATION SERVICES

The Executive Volunteer Corps (in New York City and other areas) and S.C.O.R.E. (Corps of Retired Executive, funded by the S.B.A. of the federal government) are two of the agencies staffed by retired executives who volunteer their services to help people start a new business or improve the functions of an operating one, without charge.

Guidance is offered in the use of funds, preparing plans, securing licenses and registrations, setting up the legal form of business, agreements between the parties, or anything else deemed important to the applicant. Where legal advice is needed, the applicant is referred to the Legal Referral officer of the local Bar. Where accounting professional advice is needed, the C.P.A. organization offers help at minimum charge. All facts are kept confidential.

The federal government has other agencies who offer assistance by mail, and the Small Business Administration, which also gives personal conference advice in offices throughout the United States. Many helpful pamphlets on business are offered free.

Almost every state has a Department of Commerce, which offers many types of business advice as well as helpful pamphlets. (California, New York, Connecticut, New Jersey, Florida, and Pennsylvania are especially recommended.)

For advice on locations and population, Chambers of Commerce, state and local, are helpful.

Z. RETAIL STOCK TURNOVER RATIO

Merchandise Kind of Store	Inv. Turnover	Year Net Proift %	Net Profit % on Net Worth
Childrens-Infants	3.5	4.8	18
Mens and Boys cloth'g & furn.	3.6	4.5	17
Department stores	4.6	2.0	9
Family clothing stores	3.3	5.1	16
Furniture stores	4.4	4.4	16
Hardware stores	3.3	4.5	16
Auto and home supply	5.1	4.3	22
Household appliances	5.1	3.6	20
Jewelry	2.4	7.7	20
Misc. general mdse.	4.0	4.1	14
Paint, glass, wallpaper	6.1	5.5	25
R dio and TV	4.9	4.0	22
Retail nurseries, lawn garden supplies	5.6	4.5	19
Shoe stores	3.3	5.2	20
Variety stores	3.2	3.7	13
Women's ready to wear	4.5	5.0	19
Grocery stores	15.4	1.8	20
A Ratio of	Av. Mo. $\dfrac{\text{Inventory}}{\text{Net Sales}}$	$\dfrac{\text{Net Profit}}{\text{Net Sales}}$	

*Reprinted by special permission of *Dun's Review* October 1979. Copyright © 1979 Dun & Bradstreet Publications, Inc.

GLOSSARY

Absentee Management. Makes retail stores difficult to control ... gives small stores locally run an advantage. (Chapter 1, 2)

Accounts Receivable. A record of amounts owed you ... a monthly listing, schedule. (Chapter 11)

Ace. Active Corps of Executives ... a free service of executive aid to business. (Chapter 1)

Accrual. The system of accounting required for all business with inventory. Book entries govern finances as the transaction occurs (not when cash changes hand). (Chapter 11)

Account Books, Accounting. The system of totals of the business transactions recorded in the basic journals and ledgers for time periods ... usually checked and summarized in financial reports by a C.P.A., Certified Public Accountant. (Chapter 11)

Advertising. A message to your public that is paid for by you to induce interest in your store. (Chapter 6)

Aids. Artwork, layouts, point-of-sale signs supplied by manufacturers, to aid the sales.

Allowance. Ad money from the makers usually based on a percentage of of the goods bought by the retailer contemplating an ad program. Also may be a part-payment of the ad expense.

Campaign. A series of ads sometimes part of a national program where manufacturer and retailers coordinate their ads.

Response Classified. A system of letter classifications (X,Y,Z) expecting a different response from ads differing in the copy and items.

Agency. Experienced professionals you hire.

Budgets. Funds for particular or regular ad purposes.

Age Discrimination in Hiring. 1967 Federal Act prohibiting such acts by firms larger than twenty-five employees, in interstate commerce. It protects the civil rights of people aged forty to sixty-five. (Chapter 7)

Agreements. Partnership and stockholder contracts governing their business relationship. (Chapter 4 and Appendix M)

Anticipation. An incentive percentage discount for payment of an invoice before it's due date. The interest differs with firms and money conditions.

Arbitration. Agreement by parties to allow an outside party to solve their differences. American Arbitration Ass'n sometimes made a part of agreements for this purpose, assess damages etc.

Articles of Partnership. The document which registers the firm as a going business with the local, usually county, authority. The name may be a D.B.A.— *doing business as*—and the partners are liable personally to creditors. Differs from *partnership agreement which governs conduct of partners with one another.* (Chapter 4, Appendix M)

Assets. The property, stock, and other interests of the firm as opposed to liabilities (what it owes). *Fixed* are those assets used to operate the business; *current* are those that will be turned into cash in normal course of operations, this year. (Chapter 11)

Assortment. The tactical breakdown of your stock-for-sale into categories, sizes, colors, season and style to appeal to your customers. (Chapter 5)

Auctioneer. An independent agent who sells property to the highest bidder price, for the owners or the receiver (court appointed), usually on commission.

Automatic Mark-downs. A system of reduced pricing during a period of time as merchandise ages in stock. Made famous by Filenes, Boston, Mass. in their basement. (Appendix B)

Backorder. Occurs when supplier doesn't fill your order completely and ships the balance later. Some firms refuse backorders because of extra shipping costs.

Bad Debts. Those amounts owed now which are considered uncollectible which are charged off against profits.

Bait and Switch. An unethical practice of using bait merchandise as a come-on only to almost refuse sale of it in an attempt to get customer to buy other more profitable goods. (Chapter 6)

Balance the Books. The accounting process of totalling in which assets are balanced against a total of liabilities (current and long term) and net worth (capital). Usually done at year end. A balance *sheet* is this summary. (Chapter 11)

Bank Loan. The normal source of *debt* borrowing for stores whether long-term, or short-term usually requiring interest payments and principal repayments on a regular schedule. (Chapter 3)

Bankruptcy. The insolvent condition of a firm's finances when either the debtor or his creditors do not want to continue in this condition. The Federal Law calls for meeting of creditors, appointment of committee to represent them, receiver for the debtor's assets, and decisions how best to re-coup some of the debt. Bankruptcy can be personal, too, with some of the minimum personal assets of the debtor exempt from the creditors.

Bartering. The exchange of property without cash, or the exchange of any other thing of value, (services, etc.) for property. (Chapter 11)

Bill Of Lading. The document accompanying a shipment which describes and identifies it for all parties. A signed copy from the freight forwarder is evidence that the shipping company has sent the shipment on it's way. This is often the point at which title to the goods changes hands, and any loss thereafter is the problem of the receiver.

Basic Stock List. The model stock of minimum quantities of the assortment to be maintained at all times.

Bonus. Special extra payment made to employees for unusual effort on behalf of firm, or unusually high profits which management wants to share with employees. (Chapter 7)

Book Inventory. The figures representing the total of the stock by taking the actual inventory, adding all merchandise that has come in, adjusting for all markdowns, and subtracting all goods sold. If an actual physical stock-count is now taken, the stock losses from pilferage should represent the difference between the book and the actual. (Chapters 3, 5, 8)

Box Stores, Box Sales. Featuring regular or special sale days of selling multiples, full boxes as packed, dozen or half-dozen of an item with appropriate prices. (Chapter 6)

Brands. An established name on an item which lends an incentive to the customer to buy for quality, fashion, designer name, or any combination of reasons. Brand names lend a store a quality image. (Chapters 5, 6)

Boot-Strap-Financing. Starting a business with a tiny amount of capital, and by buying only quick turnover items succeed in accumulating enough to grow. Today's business climate does not give much chance to pull one's self up by the bootstraps because there are so many cash deposits, licenses, and prepayments necessary in addition to the cash (before delivery) needed for small quantity suppliers. (Chapter 3, Appendix A)

Budgets. The sums planned as expense in operating costs of running the business for better control of expense. (Chapter 3)

Bulk Sales Laws. Laws intended to control the sales of entire stocks of a business in one bulk sale, to prevent defrauding creditors who might be entitled to an interest in the proceeds. A buyer of such a stock must note whether these laws were heeded. State sales tax laws must also be noted (Appendices K, L)

Business Broker. A professional who sells a business for a commission fee. When you request one to find a business for you, you must arrange the fee beforehand. (Chapter 1)

Business Life Insurance. An insurance policy on the life of active participants to ease the handling of the ownership in case of death. It sometimes will pay the owner's estate in exchange for his or her share of the business which is then retired. (Chapter 10, Appendix M)

Business Strategy. The plans for merchandising operations which are calculated to succeed in making more profits and growth. (Chapters 1, 2)

Business Interruption Insurance. Part of the comprehensive fire insurance policy which covers the firm for loss of profits until the repaired store is ready to resume operations. (Chapter 10)

Buy-Back Agreement. A safety clause inserted into agreements to allow rescinding of the agreement to sell a business (or part of one) under certain conditions that make it unwise for the parties to continue with it. (Appendix K)

Buy-Sell Agreement. Usually a part of a partnership (or stockholders) agreement between themselves to offer the other partner his share of the business, first, before offering it to any third party. A price may be set based upon certain key company figures. (Appendix M)

Buying Urge. A customer's motivation to buy. It may be a seasonal need, style, price, any other variable. (Chapters 5, 6)

Calendar Year. Operating the accounting in the calendar year for profits and taxes as contrasted to fiscal year. Also, sales planning according to the calendar and holidays. (Chapters 3, 5)

Capital. The total sum invested in your business, later also called "net worth." (Chapter 3)

Capital Gain. When property is sold for profit that has been held for more than the minimum year period the profit is taxed not under regular profit tax percentages but under the lower percentage of capital gain. (Chapter 11)

Cash System. Cash is the system of accounting required in a business that has no inventory, a service business perhaps. All transactions are accounted for only when cash changes hands. (Chapter 11)

Cash and Carry. A store's special terms while offering unusual value for a particular event . . . cash only (no charge cards or other credit), no delivery, or other service. (Chapter 5)

Cash Discount. Goods are sold under vendor's trade discount and cash discount usually added together, so that payment has a specific due date. If the invoice is not paid by that date, the cash discount is lost and the payment is due NET, no discount. The courts have ruled that the trade discount may still be deducted in late payment. (Chapter 3)

Cash Flow. The ebb and flow of actual cash that occurs in any business as money from sales and other income flows in, and other cash is paid out regularly for operating expenses of the business. It is projected on a chart for the period of time to come to plan for its supply. (Chapter 3, Appendix V)

Cash Value. In insurance policies it is the amount to be paid in the event of a loss. It is the original cost less the depreciation normal for the period since acquired. (Chapter 10)

Cash Terms. Usually means payable without any discount at due date, "net, 10EOM"–payable the 10th of the following month, or "net 30"–due to be paid 30 days after date. See also C.O.D. and C.B.D. (Chapter 3)

C.B.D. The cash required before the delivery of goods will be made.

Ceiling Price. In times of great price rises due to wartime shortages, the government imposes ceiling prices to control profiteering, etc. In recent years ceiling prices were imposed on gasoline. (Chapter 5)

Chamber of Commerce. An association of business executives of an area who work out beneficial legislation to encourage and benefit commerce of the area. It is a good source of local population data. (Chapter 1)

Charge Account Customers. An "in house" charge for patrons that has become very costly for stores to administer. Customers have a more personal feeling for stores with it. Most small stores have dropped it in favor of bank cards. (Chapters 5, 7)

Charter of a Corporation. States where a corporation applies will charter a corporation according to their particular laws. The charter states the names of the incorporators, address, purpose and types of business it will conduct, and stock shares to be issued. (Chapter 4)

Checkbook for Business Bank Account. An excellent source of a primary business record confirming income deposits, paid out expenses and often salary and wages as well. (Chapters 3, 11)

Check Cashing. A good service, cashing payroll checks with a well-planned routine for safety, bringing in customer traffic. (Chapter 9)

Closed Corporation. Stock held by few people, not available to the public. (Chapter 4)

C.O.D. "Cash on Delivery"—payment for goods when they are delivered.

Co-insurance. A term used to describe the way fire insurance policies are written. Most policies call for co-insurance at 80 percent and as long as your policy face value is 80 percent of the total value of the property you are fully covered. If you are insured for less and you suffer a loss, you will not recover the full amount of the loss. (Chapter 10)

Collateral. Property pledged to guarantee repayment of a loan. This collateral property is forefeited in the event loan terms are not met. (Chapter 3)

Collective Bargaining. 1935 Labor Relations Act establishing workers the right to organize into unions and to bargain collectively with employers. Other later legislation has reinforced this right. (Chapter 7)

Compensation. The right of workers to monetary compensation for injuries suffered on the job. States require insurance policies to cover these injuries and detail payments and conditions. Many states have their own fund to control the coverage and effect some premium savings. (Chapters 7 and 10)

Comprehensive Business Plan. The overall plan concerning the details, funds, aims, strategy, merchandise, location, owners, and their expertise—everything necessary to tell the story to a lender to convince him that the money will be wisely invested. It contains financial data from the past and projections of cash flow, profit and loss, balance sheets, capital expenditure estimates, etc. (Chapter 3)

Consignment Selling. Selling to a retailer with the understanding that in the event the goods is not sold by him in the time period, it may be returned for credit. Very little of this is done any more, and those firms that sell on consignment are usually charging the additional costs in the price charged for the goods.

Consumer Affairs. The local city department of licensing to control business activities, restrict certain use of property, street peddlers, cafes, locksmiths, construction (expertise), etc. (Chapter 4)

Contracts. (See specific type—Franchise, Labor, Partner etc.)

Convenience Stores. Carry pickup items not usually requiring shopping or selecting ... the very staple groceries, dairy basics, delicatessen items, papers, candy, etc. in long-hour schedules ... some franchised.

Corporation. An artificial creation chartered by states to operate a business with limited liability of the owners, whose portion of ownership is represented by shares of stock. Corp., Inc., and Ltd. (limited) designate this status. (Chapter 4)

Sub-Chap "S" Corp. Special restricted smaller stock company, where yearly profits are untaxed as a corporation ... but only to owners individually.

Co-Signer. A lender who requires more security to guarantee repayment of a loan often requests another person's guarantee. The third person will "co-sign" the document and be liable if the original borrower defaults. (Chapter 3)

Credits. The funds owed to you.

Credit Bureau. An agency that monitors the personal reliability of consumers in an area by using information supplied by their store members, banks, etc. Information relative to repayment of debts, criminal activity and other may be on file for use by subscribers to the service. (Chapter 3)

Credit Agency. Evaluates the credit worthiness of a business by accepting their CPA reports and checking reliability of timely payments with companies who sell this firm. This information is provided to subscribers to their service who decide an appropriate credit line. (Chapter 3)

Credit Line. The amount of credit for merchandise that a vendor (supplier) limits to a new customer. (Chapter 3)

Crime Insuance. Any policies which protect the business against losses by crimes against the business. Burglary, Robbery, Embezzlement, etc. 3-D crime policies protect against all kinds. (Chapter 10)

Current Assets. That property owned by the business which will normally become cash in the course of business this year. (Fixed assets are those used to operate the business—fixtures, register, auto, etc.) (Chapter 11)

Dating Bills. Invoices for supplies or merchandise are normally "dated" to require payment by a certain date later. These bills which are dated on or after the 25th of the month are considered to have been shipped on the first of the following month, thereby delaying the expected payments (E.O.M.—End of month terms) until the following month. This does not apply to invoices that require payment in a given number of days—10 days, 30 days, 60 days. A vendor may offer longer payment terms by marking the invoice "as of (date)" and store payment may be delayed to correspond to this dating. (Chapter 3)

D.B.A. Doing Business As, a registration of a single proprietorship, or partnership to do business under an assumed name (not corporation) by filing
with the county clerk where located. The name may, if desired, be called
"company." Responsibility for using a name already operating is with the
new owners who should search all telephone directories to make sure
their's does not conflict with a name being used. (Chapter 4)

Debt Loans. Those loans given to a business where the lender contracts to
receive regular repayments of interest (and principal) over the period of
the loan. Where security for the loan is not the transfer of equity (corporate stock) to the lender . . . an Equity Loan. (Chapter 3)

Debtor. One who owes an obligation or debt.

Default. Failure to pay an obligation, loan or any other contract in the terms
specified. (Chapter 3)

Designer's Merchandise. Items whose brands carry the name of a known designer. The consumer may view these products as status items. (Chapter 5)

Depreciation. The normal lessening of value of property over a time period. On
fixed assets of a company which may not be charged against income
totally in the year acquired, there is an allowable time schedule of yearly
depreciating which may be charged against income, so much each year
until the entire cost has been so charged. If this asset is sold after that
time, the price gained is a profit to the company. (Chapter 11)

Discounting Your Bills. Paying on the due date so that you may subtract from
payment all percent cash discounts due you for the timely payment.
Doing so insures a better credit rating. (Chapter 3)

Direct Mail. An effective merchandising method done by notifying a given mailing list of customers of your offerings, having them place orders for cash,
check, or charge card, and shipping the order to them by mail, U.P.S. or
other carrier. (Chapter 6)

Disability Insurance. Relates to payment to employees of salary benefits when
their injuries sustained were not job-related (compensation). Some states
require employers to carry such a policy and it is offered as part of the
"State Insurance Fund." (Chapter 7)

Discrimination in Hiring in Federal Legislation. Forbids hiring or not hiring
someone because of race, color, religion, national origin, sex, age, etc.
It is an extension of the Civil Rights Act of 1964. (Chapter 7)

Distributors. Usually represent a producing factory by stocking a line of goods
and selling and delivering to retailers or others in this area. They usually
specialize in a particular category of goods but may carry more than one
line (brand).

Door-Busters. Goods advertized at such an unusual low price that customers are
expected to try to "break down the doors" to the store to buy them.
Similar to "loss-leaders." (Chapter 6)

Dun and Bradstreet. The famous credit agency located in New York, N.Y. that handles a large percentage of the credit evaluation for member suppliers selling to retailers. They publish annually a large book of listings evaluating net worth of a business and their opinion on how promptly bills will be paid. (Chapter 3)

Drop-Shipments. When a retailer buys quantity of a given item (packed as assorted by the factory) from a wholesaler or jobber, this middle-man will offer some price concessions, or dating, to the retailer and "drop-ship," directly ship the full cartons to him from the factory.

Embezzlement. The crime of larceny, taking property unlawfully when you have been given custody of it. (Chapters 7, 10)

Employees. Employees wages are governed by both State and Federal regulations, which often change. These changes are sent to employers once they have been registered with the U.S. Income Tax Bureau on form SS4 (10-67) at the nearest I.R.S. office, and the FICA regulations for Tax withholding and Social Security deductions as well. If any person performs labor for your business as a "non-employee" and earns over $600 in a year you must file a #1099 NEC notifying I.R.S. of this persons payments, when you file your firm's yearly return. See Employees, Chapter 7, Personnel.

Entrepreneurs. People willing to take a chance with their own money to build a success in a new business with their own imagination.

E.O.M. Terms. End of month terms are stated on the invoice for goods you buy in certain trades and apply to the due date for payment of the invoice. Any invoice marked "net 10 E.O.M." is payable on the 10th of the next month, net cash. If the invoice calls for 8% 10 E.O.M., or any other percentage, you may deduct that percentage when you pay the invoice on the 10th of that next month. Any merchandise sent and billed after the 25th of the month is considered to have been shipped and billed the first of the following month (to give buyer time to pay the invoice). Chapter 3)

Equal Opportunity. The Federal Credit Act of 1975 forbidding the refusal of credit to anyone for reasons other than economic. (Chapter 9)

Equity Financing or Loans. Involves the use of the owner's equity in the company, usually shares of stock, which are transferred to the lender who hopes for great increase in value of the shares over a period of the next few years. This type of loan is usually made by venture capitalists who take the greater risks lending to a new company in the hope of this three or four time gain in value. The company is not, however, burdened with the regular repayment schedule of the typical debt loan. (Chapter 3)

Escape Clause. The provision in a partner or stockholder agreement which provides for a rescinding and refunding of the original capital in the event that they do not get along. (Appendix M)

Established Business. One alternative to opening a new business, which requires a lot of special skills, is to buy an established store where the total price includes stock and fixtures, and the premises are ready to operate. The final price is known when you buy it. (Chapter 1, options)

Excise Taxes. Levied by the Federal Government on certain products, tires, aviation fuel, etc. and are collected by manufacturers and retailers and added to the price separately. There are forms to be filled out and funds collected turned over to Federal Reserve through your bank.

Expenses: Fixed and Variable. All those operating costs not including the payments for the goods you sell. Fixed are those such as overhead—not under your control; variable are controllable to increase or decrease when you need more or less operating help, advertising, etc. (Chapter 8)

Expansion. Decision of management which requires understanding the movement of dollars into profits under your controls. It is a plan which does not overextend company finances.

Factors. Provide cash to suppliers after they have shipped to retailers (upon credit approval of factor) and have stamped an invoice to make payment directly to the factor. Contracts with suppliers are either "with recourse" or not, seeking repayment of funds from supplier if retailer fails to pay the invoice. The rate of interest charged by factors is over 25 percent and they are known to add extra days to the term of interest by delaying payment to supplier. (Chapter 3)

Fair Trade Laws. Passed on the assumption of a property right in the brand name which could be diminished by price cutting. They were abolished in the 1970s. (Appendix O)

False Arrest. The charge made against another person or a store if held under a charge of having committed a crime such as theft, and it includes a suit for damages. Employees must be certain that a crime has been committed before accusing anyone. (Chapter 9)

Federal Reserve Figures. Made public monthly and quarterly based on the sales figures of different department and specialty stores matched to last year, by department. These are valuable to compare because even if your figures are behind your last year's you may have the satisfaction of your loss being less than the federal reserve district of which you are a part. (Chapter 8)

Fidelity Bond. Bought from an insurance company who will guarantee the integrity of a person working in a position of financial trust. The company investigates the employee. (Chapter 10)

FIFO. The accounting method of evaluating inventory—First In, First Out—which is to a firm's disadvantage in periods of inflation and leads to a higher taxable profit on the theory that the latter, higher-cost stock is still in the inventory taken at year's end. During inflation they prefer LIFO. (Chapter 11)

Fiscal vs. Calendar Year. Gives a more appropriate time of a store's year to take inventory and close the books figuring taxable profits. Most stores prefer the end of January since that gives them adequate time to look over their stock, take markdowns, run clearance sales, and get ready for counting their stock in a period not nearly as busy as the end of December. Any bonus or salary payment made in January, when all of the financial facts are confirmed is not taxed to the individual until next year. (Chapters 5, 8, 11)

Financial Statements. Summaries of the operating data, usually prepared by the accountant, to apprise interested people of comparative figures on which a judgment of financial health may be made. (Chapter 11)

FICA. Initials referred to in federal laws that requires employers to deduct income taxes and social security from wages as the payroll is prepared and turn it over to the local bank with papers filled in with data. It requires employers to pay over a matching sum of social security amounts deducted from all employees. (Chapters 7, 11)

Fixed Assets. Those assets owned by the business which are used to operate the business. These assets are depreciated at a regular rate per year and this amount is a deduction against profits for tax purposes. (Chapter 11)

Flea Markets. An open table-selling cash market where many vendors sell assortments of different items presumed by customers to be lower than regular prices in stores. New and used, old style and novel, lowest price and medium to high priced goods varies from market to market everywhere that good traffic may be attracted. Table locations for vendors vary in rental by location and there seems to be a satisfactory profit showing. It is doubtful that a full accounting of sales tax or profit taxes is made by most of the participants. (Chapter 1)

Franchises. Grant of the right to operate a business in the style of the franchisor company. The franchisee, for a down payment fee, is trained to operate in this manner, with supplied merchandise, fixtures, etc. The franchisee pays a percentage of sales monthly. (Chapter 1)

Franchise Tax. Usually a state tax for the privilege of operating certain businesses. Some states have a minimum corp. profit tax which is similar. (Chapter 4)

F.O.B. Free on board, which indicates the point at which the buyer pays all expenses of shipment; that is, the F.O.B. point transfers the sender's duties to the receiver. (Chapter 3)

Fringe Benefits. Those extras given to employees beyond salary; most are not guaranteed by labor legislation. Some of them are paid vacations, hospitalization and health plans, retirement plans, discounts for purchases, etc. (Chapter 7)

Gimmick. An unusual and different appeal, a novel presentation. (Chapter 1)

Glass insurance. A policy covering front plate glass, doors, showcases, etc. against breakage. It is quite expensive and has been discarded by many stores. Coverage includes frames, lettering, trim. (Chapter 10)

Going Out of Business Sales. The response of the public to these funeral events is legend and most communities have license requirements to assure authenticity. There is considerable abuse, however, as promoters buy a well-respected name store and run a lengthy sale, bringing in their own old stock from auctions, etc. as if it was from this store. (Chapter 2)

Going Public. The process of opening the right to buy the stock of a privately held (family) corporation to the general public, usually following the S.E.C. regulations.

Gross Markup, Gross Margin, Gross Profit. Interchangeable terms for the difference (in dollars) between what the retailer pays for goods and the selling price (Chapters 2, 5, 8)

Grand Opening. The promotional party preparation to get local patrons turning your way. Make it fun for customers and employees. It includes doorbuster values, games, prizes, etc. Take down names for mailing list. (Chapters 5, 6)

Growth. Is your first goal toward the success for your store and your life in the community. This brings profits which allow expansion and more. (Chapter 8)

Handbill. Attractive colorful printed matter to be handed out in a strategic area to notify passerby of new offerings. Sometimes mailed with monthly statements to your own customers (Chapter 6)

Health Insurance Policies. A fringe benefit for your employees which is an approved business expense if all are covered, not just owners. (Chapter 10)

Image. The customer's view of the store—an impression, not always factual, which affects shopping loyalty to you. (Chapter 6)

Instinct. A valuable asset added to background knowledge of the merchandise, storekeeping, communicating knowledge, artistic flair, and a willingness to work the schedule that patrons demand.

Interest. The charge a lender demands of a borrower for the use of the money. (Chapter 3)

Income Statement. Also referred to as a "profit and loss" statement, it summarizes the results of the operation for a given period. (Chapter 11)

Index of Business Information. Found in the library files of the Wall Street Journal or the New York Times.

In House Credit System. An installment type credit system (traditional old type) or a charge account has been approved and registered, and is attended by the stores personnel. An expensive process. (Chapter 9)

Initial Markup. The opening gross markup, the percentage made when dividing your gross profit (subtract cost of goods from selling price) by the total selling price. (Chapters 2, 5, 8)

Installment Credit Accounts. The traditional in-house weekly payment plans where by the merchant remained close to his debtor-customer, seeing him often so that he had the chance to add another bill on to the account every time he made a payment. (Chapter 9)

Institutional Ads. Calculated to improve the image of the store, to interest customers in a new development in the store's merchandising, or to secure a loyalty through some community project. It has a long term effect. (Chapter 6)

Interior Displays. Very important parts of your presentation affecting your merchandising effort when used strategically near heavy traffic areas to sell particular stock. (Chapters 2, 6)

Inventory. Sometimes used interchangeably with stock, it also means the physical counting of your stock. Inventory is taken (at least) once a year at the end of your fiscal year. (Appendix R)

Irregulars. A grade of quality just below perfect (or first quality, that other makers call their best). Irregulars are said to have tiny unnoticeable defects in appearance and wearing ability.

Jobbers. Middlemen buying from manufacturers and importers and reselling to retailers. The usual operation is one that buys a great many lines to service retailers in most of their needs for their patrons. (Chapter 1)

Journals. Basic books for recording everyday transactions in a way similar to a diary; one journal is used for income, and another for expenses. These figures are then broken down into more usable information in ledgers. (Chapter 11)

Keystone Method of Pricing. Used extensively in the jewelry trade, it is a 50 percent retail markup, double the cost to get the retail price. You occasionally hear "triple" keystone, meaning three times cost.

Kooky Styles. Strange, illogical trends without precedent or taste of the traditional. (Chapter 2)

Labor Legislation and Federal Laws. They include:
  1935 Wagner Act: right to bargain, unfair practices.
  1938 Fair Labor Standards: wages, hours, overtime.
  1963 Equal Pay Act: prohibits discrimination for sexes.
  1964 Civil Rights Act: prohibits discrimination for race, religion, color or national origin.
  1967 Age discrimination.
  1970 OSHA—Occupation safety and health standards. (Chapter 7)

Lading. Bill of Lading is the document that describes all details of the shipment that it accompanies. (Chapter 9)

Lease. Your written, binding contract with the landlord for the use of space for your given term. See Chapter 2 and use an attorney.

Liability Insurance. A primary policy to protect your business against suits by persons hurt while on your premises. Noncustomers, delivery people, anyone can sue you. The large face amount of policy coverage is little more than lesser amount, and it is a better choice. (Chapter 10)

Lien. Is a legal hold on a piece of property awaiting the discharge of a debt. Once paid, the lien is discharged.

L.I.F.O. Last In, First Out, it is the accounting theory of inventory evaluation used to good advantage in inflation periods because the higher priced (last acquired) goods was deemed to have been sold and no longer in the inventory. Lower priced goods left meant a lower valuation on the inventory now, less tax to pay. (Chapter 11)

Life Insurance. A fine addition to a partnership or stockholder agreement, paid for by the business which would go to the estate of the deceased partner in exchange for his interest in the company. The share is retired or sold to other parties with ease. (Appendix M)

Life Styles. An environmental variable that affects consumer buying habits and offers new challenges in merchandising. (Chapters 2, 5)

Limited Partner. All partners are general partners and fully liable for the debts of the business unless they have filed a "limited partner" form with the county clerk and have a signed understanding with the other partners. The limited partner may not participate in management, but collects his share of profits. Liability generally, see Chapter 4, Form of Business. (Chapter 4)

Liquidation (of a business, stock and other assets). Often requires conforming to the Bulk Sales Act of your state. If you owe no debts and have no creditors of any kind, you may liquidate a noncorporate business without asking anyone. It is probably wise to cancel your DBA registration and notify the Sales Tax Dep't. as well as a final return to I.R.S. Use the form to cancel your corporation charter with the Secretary of State. (Chapter 4)

Liquidity Ratio. The relative figure of your liquid current assets (money or will be) over the figure of the current liabilities. (Chapter 11)

Loans. More readily granted to business operators who present a comprehensive business plan. In this way the lender can have confidence that the loan re-payment schedule fits well into the scheme of sales and projected profits. (Chapter 3)

Long Term Gain. Profit made on property held for more than the one year period. The percentage of tax paid on it is less than ordinary profit. (Chapter 11)

Losses. Long-term losses may be charged against long-term gains on a dollar for dollar basis, but not the same against ordinary profits or short-term gains. (Chapter 11)

Loss Leaders. The supervalues you use to bring in traffic on special sale days. Often they are currently in good demand at regular price, and the cutting of price below your own cost is sure to be interesting enough to bring in trade. (Chapters 5, 6)

Mama-Papa Stores. An American tradition and how many of our giant department stores started. Husband and wife team up in a small store with good ideas and steady growth. Today's typical example is Caldor Discount Stores, less than twenty years old, almost fifty stores, bought out by Associated Drygoods Corp. in 1981. (Appendix B)

Maintained Markup. The actual markup remaining in the season when markdowns, discounts, and other diminishing items are subtracted. (Chapters 2, 5, 8)

Markup. The difference between cost and selling price. Also called gross profit (Chapters 2, 5, 8) or Markon. When referred to in percentage, you divide the profit by the retail. Manufacturer's markup is figured on the cost.

Management Training. A most potent incentive to good employees whom you wish to reward and encourage. It allows individual responsibility, encourages decision-making. (Chapter 7)

Manufacturers Representative. Usually an independent salesman who works on commission without overhead input from the maker. He may carry other lines. (Chapter 5)

Marketing. A common expression for how a new product is to be packaged, packed, and shown to potential customers with the known price and delivery established by the factory potential. Although this usually refers to manufacturers, a study of an additional or altered market for a retailer may be the means of growth. (Chapters 5, 6)

Mergers. A kind of business marriage whereby the stock of one corporation (may be other form, too) is exchanged with the other, with the approval of the stockholders, forming one company. (Chapter 4)

Merchandise Your Stock In-trade. The merchandising process of thinking and planning the strategy of operating which satisfies the trade, while making good profits and achieving healthy growth. Merchandising requires good controls. (Chapter 8)

Minority Owned Business. As referred to in federal law to aid small business, it is a business that is more than 50 percent owned by ethnic minorities or the handicapped. (Chapter 3)

MESBICS. Minority Enterprise Small Business Investment Companies set up to fund ventures of these minorities when approved. (Chapter 3)

Motivation. In personnel including managers in training is one of the important leadership assets to acquire. (Chapter 8)

National Labor Relations Act (Wagner Act). Gave employees (1935) the right to organize, collective bargaining machinery, and the National Labor Relations Board. In 1938 the Fair Labor Standards Act established minimum wage, hours, overtime pay, and limited child labor. (Chapter 7)

National Retail Merchants Association. The well-established trade group for retailers, who, for a membership fee, lobby in Washington for favorable legislation, send out advice on operating methods, offer a yearly convention to confer with member stores, and send out a helpful monthly magazine, *Stores.* (Chapter 1)

Net Dating. When an invoice is paid (on the due date) and there is no discount to be deducted, either cash discount or trade discount. (Chapters 3, 5)

Net Profit. The profit that remains after all expenses are deducted from the net sales and other income. Any increase in the value of your inventory since your last year-end inventory becomes an additional net profit. (Chapter 11)

Net Worth (or Capital). The remaining figure when you have deducted all liabilities from the assets of the business at this particular moment. (Chapter 11)

Niche. The opportunity, the need of the area, the kind of opening an entrepreneur seizes upon because it makes his or her offering distinct and better than existing stores. A study to find this need is worthwhile. (Chapter 1)

Non-store Retailing. Offers growth while remaining in the relatively same overhead physical expense. Selling by mail, phone, catalogue, door-to-door, vending machines, can be very productive. (Chapter 5)

O.C.R. (Optical Character Recognition). A growing method of ringing merchandise at the register by passing a wand over the code printed on it. (Chapters 8, 9, 11)

Occupancy Tax. A charge is 2½ to 5 percent of the rent in all commercial properties in New York City. (Chapter 4)

On-the-Job Training. The expertise required for store owners in certain kind of stores that require unusual presentation. For most stores it is superior to schooling, book advice, or help from professional buying offices. (Chapter 1)

One-price-System. Marketing and maintaining a price firmly as you sell goods in your store. In most of the world's stores the opening price is rarely the selling price as the merchants and customers spend time haggling over it. In the U.S., firm prices, except for antiques, have been the rule for the last hundred years.

Operating Expenses. Every expense both fixed and variable, but not the cost of the merchandise. (Chapters 3, 8, 11)

Operating Loans. The usual cyclical funds placed at the readiness for stores' use as needed, in the regular course of business, by their bank. Planned a long time ahead, this loan is forecast yearly and avoids a cash crisis when a heavy inventory for planned sales is needed. (Chapter 3)

Operating Budgets. Those budgets related to different costs of doing business—advertising, employees, or any expense that is variable and benefits from control. *Cash budget* is forecasting the cash flow, matching the need to supply and arrangements to supplement what will be short. (Chapters 3, 11)

Open Order. An order that has not been filled by the supplier and has not been cancelled by the store. (Chapters 3, 5)

Open-To-Buy. That figure to fill the needs of the store for the coming period—a buying budget—based on a forecast of sales. (Chapters 3, 5, 8)

Order Checking. The process connected to goods coming into the receiving department of the store to prevent a receipt of goods other than is still wanted. The order, if completed by the shipment received, is marked and filed away. (Chapter 9)

Options. Are choices to be made by decision of the lessee to stay on for a further term, under terms and conditions granted in the lease. If the store owner-lessee decides not to accept the option, the tenancy ceases at the end of the original term. (Chapter 2)

OSHA. The federal legislation Operating Safety Health Act which controls working conditions in certain types of workplaces. It requires regular reports if there are over ten employees. (Chapter 7)

Outs. Out-of-stock list kept handy to make sure the stock fill-in needs are pursued. (Chapters 5, 6)

Outdoor Advertising. Billboards (now under severe restriction by both federal and state laws) suitable for institutional copy or branded goods sometimes part-paid by vendor. (Chapter 6)

Over-Bought Condition. An especially serious situation in a new store when the traffic has not developed, and cash will be needed for other goods. This impedes cash flow because the ideal assortment is not maintained. (Chapters 5, 6)

Overhead Expenses. Those expenses connected with the premises, rent, utilities, phone, heating and so on. It may include maintenance.

Owner's Equity. The value of the owner's share of the entire business. Venture capital lenders offer equity loans for some of the owner's equity (shares of his stock) which lenders then hold for a few years in hopes of a rise in value several times the original price of the shares. (Chapter 3)

Partner Agreements (stockholder agreements in a corporation). Legal documents that are absolutely essential when two or more people join in business together, regardless of their family relationship. (Appendix M)

Party-Plan Selling. Nonstore selling whereby the operator invites friends to a party at home showing special merchandise for them to buy. The jobber or retailer supplies the merchandise and a method.

Part-time Employees. Possibly a very effective solution to the experienced personnel need, and the cost is less. The short needed-hours schedule is satisfactory to employer and employee. (Chapter 7)

Payroll vs Non-Payroll. Many small stores have certain work performed for them on a non-payroll manner thereby saving the cost of social security matching percentage, vacations, and other fringe benefits. If it is logical for this worker to bill the store for the work as an independent contractor, it can be done. If I.R.S. doesn't approve, it is a responsibility of the store owner, who if wrong is responsible for the social security of the employee as well as the store's share. (Chapter 7)

Percentage of Sales Method. The most common gauge for planning expense budgets of all kinds and for comparing these ratios with other years and other like stores. In advertising planning there are other factors, too. (Chapter 6)

Perpetual Inventory. A continuous entry system taking the physical inventory count, adding new invoices, and subtracting markdowns and monthly sales so you have a book figure to compare with an actual stock count to apprise you of a shortage. (Chapters 5, 8)

Personal Selling. Done by well-trained employees it is a very great advantage to you in a small store over the chain stores, discount, self-selling, and even the understaffed department stores. The experienced specialist/salesperson can produce far more sales volume in certain lines. They get paid base salary and commission. (Chapter 7)

Personal Finance Company. One of the poorer sources of loan funds because of the traditional high interest rates charged. Banks today are expected to approach those high rates, but they are favored because they are more adaptable for retailers. (Chapter 3)

Personal Living Budget. The personal living fund you perceive as necessary to carry you along before the store produces a profit for you to live on. (Chapter 3, Appendix X)

P.O.S. Systems. Those machines (Point of Sales) which record the transactions in a more detailed manner than traditional registers. They are especially effective when the data is fed into computers for informative printouts to management and automatic stock replenishment. (Chapters 2, 8, 11)

Point-of-Purchase Displays. The visual selling points of your floor or windows usually supplied by the manufacturers and sometimes timed to match national advertising campaigns. (Chapter 6)

Premises. Your entire place of business, front, selling floor, stockroom, office. (Chapter 2)

Price Discrimination. Extra discounts or ad allowances to stores. Forbidden under federal legislation, it nevertheless continues uncontrolled. Price fixing is allowed for liquor and other items when in the public interest. (Chapter 6, Appendix O)

Primary Trading Area. That major area from which most of your trade comes. It is important in considering the coverage of media. (Chapter 6)

Principal of a Loan. Is the original sum loaned to the borrower. (Chapter 3)

Private Brands or Private Label. That merchandise which is packed in an exclusive packing for the store (or jobber) which seems to indicate to the consumer that the quality is under your control. In some cases large users or department store groups order a superior quality packed this way to enhance their image of quality overall.

Product Liability Insurance. Covers your vulnerability to suits for damage when a product you make (or is privately packed as though you made) injures someone. (Chapter 10)

Profit and Loss Projections. Predict financial details of the business to creditors and other interested people, including owners. They are usually prepared by a C.P.A. (Chapter 11)

Promissory Note. The written evidence of a loan which details the amounts and terms of repayment. (Chapter 3)

Promotion. An activity to stir up extra business by changes in price, or other advantage, to urge more buying by different assortments, or displays, usually accompanied by ads to notify customers. (Chapter 6)

Promotional Allowance. Offered to retailers by suppliers is it, a percentage of the order to induce the retailer to play up the sale of the goods by ads or other promotional method. (Chapters 5, 6)

Public Adjuster. A professional advisor to those who have suffered a loss covered by insurance. He or she works on a percentage of the recovery, knows the policy language so as to get the maximum recovery, knows the company representatives who cooperate, and hopes to get enough to cover the cost of his or her services. (Chapter 10)

Public Corporation. One in which the stock shares are available to be bought by the general public. Public corporations try to conform to special regulations which make their shares available on major stock markets. (Chapter 4)

Public Service Ads. Aimed at an image of the company emphasizing public service rather than a commercial one. (Chapter 6)

Public Relations. Are the subtle ways of becoming a known, well-liked business through stories of human interest about the business or its workers. It is far more effective than advertising to improve the image. PR professional for a fee can find this interesting story to interest the public. (Chapters 1, 5, 6)

Push-Money. (P.M's) Special incentives to store personnel to sell less desirable or leftover goods. It helps keep stock clean. (Chapter 7)

Quantity Discounts. Special discounts to a store keeper for buying wholesale-lot quantities, which are usually too large for easy consumption. Until the store has a good traffic and can draw well promotionally through advertising and displays, a small store will benefit more from assortment. (Chapters 5, 6)

Quick-Ratio. Current assets minus the inventory has been termed *quick assets.* Quick assets divided by current liabilities is quick ratio (liquidity). (Chapter 11)

Rack-Jobber. One who supplies and services racks that display his goods by taking inventory and filling in stock as needed. He will sometimes replace unsold stock with other goods. The rack and the goods are in his packaging name. (Chapter 5)

R.O.G. Receipt of Goods dating on an invoice requires payment of the invoice on that day.

Regular Terms. Those traditional payment terms which a particular trade is offered for customers who pay bills on time. If you have no credit line you must pay cash before or at time of delivery. (Chapter 3)

Rent. Is the fee charged per month for the use of certain property for the time period called for in the lease, and under other terms named therein. (Chapter 2)

Resale Certificates. Issued by the state sales tax office to authorize a business to purchase any goods they will resell without paying the sales tax. The other certificate by the sales tax department is authorization to collect and pay over to the state the required tax on certain items. Retailers need both. (Chapter 4)

Resident Buying Office. Offices in large cities offering client stores a place to work while they shop lines for their buying needs. They offer these clients advice on comparisons of suppliers lines and will buy for them when authorized. There is a regular monthly fee charged by these offices as part of a yearly contract. They have seasonal meetings where stores exchange ideas and a showing where sample lines are shown. (Appendix P)

Restrictive Lease Clauses. Hinder the lessee from using the property for any purpose except that stated in the lease. It is important to have leeway to operate in another manner if the business needs change. A lawyer can help you avoid restrictions. (Chapter 2)

Retail Calendar (for sales projection and advertising plans). Denotes holidays that affect your business. It helps you plan for personnel schedules and know when to buy more stock, arrange for loans, and make important management decisions. (Chapters 3, 5, 6)

Retail Method (of computing profit/percentage). Dividing the profit (your cost subtracted from retail) by your retail price, to compute the profit/percentage. (Chapter 2)

Revolving Account. One that may be added to at any time while there is still an open balance on it. Banks make a similar pre-arranged cyclical loan plan with stores who need money during certain seasons of the year. (Chapter 9)

Robinson-Patman Act of 1936. Originated to prohibit price discrimination. Much of the philosophy is outdated and the price-cutting methods of retailers on branded goods are no longer restricted since the 1976 demise of Fair Trade. (Chapter 6)

Royalty. A fee for the use of property, sometimes a given sum for a time period, other times a percentage of the business done by the user.

Running Money. That cash on hand necessary to pay all current costs of doing business with a little extra in case of unexpected problems. (Chapter 3)

Sales Below Cost. Still forbidden in a few states even though fair trade price maintaining has been abolished (1976). (Appendix O)

Sales Planning. The primary management function as a business projects operating controls. (Chapters 3, 5)

Score. The federally funded Service Corps of Retired Executives who will aid small business with advice. A city-sponsored similar organization is the Executive Volunteer Corps, and ACE. (Chapter 1, Appendix Y)

Seasonal Loans. Those needed by retailers at busy times of the year, every year. They are arranged for a long time in advance. (Chapter 3)

Seconds. A grade of merchandise below perfect (first quality). In drygoods, sheets, pillow cases etc. it is one grade below perfect . . . in hosiery and other wearing apparel it is below "irregulars." It is a substandard grading which depends very much on quality standards of the maker.

Securities. Valuables such as shares of stock of a corporation. These are usually not protected under the burglary policies unless specifically named or under the 3D type of overall coverage.

Self-service Retailer. Puts everything out on display, has fixtures and tables that offer the customer easy self-selection. Very little or no advice is available, prices and sizes are easy to read. (Chapters 5, 8)

Selling Agents. Independent representatives paying their own expenses who work on commission based on the sales made for their factory source. Some agents represent several lines. (Chapters 5, 8)

Service Business. One that exerts a treatment or repair on property owned by the customer. Service businesses may do repairs, cleaning, or household chores on another's property, or personal treatment on hair, skin, or body. (Chapter 2)

Shares. The units of ownership in a corporation. They have a nominal "par value" which bears no relationship to the actual traded value. They may be sold privately at any price agreed, or on a public stock exchange where a value is recorded on a daily basis.

Shipments. From suppliers become the property of the buyer as soon as in the hands of the carrier if the order is "FOB supplier," and buyer pays the freight. If it is FOB store, the buyer-store pays no freight and becomes the owner when he signs for receipt of the shipment. (Chaper 9)

Shopping Centers. Groups of stores in a single area run as a unit for one owner (individual or corporation). They feature auto parking, group advertising, and in some cases waterfalls, scenery, covered walks, and fascinating novelties to interest shoppers in addition to the store goods. The larger malls are "anchored" by department stores, discount stores, or other giants whose traffic is shared by all. (Chapter 2)

Shoplifting. The crime of stealing goods from the stores during shopping hours. It is a temptation for amateurs when poor supervision is noted, and always a store problem when professionals do it. Because it has become the source of so much loss, the judges are treating it more sternly. (Chapter 9)

Shortage. The difference between the book inventory, as kept in a perpetual inventory book, and the actual count of the stock when taken. Store shortages 30 years ago used to run 1 to 2 percent. Today they may run as high as 7 percent of sales. (Chapter 8)

Signs. Outside the store are the responsibility of the store owner even if on the premises at the beginning of the lease. They are important to your outside display and help with identity. (Chapter 2)

Silent Partner. One who does not participate in the active management of the partnership business. A silent partner may be limited in financial responsibility if he or she follows the limited partner regulations and properly files in the county of operation. (Chapter 4)

Skimming. The taking of a portion of the sales as one's own and not reporting it as income. The IRS and other taxing authorities consider it fraud punishable by jail terms, fines, penalties, and interest on the tax due. It is a retailer's favorite way of cheating and hard to detect. (Chapter 11)

Snob Appeal. Product lines with prices way above the expected range, arrogant customer treatment in the stores, and very little of the original small-store charm. It still sells in great volume in many of its stores (some franchises) by name appeal. (Chapter 5)

Sole Proprietor. A single person starting in business who may use his or her own name without any registration, or file in the county for a D.B.A. (doing business as) using a chosen name, even calling it "company" if desired. To go out of business the sole-propietor need only to pay debts and landlord and close up. He or she pays income tax on the company profits as his or her own, and is personally liable for debts of the company. (Chapter 4)

Specialty Store. Originally a stock consisting of many lines of one class of item. Many consumers think of a specialty store as one carrying items of sportswear and accessories. (Chapter 5)

Standard Form Lease. One preprinted, leaving room for the names of the principals, dates, etc., and for options, but features clauses normally tilted in favor of the interest of the landlord. Lawyers are aware of this and use the open spaces to give the tenant-client a better deal. (Chapter 2)

Staples. Wanted items of customer interest that remain so over long periods without change. They are on the basic stock list never to be out of stock. (Chapter 5)

Stock. Another name for inventory, the goods you sell in the store. Stock is also the ownership of a corporation broken into pieces called shares of stock. Turnover of stock is the number of times the average value in dollars is sold out and rebought, the average value into the yearly sales volume. (Chapters 2, 4, 5)

Stockholder Agreements. The essential contracts between co-owners which governs their input, their working arrangements, and any foreseen change in their status in the future. It is the same as a partnership agreement but covers the corporate form of business. (Chapter 4, Appendix M)

Store Policies. Those policies by management to deal with returns, exchanges, and refunds to customers as well as any special request for goods or services, and store hours. Policies also affect discounts to employees and special citizen groups including charities. Rules for employees and fringe benefits are part of policy. (Chapters 5, 7, 9)

Straight Salary. The usual pay for store employees, which doesn't take into account the amount that an employee has sold. In a certain few merchandise categories expertise in handling is a very important factor and commission is expected on top of base salary. (Chapter 7)

Sub-Chapter S Corporation. One which is not taxed as a corporation because all profits are charged as income to the stockholders relative to their interests. No stockholders may be foreign nationals, up to ten stockholders, one class of stock, no more than 80 percent of income from outside U.S., and other restrictions (Chapter 4).

Suppliers. Those firms that offer goods to the retailer for the stock in trade. They may be manufacturers, distributors, jobbers, importers, wholesalers of any type, or even retailers who are able to supply goods at a price which fits the store merchandising. (Chapter 5)

Surety Bond. One that must accompany certain bids to supply goods or services to government agencies, to guarantee performance. (Chapter 10)

Tactics of Management. Should be varied, and hopefully creative and changed as time goes on. The inventive input of a merchant who sees his strategy go with the flow of change and be successful in attracting the trade he has uncovered, is rewarded both financially and philosophically. (Chapters 1, 5).

Target Market. That specific group of people to whom you want to sell your products. This group should always be in mind in your planned thinking about the details of your story, the strategy, the financial budgets, the merchandise categories, etc. (Chapters 1, 2, 5, 8)

Taxes of all types, for all forms of business are discussed in Chapters 4, 7, 11.

Technology of Retailing. Is forcefully reminding us that there are new ways to control our inventories, keep basic stock available for sale at all times, mark goods according to plan more quickly and accurately, and keep a constant eye on the flow of cash. Electronic data processing is available at lower cost each year, POS terminals ring up sales and give a more accurate breakdown of what was sold and what needs to be reordered, and management has more data available to plan for the future. (Chapters 8, 11)

Terms of Sale. Include trade discounts, cash discounts, or payment with no discount (net), with term of payment time stated. There may be a CBD (Cash Before Delivery), COD (Cash on Delivery), Cash ROG (Receipt), 10 days, 30 days, 60 days, or EOM End of Month with days specified. Any invoice dated the 25th or later in the month, on EOM terms, is deemed to have been shipped the first of the next month for payment time period. Thus net 10 EOM means pay the bill next month by the 10th. (Chapter 3)

Textile Federal Legislation. Requires manufacturers to label the fiber content on garments and use an identifying number. (Chapters 4, 7)

Title. Ownership of property. In real property land or buildings you have the title searched before you pay for it in order to insure the fact that you get "clear title." "Title companies" search the records of ownership prior to the last owner before they offer you a policy to guarantee the title to what you are buying. Title to an order of goods you buy passes to you at the FOB point named in the order. (Chapters 7, 8, 9)

Trade Discount-Cash Discount. Every kind of merchandise you buy has a customary trade discount. In women's clothing mostly 8 percent, in men's wear 2 percent, 3 percent or net. Courts have ruled that even if a store does not pay on time, they do not lose the entire trade discount although they lose the part of the percentage considered cash discount for paying on time. When accounts pay after the required time period, they usually deduct the entire discount anyway, and a dispute arises. (Chapter 3)

Trading Area. The limited geographical boundary from which a store is expected to draw its regular trade. As time progresses and a store becomes known for special values, assortments, brands, or any outstanding appeal, its trading area enlarges. Mail and phone orders come from far off. (Chapters 5, 6)

Travel and Entertainment. A deductible expense of the firm. To foster a business, to pay for the expense of any activity necessary to run the business, for any travel connected with its operation.

Trend. A factor to be noted in planning and projecting the sales and expenses of the coming season. (Chapters 3, 5)

Truth in Lending Federal Legislation. Restricts the type of questions that may be asked a prospective borrower or one seeking credit. Credit information about any borrower who has been turned down must be available to the borrower.

Turnover. The ratio of the average inventory of the store (retail value) divided into the retail net sales for the year. This is the number of times this stock is sold and rebought during the year, each turnover producing a profit which will show up in the year result. (Chapters 2, 3)

Unfair Labor Practice. Forbids employers from impeding employees from discussing joining a union, or any other move against collective bargaining. The hearings concerning employer's conduct are bad public relations. (Chapter 7)

Unique Concept. Is the eagerly sought special factor you add to your merchandise presentation or service to create a special impact on your trade that begets loyalty and interest. (Chapters 1, 2)

Unit Control Systems. Have evolved in recent years with E.D.P. (electronic data processing) computer printouts for the buyers aiding their fill-in purchases, especially helpful in spotting the "hot" numbers when the buyers are not on the selling floor. POS registers have the direct input. (Chapters 5, 8 11)

Under-Capitalization. A strong source of problems that sometimes leads to the downfall of an otherwise well-run business. The market of suppliers will not give you the advantage of the best sources, unusual values for cash will not be acquired, and banks will not be favorably impressed with your needs for seasonal regular short-term loans. (Chapter 3)

United Parcel Service. A public delivery system for packages under 50 lbs., far more reliable and less expensive than Parcel Post.

Universal Credit Plan. One that includes all the present bank cards and the travel, entertainment cards (American Express, Carte Blanche, Diners).

Variable Expenses. Those that naturally vary with different times of the year, and other years, but most important vary by the intent of management decision to operate with the needs of business. (Chapter 8)

Vendors. People who sell. Your vendors are your suppliers. Vendor relations are best maintained by paying invoices on the due date. Apply for a credit rating early enough to give the vendors time to allow you a credit line for your first purchases. (Chapters 3, 5, 8)

Vending Machines. One of the many non-store retail opportunities. Placement in good locations and physical security are primary problems. Special licenses required in many areas.

Venture Capital Lenders. Do not favor retail stores. They look for good management, good products, and an opportunity to invest in a producing company where their money has a chance to multiply three or four times in a few years. They hold capital stock as security and sell it back at a profit. They may be private individuals, groups sponsored by associations, opportunistic funding semi-banking types, or be government sponsored, as in the case of the Federally funded SBICs, small business investment companies or MESBICS, set up under S.B.A. for minorities. (Chapter 3)

Volume of Sales. The key figure on which all ratios and planning are based. The first planned figure for sales volume is the most difficult; but by following the suggestions made in planning Chapters 1, 2, and 3 and using the charts of year's sales calendar, an approximate usable figure may be reached. (Chapters 1, 2, 3)

Warranties. The promises you make to customers concerning the quality and wearability of your goods. It may be a promise to replace goods, make full refund, repair them, or any other. Your reliability begets loyalty. (Chapter 5)

Water Damage (except from Cyclone–windstorms, etc.). Is not covered in fire policy with extended coverage. Sprinkler damage must be covered in a separate policy, unless during a fire. (Chapter 10)

Wear and Tear. An important element in the depreciation of fixtures and other fixed assets that you depreciate yearly, charging it against profits. (Chapter 11)

Well-Rated Accounts. Those accounts whose record of payments of invoices is good and whose continued success in growing and increasing net worth has reduced any credit risk to a minimum. (Chapters 3, 5)

Window Displays. Your face to the traffic. Give the passerby a glimpse of your offerings, prices, ways of doing business, and it may be the magnet that creates an interest. Professional window trimmers are sought-after; they charge more, and they are worth it. (Chapters 5, 6)

Withholding. Is the general reference to the requirements of governmental taxing authorities regarding social security and income taxes deducted from employees salaries separated and paid over regularly to these agencies. (Chapters 7, 11)

Wholesaler. Is the general term given to those middle-man firms who buy from manufacturers, importers and other sources and serve retailers with a variety of lines of goods with prompt delivery from stock, in small quantities, at a price 20 to 25 percent above a factory price. In some cases special pre-season purchases of wholesalers give them a lower price on certain items allowing them to resell at close to the factory price. Wholesale price is supposed to mean that given to quantity buyers, but when advertised by retailers, it is not always so.

Wool Products Labelling Act. Requires manufacturers to label the proper percentages of wool and other fibers, the percentage of virgin or reused wool, etc.

Working Capital. Your current assets less your current liabilities. The ratio with sales indicates efficiency. (Chapter 11)

Workmen's Compensation Insurance. Required in most states if you have one employee. It covers job-related injury. (Chapters 7, 10)